THE FAMILY TREE

SCOTTISH

GENEALOGY GUIDE

THE MI...

Stower Head
The Aird

Moor Forest
Knockfin Kildonan
Berrydale
rd of Caithness

More H[d]
Loch Shin
Larg K Dunrobin
RogartK
Loth h[d]

L.Asynt
Loch Broom
Coiyach
Dunclain
Goldspie
Frith of Tain or Dornoch
Tarbetness

ebuck H[d]
Little L.Broom
Rea Head
Ewe
Loch Broom R
Kincardine
Dornoch
Creech
Tain
Fearn
MURRAY FRITH
Burgh Head
Orainie
Seymouth
Port Nockie
Cullen
Portsoy

L.Gerloch
L.Torridon
Rona
L.Maye
Loch Maye
Ben Wevis
Dingwall
Beauley
Fortrose
Cromarty
Fort Geo
Nairn
Calder
Forbes
Dallas
Elgin
Keith
Fochabers
Banff
Foggylone
Rothieman

30
Applecross K
Loch Garron
Garron
L.Monar
Killorie
Kirkhill
Inverness
Dores
Daviot
25
Moy
24
Ardeclach
23
Inveraven
Glass
Fergus
Gartley
22
Invern

28
L.Maddy
L.Alfarig
Glen Urquhart
Kilmore
Loch Ness
Boondartul
Boteskine
Aviemore
Kincardine
Cairngorm
Tomantoule
Kirkmichael
Kearn
Tullynede
Fough
Lamphan

Military Road
Duach T.
Fort Augustus
Keiguste
Duthill
Braemor
Tarland
Charlest
Kincardine

L.Hourn
Lochand
New K of Laggen
Old K
Castletown of
21
Wells Birss

L.Nevish
L.Arkeig
Caledonian Canal
Kirktown of Clova
L.Ethnots
Fettere

P. of Slate
L.Eye Sl[?]
L.Lochy
Kilmanivag
L.Laggen
L.Bright
Spittle of Glenshee
Kirkmichl
Kirktown of Isla
Contachie
Brechin

Egg I
L.Eil
Kippaly
Ben Nevis
Fort William
Strowan
Blair Atholl
Moulin
Logierait
Allyth
Blairgowrie
Farfar
Aberlemno
20

Ardnamurchan
L.Shiell
Ardgowar
Moydart
L.Rannoch
K Rannoch
Dull
Glammis
Cupar of Angus

Morvern
Appin
27
Arnachatton
Bonawe
Glenorchy
L.Leven
Georges H.
Fortingal
Kenmore
Loch Tay
Dunkeld
Kinclaven
St Martins
Scone
Dundee
River Tay
Button
den Bay

I of MULL
Murkearn
Kilchrenan
Glenorchy
Imshall
Clifton
Killin
19
Monzie
Methuen
Perth
Dunmail
Briol
St Andre

Kilmore
Kilmil ford
Inverary
Strahur
Eilmichael
Balquhidder
Callender
Coprie
Mathill
Auchterarder
Dunning
Newbu
Crieff
Blackford
Dumblane
17
Kinross
Falkland
Piglot
Large
18
Wemys
Crail
Fife
Anster

Ben Lomond
Thornhill
14
L.Lomond
Buchannan K.
Dumbarton
Stirling
16
Alloa
Clackm
Kincardine
Dunfermline
Kirkaldy
Dysart
Frith of Forth

Loch Fyne
Kilfinnan
Killsyth
Canal
Glasgow
airdrie
15
Falkirk
Linlithgow
Queensferry
Anghorn
Du

Skipness
Butel.
Paisle
Port Glasgow
Greenock
Renfrew
Hamilton
Lanark
Carstairs
Carnwath
Edinburgh
Musselburg
Dalkeith
Gifford
Middleton
Herriot
Channelk
Catfra Mill
Longfor

Ardmore
Gia I
Killear
Kilmarnock
Dalry
Largs
Muir K
Machline
Strathaven
Douglas
Carmichael
Lamington
Biggar
9
Linton
Eddleston
Peebles
Lyne
Lander

Ballachinten
Holy I.
Ave
Tundonald
Greenock
Muir K
Carmichael
Tweedsmuir
Yarrow
10
Galashiels
Selkirk

THE FAMILY TREE

SCOTTISH

GENEALOGY GUIDE

How to Trace Your Family Tree in Scotland

AMANDA EPPERSON

**FAMILY
TREE
BOOKS**

CINCINNATI, OHIO
familytreemagazine.com/store

Contents

Introduction

I know who my Scottish immigrant ancestors are. Do you?

A clarification: I know who they are on my mother's side. They came to America in the 1920s and are all easily traced in US and Scottish records—at least to the early nineteenth century. But the Scottish ancestors on my *father's* side are an entirely different story. In fact, I don't even know if I have any. However, his DNA results (and the fact that his earliest ancestors were in the American colonies before 1700) strongly suggest that Scots are in my paternal line somewhere. However, they will be much more difficult to trace.

Whether your Scottish ancestor came to America yesterday or in 1714, you will need to develop skills to trace immigrant ancestors through time and confirm their identity in both countries. This can be a daunting task, especially if you seek a colonial immigrant.

Luckily, we are living in a "golden age" of genealogy, with more and more sources coming available online every day. And with many of them indexed and keyword-searchable, it's never been easier to access them—although I don't think any algorithm will be able to search all at once for the great variety of spellings for surnames like McGillivray and Fenningham.

This book will help you trace your Scottish ancestry—no matter when your ancestors arrived—whether you are a novice or an experienced researcher. We'll walk you through the steps of discovering your ancestor's homeland in American records and introduce you to Scottish history, migration patterns, and all kinds of records (church, civil, military, and more). In the following pages, you will learn how to access many of these documents online, helping you identify your ancestors and discover the world they lived in.

With diligence and with luck, you too, will be able to say, "I know who my Scottish ancestors are and where they came from"—or, at least, one of them.

Amanda Epperson, PhD
Cleveland, Ohio
May 2018

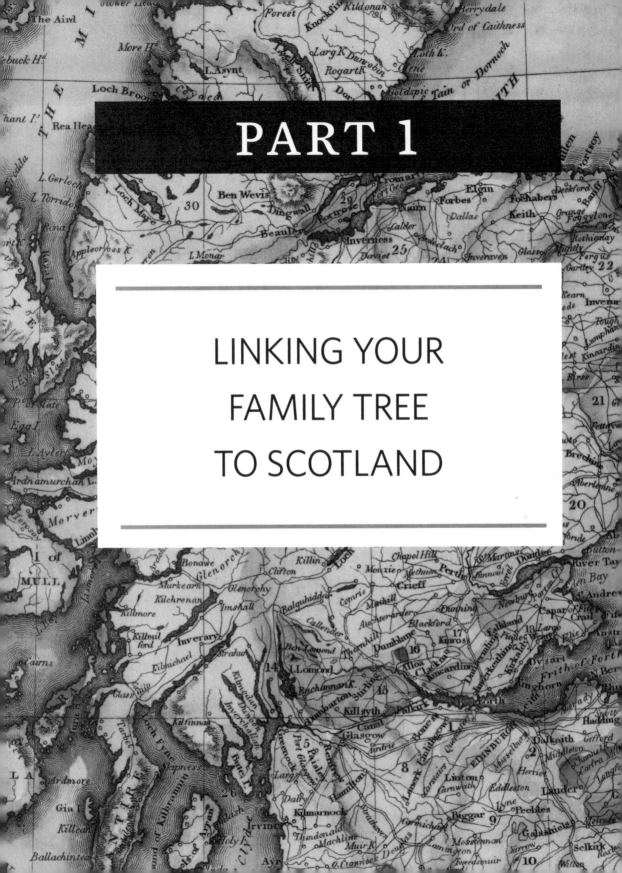

PART 1

LINKING YOUR FAMILY TREE TO SCOTLAND

1

Discovering Your Scottish Heritage

Tartan, kilts, bagpipes, and the Loch Ness Monster instantly bring Scotland to mind, whether you have Scottish ancestry or not. You may be aware of your Scottish great-grandfather and are eager to uncover his Scottish origins. Or perhaps you simply feel connected to Scottish music or the sound of Scots Gaelic and are hoping to share a genetic connection with this fabulous country. While the overall numbers of Scots who have immigrated to the United States may be small compared with other ethnic groups, Scottish Americans (including John Witherspoon and Andrew Carnegie) have had an outsized influence on American culture and business. And because Scots immigrated to the United States for more than three hundred years, you may very well have Scottish ancestry hidden somewhere in your family tree (image ).

This chapter provides a brief introduction to the history of Scottish immigration to the United States. Knowing the circumstances surrounding your ancestors' arrival in the United States can provide insight into their lives and reasons for departure. This chapter also features a brief summary of Scottish cultural activities maintained by Scottish Americans, allowing you to experience your heritage and honor your ancestors in new ways.

My grandfather, William Keir Hood, prepares to play the bagpipes at an event in Cleveland, Ohio.

IMMIGRATION TO THE UNITED STATES

Scots have been coming to America since Colonial times, and many Scottish immigrants have played an integral role in American history. Here, we'll outline some of the broad trends in Scottish immigration to the United States. See chapter 4 for more on Scottish history.

Scots in Colonial America: 1600s–1700s

Scottish American history began in the seventeenth century. Few Scots came to the Americas in the first half of the century because emigrating-minded Scots had better opportunities closer to home, most notably in Ulster (see the sidebar on Ulster-Scots).

However, this situation changed mid-century, when many Scots were forcibly removed from their homeland to the American Colonies. After being defeated by the English commander Oliver Cromwell in 1650 and 1651, captured Scottish troops were

A Brief History of Ulster-Scots, or Scots-Irish

In the early 1600s, the English government sought to solve the "Irish problem," hoping to curtail Catholic influence in Ireland. After the English suppressed a series of rebellions in Ulster, a province in the north of Ireland, the region was left largely unpopulated, allowing England to settle Protestants in the area. The government created the Plantation of Ulster, a scheme to settle English and Scottish Protestants in Ulster.

Private landlords arranged for Protestants to move into Counties Antrim and Down in Ulster. County Down was divided between Scots Hugh Montgomery and James Hamilton, both born in Ayrshire, Scotland (where Scottish emigrants to Ireland would later come from). Likewise, the largest landholders in County Antrim were Arthur Chichester (an Englishman) and Randal MacDonnell (a Scotsman). Most settlers to Chichester's portion of land came from his native Devon, England, while MacDonnell (though a Catholic Highlander) sought most of his tenants from Protestant Lowlanders.

One year later, the project expanded to include the Irish Counties of Armagh, Coleraine (present-day Londonderry), Tyronnel (present-day Donegal), Tyrone, Fermanagh, and Cavan. In part because Scotland was much closer to Ulster than England, Scots soon outnumbered English settlers 20:1. Scottish migration to Ulster was largely complete by the early eighteenth century, when about 600,000 people of Scottish descent lived there.

However, not all the Scots-Irish or Ulster-Scots (as they came to be known) remained in Ulster. In 1718, the Ulster-Scots emigration to the America colonies began. Some estimates assert that upwards of 250,000 people from Ulster settled in the thirteen American colonies between 1718 and 1775. Emigration from Ulster to the United States continued to be significant throughout the nineteenth century.

Given this unique history, you'll need a different set of tools to research your Ulster-Scots/Scots-Irish ancestry. This book focuses on finding your ancestors who came directly from Scotland to the United States. For more information on tracing your Ulster-Scots ancestors in Ireland, see *The Family Tree Irish Genealogy Guide* by Claire Santry **<www.familytreemagazine.com/store/the-family-tree-irish-genealogy-guide>** or download the Scots Irish Genealogy Crash Course web seminar **<www.familytreemagazine.com/store/scots-irish-genealogy-crash-course-ondemand-webinar>**.

transported to Massachusetts, Maine, and New Hampshire. In these Colonies, they were sold into indentured servitude for seven-year terms.

The first Scottish American organization, the Scots' Charitable Society, was founded in Boston in 1657 to help the Scotsmen whose term of indenture expired that year. Covenanters, Presbyterians who were ardently opposed to government interference in the Church of Scotland, were also transported to the Americas during a period of religious turmoil in the 1680s.

Other Scots came to the Americas under their own free will. Scottish merchants operated throughout the American Colonies in the mid- to late-1600s, though they may not have been permanent residents. The Navigation Acts, passed by the English Parliament, forbid the Colonies from trading with any European countries besides England. Since Scotland was treated as foreign for the purposes of these laws, any direct trade between Scotland and the Colonies was illegal. Still, contemporary records suggest Scots regularly smuggled goods out of the Colonies.

Other voluntary emigrants settled in the colonies of East Jersey (now part of New Jersey) and Carolina. The proprietors of East Jersey, several of whom were Quakers, received their charter in November 1683, and the new colony attracted immigrants from all over Scotland. Charleston in Carolina became another highlight of Scottish immigration after a nearby settlement (Stuart's Town) was founded by Covenanters, then destroyed by the Spanish just two years later. The Stuart's Town settlers relocated to Charleston or the northern colonies.

In 1707, the separate nations of England and Scotland formed a political union creating the United Kingdom of Great Britain. After the Union, Scots were able to trade with and settle in British territories. As a result, Scottish migration to the American colonies began in earnest in the 1730s and reached its height after 1760. By 1790, Scots had settled in every colony from Maine to Georgia and (by some estimates) represented just over 5 percent of the population.

Two trends stand out about the experience of the Scots in Colonial America. Highland Scots (from the northern and western part of the country) tended to settle in frontier regions like the Cape Fear Valley in North Carolina, the Mohawk Valley in New York, and Darien in Georgia. Lowland Scots (from the southern and eastern part of the country) often settled in the more established parts of the colonies and frequently gravitated to the growing urban centers of New York City, Philadelphia, Boston, and Charleston. Additionally, educated Scots, both Highland and Lowland, were overrepresented in Colonial government and the fields of religion, education, and trade. These well-educated merchants, religious figures, and educators were often unable to find work in the homeland, so they

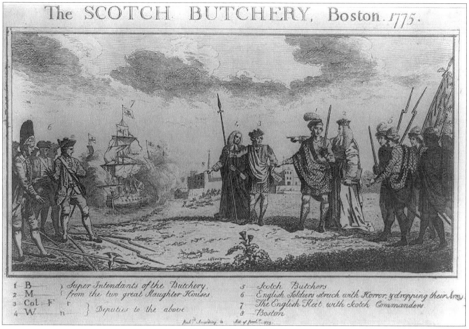

B

The SCOTCH BUTCHERY, Boston. 1775.

1 B——— } Super Intendants of the Butchery, from the two great Slaughter Houses	5 Scotch Butchers
2 M———	6 English Soldiers struck with Horror, & dropping their Arms
3 Col. F——r } Deputies to the above	7 The English Fleet with Scotch Commanders.
4 W———n	8 Boston

This 1775 cartoon depicts Scottish Lords Bute and Mansfield (center-right, numbered 1 and 2) directing troops in traditional Highlander dress (right, numbered 5) to inflict a "Scotch butchery" on British troops and the people of Boston. Meant to drum up fear in the hearts of colonists, this is an example of the Scotophobia that existed prior to the American Revolution.

followed their Scottish brethren across the Atlantic. Simply put, many Scots needed to leave Scotland to earn their keep, and they were willing to do so.

As you might expect, all emigrants from this time period reached the Colonies by sailing ship, but their method of departure depended upon their circumstances. Highlanders from the same parish often sought their fortunes together in the New World, traveling in large groups. More commonly, individual extended family groups left together: patriarch, his children, and their spouses and children. Generally, these groups, large and small, paid for their own passage. Others were forced from Scotland. The Scottish government continued to transport convicts to the Americas (though Scottish courts sent considerably fewer than the English). A number of Scots indentured themselves, binding themselves to serve a master for a certain number of years in exchange for passage and (if they were skilled) an annual salary. Many Scots were actually indentured in London, having travelled to the metropolis to seek a living and deciding to emigrate to the colonies only after they were unable to find a living.

In this age of sail, most cities along the eastern seaboard served as ports of entry for immigrants. Scots arrived in New York, Boston, Philadelphia, Charleston, Savannah, and many others. Toward the end of the Colonial period, Philadelphia became the most common port of entry for Scots arriving from Europe. Immigrants would travel from these port cities to their ultimate destinations, either over land or by local ships.

While the average Scot probably did not face any outright discrimination during the eighteenth century, they often were looked upon unfavorably. This feeling in the Colonies mirrored a similar trend in England, where both nations were still adjusting to the effects of Union. This disfavor was exceptionally strong in the Chesapeake area, where many Colonial planters resented their indebtedness to the Glasgow tobacco merchants.

This resentment boiled over in the already contentious climate in Colonial America, and Scottish immigrants played a large role in stoking the flames. At the outbreak of the American Revolution, ten of the thirteen Colonial governors were Scottish, and both the English and Loyalist Americans scapegoated the Scots as the cause of the war (image **B**). In the first draft of the Declaration of Independence, Thomas Jefferson wrote of "Scotch and foreign mercenaries" that had been sent to "invade & deluge us in blood," likely referencing German Hessian and Scottish Highland soldiers who had been recruited to defeat the rebelling Colonists. However, Scottish-born members of the Continental Congress, particularly John Witherspoon, objected to the negative characterization of their homeland. Ultimately, the reference to "Scotch mercenaries" was removed from the final document.

After the conflict was over, Scots had to decide whether or not to live in the new nation. Many Highlanders (who had come to the Colonies in the 1760s and 1770s) were, like other recent immigrants, Loyalists, and left the United States at the end of the war. Roughly half of the Highlanders in the Cape Fear and Mohawk Valleys left after the War, heading for Canada, the Caribbean, or Scotland. But the other half stayed—determined to make peace with their neighbors and the new country.

The 1800s: A "Century" of Emigration

Though many Scots came to the United States early in the country's history, immigration came to a standstill between 1775 and 1820. Immigration was made difficult due to the American Revolution (1775–1783) and War of 1812 (1812–1815) on the US side, in addition to the French Revolution (1789–1799) and Napoleonic Wars (1803–1815) on the European side. Afterwards began what is known as the "century" of immigration, lasting roughly from 1820 until 1930. This time period saw millions of people migrate across the world, especially from Europe to North America.

Scotland was particularly affected by mass emigration. Scotland's population grew between 1841 and 1921, but it lost between 10 and 47 percent of its natural increase per decade and saw its population decrease between 1921 and 1931:

Year	Scottish population
1841	2,620,184
1851	2,888,274
1861	3,062,294
1871	3,360,018
1881	3,735,573
1891	4,033,103
1901	4,472,103
1911	4,760,904
1921	4,882,407
1931	4,842,554

In terms of emigrants as a percentage of the homeland's total population, only Ireland and Norway lost more of their populations to emigration during this time period than Scotland.

However, the actual numbers of Scots in the United States were quite small compared with other immigrant groups, especially in individual communities. For example, Germans flocked to the Midwest, where they greatly outnumbered Scots. In 1850, Germans in the city of Cincinnati outnumbered Scots in the whole state of Ohio 7:1.

People from all over Scotland settled successfully in every region of the United States during this period. They continued to settle in New York City and Philadelphia, established farms in Ohio and Wisconsin, and built adobe homes in California

No matter where they went, Scots—who were white, English-speaking, and Protestant—tended to be "invisible" to the rest of society, a phrase first used to describe them by historian Charlotte Erickson. Scots and other British immigrants were seen as more able to assimilate into American culture than other, non-English speaking European populations. However, their ability to speak English masked the vast differences in the social and political structure of the two countries, as well as the difficulties these immigrants faced in their new homeland.

In the first half of the nineteenth century, most Scots who immigrated to America came in family groups and moved to rural, farming communities from the Northeast, the Central Belt, and the Border regions of Scotland. They often chose their destination from a guidebook or at the suggestion of those who had previously settled in the United States.

Many were urban people who thought farming would be a better life, or farmers seeking an improved quality of life.

This changed somewhat in the second half of the nineteenth century, when many more single men and women came to America. As the second Industrial Revolution took off in the United States, booming factories required more employees, and Scots had several advantages over other immigrant groups coming to America at this time. First, many had the advantage of heavy-industry experience. Second, they were fluent in English, literate, and numerate due to the excellent education system in Scotland (again, especially as compared with other countries). These factors meant that Scots were able to acquire better jobs and command higher wages, especially in management roles (such as in coal mines).

The last period of significant Scottish migration to the United States occurred in the 1920s. This migration might have been larger if it hadn't been for the restrictive immigration acts passed by the US Congress during this decade. After the first quota act of 1921, immigration from the United Kingdom was reduced by almost 20 percent. After the Scottish economy (which had depended upon heavy industry like shipbuilding in World War I) collapsed, Scots still found the United States an attractive destination. By 1930, the Scottish-born population in the United States had increased by almost 100,000 over that of 1920, increasing from 254,570 to 354,323.

SCOTTISH TRADITIONS AND CULTURAL INFLUENCES

All things Scottish have become increasingly popular since the release of the successful films *Braveheart* (1995) and *Brave* (2012), as well as the television series *Outlander* (first aired in 2014). However, Scottish Americans have actively maintained and promoted Scottish culture in the United States for centuries. They have formed organizations, hosted dinners, and held sporting events. Shops in America sell imported goods like tartan fabrics and chocolates. Learning about these various cultural events and symbols will help you more greatly appreciate your Scottish heritage.

Scots and Scottish Americans also celebrate their heritage through traditional dress. The kilt, the traditional garment for Scottish men, is popular at Highland games (see the later section), weddings, and other special events on both sides of the Atlantic. In Scotland, the kilt (first worn in its current form 270 years ago) is also the favored garment for supporters of Scottish sports teams.

Tartan, a checkered pattern of multiple colors, has been associated with Scotland (especially the Highlands) for many centuries. Since the early nineteenth century, families or regions have adopted particular setts (patterns), though there are no rules limiting who may wear which tartan pattern. If your family doesn't have a tartan (or you don't like

Famous Americans with Scottish Ancestry

Scots and their descendants have been part of America for over 350 years. In this time, they have distinguished themselves in many fields, from education to entrepreneurship. While a list of famous Americans with distant Scottish ancestry would fill an entire volume, the list of those who were immigrants or the children or grandchildren of immigrants from Scotland is still impressive:

- Alexander Graham Bell, inventor
- James Blair, founder of the College of William & Mary
- David Dunbar Buick, motor car designer
- Alexander Calder, artist
- Andrew Carnegie, industrialist
- Robert Downey, Jr., actor
- David Duchovny, actor
- Malcolm Forbes, magazine editor and publisher
- Alexander Hamilton, first secretary of the US Treasury
- Patrick Henry, founding father and governor of Virginia
- Washington Irving, author
- John Paul Jones, US Revolutionary War naval hero
- William Kidd, pirate

- Jay Leno, television personality
- Douglas MacArthur, five-star general
- Jimmy MacDonald, the voice of Mickey Mouse from 1948 to 1977
- Julianne Moore, actor
- John Muir, naturalist and co-founder of the Sierra Club
- Allan Pinkerton, founder of the Pinkerton National Detective Agency
- Donald Trump, forty-fifth president of the United States
- James Wilson, signer of the Declaration of Independence
- Woodrow Wilson, twenty-eighth president of the United States
- John Witherspoon, sixth president of the College of New Jersey (now Princeton University) and signer of the Declaration of Independence

TIMELINE History of Scottish Immigration

1650 The first Scottish prisoners are transported to America after Scottish defeat at the Battle of Dunbar.

1657 The Scots' Charitable Society of Boston is founded.

1683 East Jersey, an American colony founded by Scots, is chartered.

1684 Covenanter refugees arrive at Stuart's Town, South Carolina. Spanish forces over-run the town two years later.

1704 America's first continuously printed newspaper, *The Boston News-Letter,* is first published by Scottish-born John Campbell.

1729 The St. Andrew's Society of Charleston is founded.

1730s Many Scottish Highlanders immigrate to the American Colonies of Georgia, North Carolina, and New York.

1746 Presbyterians found the College of New Jersey (now Princeton University).

1747 The St. Andrew's Society of Philadelphia is founded.

1776 Scotsmen John Witherspoon and James Wilson sign the Declaration of Independence.

1788 Robert Burns' *Poems, Chiefly in the Scottish Dialect* is first published in the United States, in Philadelphia.

1836 The Highland Society of New York organizes the First Highland Games.

1850 Scottish-born Allan Pinkerton founds his famous detective agency.

1858 The Rockford Burns Club is organized in Rockford, Illinois.

1863 Henry Chisholm, a Scottish American, co-founds the Cleveland Rolling Mill Company, the second Bessemer steel works in the United States.

1888 John Reid (and others) founds St. Andrew's Golf Club in Yonkers, New York.

1892 John Muir, a Scottish-born naturalist, co-founds the Sierra Club.

1911 Andrew Carnegie, who emigrated from Scotland as a teenager, endows the Carnegie Corporation of New York, a philanthropic foundation made of the bulk of his 145-million-dollar fortune.

1956 The first Grandfather Mountain Highland Games are held in North Carolina.

1998 Tartan Day is first celebrated in the United States.

Scotch pies (double-crusted pastries, left) and Forfar bridies (crescent-shaped pies, right) are among Scottish desserts you can sample at certain US markets and groceries.

the one "assigned" to your family), simply pick one you like. You can search all officially registered tartans from the Dress Gordon to the Edinburgh Zoo Panda tartan at the Scottish Register of Tartans <**www.tartanregister.gov.uk/search**>. Scottish Americans have also developed a ritual called the Kirkin' o' the Tartan, during which the tartan fabric and their associated families are blessed. The first one was held in Washington, D.C. in the early years of the Second World War, and churches of various denominations can host them.

Another way to get in touch with your Scottish heritage is to eat traditional foods. Scotland is particularly known for the high quality of its salmon and beef. Oatmeal, which grows well in the Scottish climate, is another staple. Some foodstuffs like shortbread, scones, Irn-Bru (a carbonated drink), whisky, and haggis (offal, suet, oatmeal, onions, and spices all boiled together in a sheep's stomach) are well known and either adored or shunned, depending upon one's taste. Other yummy Scottish fare include Forfar bridies, crescent-shaped savory pies; Scotch pies, double-crusted savory pies (image **C**); stovies, a one-pot meal of meat and potatoes; Scotch broth, a lamb and barley soup; Cullen skink, a soup of smoked haddock, potatoes, and onions or leeks; and cranachan, a dessert containing oats, cream, whisky, and raspberries.

Traditional Scottish dress features prominently in Scottish games festivals, such as this color guard at the Ohio Scottish Games in Wellington, Ohio.

Scots and their descendants in the United States have established an array of organizations to maintain their heritage and encourage interest in Scotland. These groups include clan organizations, St. Andrew's Societies, Caledonian Societies, and Scottish American Societies. These groups sponsor, organize, or attend various Scottish heritage events and holidays throughout the year. The sections that follow discuss some of the most prominent.

Highland (or Scottish) Games

Scottish organizations will put on these exhibitions of Scottish music, food, sport, and culture. As the name implies, these festivals feature athletic competitions (including caber toss, Braemar stone toss, and Scottish hammer throw), as well as contests for Highland dancing, fiddling, and piping. Many close with a "massed" band performance, in which several band groups come together to play at once. Attendees can also eat Scottish food, take dance workshops, and purchase goods imported from the United Kingdom while enjoying Scottish music and dress (image **D**). Highland Games are held variously throughout the year, though most are in the summer—find a list here **<www.asgf.org/ games-by-state/locations>**.

Burns Night

Honoring the Scots' National Poet Robert Burns, Scots have "Burns Night suppers" to commemorate Burns on his birthday, January 25. The custom spread to America by 1820, and generally contains the following:

- Bagpipe playing to welcome guests
- Recitation of the Selkirk Grace (see the sidebar)
- Bagpiping as the haggis is brought in
- Burns' Address to the haggis, followed by a toast
- A meal, usually traditional Scottish fare like haggis, neeps, and tatties
- The first entertainment: songs or poems of Robert Burns
- The immortal memory: keynote speaker delivers an address on the life of Burns
- The second entertainment: more of Burns' songs and poems
- Toast to the Lassies: humorous and complimentary address to the women present, acknowledging Burns' love of women
- Reply of the Lassies: response from the women, in which they poke fun at the men
- Final entertainment: more poems and songs of Robert Burns
- Vote of thanks to all who helped prepare the supper
- A singing of "Auld Lang Syne," a Burns favorite

If all this sounds too complicated, fear not! Burns Night suppers can vary in their length and level of detail. When I was a student in Glasgow, the graduate student club

The Selkirk Grace

Burns Night suppers nearly always include the Selkirk Grace, a prayer written by Burns:
"Some hae meat and canna eat,
And some wad eat that want it,
But we hae meat and we can eat,
Sae let the Lord be thankit!"

The Selkirk Grace has special meaning for many Scots and Scottish Americans, even without the connection to Burns Night. My family never celebrated Burns Night when I was growing up, but for many years we had a tea towel with the Selkirk Grace hanging in the kitchen. My mother remembers her father, who was born in Scotland, saying this grace with great frequency while she was growing up.

served us tiny scoops of haggis, neeps, and tatties in small Styrofoam bowls. I then rushed upstairs to eat it in the non-smoking section, where the TV was on and everyone was engrossed in their own conversations—no poems, no addresses, and no toasts. A piper played traditional tunes in the background.

Scotland is Now has an array of information about celebrating Burns Night, including recipes, links to Burn's poetry, and a forty-four-page guide to holding your own Burns supper <www.scotland.org/events/burns-night>.

Tartan Day

First held in Canada, Tartan Day celebrates Scottish heritage and the accomplishments of Scots living outside of Scotland. The holiday came to the United States in 1998, when the US Senate officially made April 6 National Tartan Day. Since its adoption, Tartan Day has evolved into Tartan Week, a seven-day celebration of all things Scottish. Celebrations vary by location, but can include parades, festivals, dinners, living history exhibits, balls, musical performances, and even group attendance of baseball games.

St. Andrew's Day

Those of Scottish heritage celebrate Saint Andrew, the patron saint of Scotland, on November 30 in both Scotland and the United States. Events celebrating St. Andrew's Day (which has been a bank holiday in Scotland since 2006) are quite varied. Several communities in Scotland (for example, Irvine, Oban, and East Lothian) hold festivals that feature Scottish food and drink, music, crafts, and fireworks. In the United States, Scottish social groups hold banquets, balls, and galas. My family celebrates with a special dinner (although some years, it is leftover Thanksgiving turkey with store-bought shortbread for dessert). You can learn more about St. Andrew and his day at <www.scotland.org/events/st-andrews-day>.

KEYS TO SUCCESS

- Immerse yourself in the immigration history of Scots to the United States. Learning about migration patterns and trends in movement from Scotland to America can provide context about their lives (and maybe even their home parish).

- Understand Scottish emigration patterns. One of your ancestral lines may have come to the United States by way of Ulster, rather than straight from Scotland.

- Learn about Scottish music, food, culture, clothes, and holidays. There's something for everyone! If you like to cook, try making scones. If you like music, listen to the songs and poems of Robert Burns. If you enjoy summer festivals, attend your local Highland Games.

2

Jump-Starting Your Scottish Research

Journeys require preparations and can make you "nervous-excited." Your journey to find your Scottish ancestors is no different. You may be excited to learn about your Scottish ancestry, but nervous about the research you need to undertake. Luckily, you can prepare for your trip in the comfort of your own home, as you must lay a firm foundation for your family tree by examining US records. As you gain experience with US records and the genealogical process, you will also gain the confidence to tackle Scottish records, many of which are similar to those in the United States.

In this chapter, we'll cover the first steps you should take in your transatlantic genealogical journey, plus share some genealogy best practices that will help get your research started on the right foot.

FIRST STEPS

Every journey (whether on the high road or the low road) begins with a single step. Genealogically speaking, this first step is starting with yourself and working backward. While this step may seem tedious, it is essential. Documenting each generation starting with yourself will ensure that you are tracing the correct family lines, saving you time in the

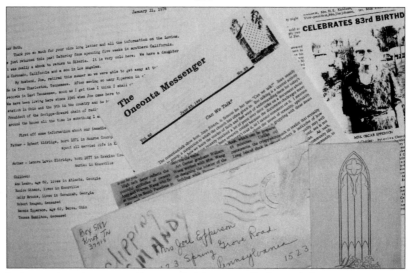

Look around your house to see if you can find documents like letters, bulletins, newspaper articles, and funeral cards.

future. And by tracing your tree backward in time, you might even encounter previously unknown Scottish ancestors. Records you find about one ancestor (such as a marriage or birth record) will help you learn about that person's parents or siblings, which will in turn lead to additional records. You'll be in Scotland before you know it!

With that in mind, let's look at the five essential steps to building a firm foundation for your genealogical research.

Step 1: Record What You Already Know

This first step involves nothing fancy—just your memory and a piece of paper. Write down all the basic information you know about yourself, your parents, grandparents, aunts, uncles, cousins, and so forth. This basic information includes each individual's birth, death, and marriage dates and locations, plus the names of your relatives' spouses and children. If you are not sure of a fact, put a question mark next to it and move on. Make special note of any clues that might lead to a Scottish ancestor—for example, a birthplace in Glasgow or a maternal ancestor with the surname Stewart. Circle these, as they'll prove useful later in your research. This foundational information will help you identify your research goals and ensure that you have identified the correct families in recent records, plus give you confidence as you begin to research the "unknown" generations.

Step 2: Find and Examine Documents You Already Have

With the info you already have in hand, you can now turn to documents to prove (or disprove) what you already know. You don't have to look far to find documents with genealogical information in them: scrapbooks, the attic, the box where you keep important papers, the back of the closet, the basement (image **A**). What can these documents tell you? How do they confirm or refute what you already believed about members of your family? What other gaps in your family's story do they fill in?

As you find and assess these documents, be sure to categorize and organize them. Take photographs or scan each before you put them away. This will help you take stock of what resources you already have, while also helping you safeguard against natural disasters like floods or fires.

Step 3: Interview Your Relatives

Now that you've mined your own memories and the "low-hanging fruit" of documents in your possession, turn next to your relatives. By interviewing your family members, you can gain all sorts of research leads while also encountering precious details that no records are able to give you.

You will be seeking two types of information in these conversations. First, ask about events that your relatives personally witnessed and are contemporary with their lives. Memories like these can help you better understand your ancestors' life and times, plus help you decide where to look for records of vital events, occupations, etc. Second, ask about traditions or family events that your ancestors know about, but did not necessarily witness themselves.

Your interview has a greater chance of success if you prepare in advance. Study the life of your interview subject and the history of any important historical events they may have lived through. If you notice gaps in your genealogical data (such as missing vital statistics), put these on your list of questions to ask.

> RESEARCH TIP
>
> **Revisit Documents**
> As you become a more experienced researcher and learn more about your ancestors, revisit your sources from time to time. You may notice a detail you overlooked before, or a fact that you did not realize was important. For example, a newly researched family line could live somewhere you've already studied, so you should revisit your sources from that place.

Be sure to make a list of your questions and general topics of discussion ahead of time—do not rely on your memory. While open-ended questions are best for eliciting spontaneous answers and memories (e.g., "What is your favorite memory of your grandmother?"), sometimes direct, closed questions are useful (e.g., "Do you recall your maternal great-grandmother's maiden name?"). If you have difficulty coming up with questions for your interview, the Center for Oral History Research at UCLA has an excellent list <oralhistory.library.ucla.edu/familyHistory.html>, as does *Family Tree Magazine* <www.familytreemagazine.com/premium/20-questions>.

Whichever questions you select, share your questions with your interviewees beforehand so they have a chance to reflect on their answers. You can also ask them if they have any family documents or photographs—or if they'd be able to identify individuals in photos you already have. The advance warning will allow your subjects to find and prepare them. You might also consider having your subjects sign a legal document regarding how your interview will be used. Will it simply be typed up and placed in a shoebox, or will you feature it in a published family history? See *The Oral History Workshop* by Cynthia Hart with Lisa Samson (Workman Publishing Company, 2009) for more.

And once you've considered what you'll ask your relatives, think too about how you'll be interviewing them. Pen and paper might suffice, but you may prefer to record audio or even video as well. Regardless of the medium, test the equipment beforehand. If you decide to use the voice memo feature on your smartphone, make sure you have enough battery and storage to last the whole interview. If you'll be using a dedicated digital or video recorder, make sure you have the appropriate memory card. Also be sure to bring a digital camera or portable scanner, as this may allow you to copy any documents or photographs that your subject has.

Step 4: Build Your Family Tree

Now that you've collected some data about your relatives, it's time to organize all those details into a family tree. Family trees, whether in print or online, will help you visual-

RESEARCH TIP

Investigate Family Myths

The oral traditions shared by our families can provide us with the breakthrough we need—but they can also lead you down the garden path. Unfortunately, you never know at the outset if a family story is accurate. Keep an open mind about the stories you hear, but treat the information they contain as *clues*, not fact.

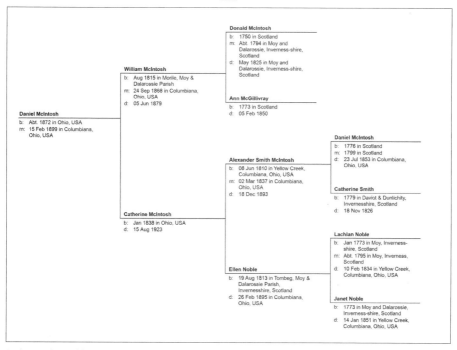

Daniel McIntosh
b: Abt. 1872 in Ohio, USA
m: 15 Feb 1899 in Columbiana, Ohio, USA

William McIntosh
b: Aug 1815 in Morile, Moy & Dalarossie Parish
m: 24 Sep 1868 in Columbiana, Ohio, USA
d: 05 Jun 1879

Donald McIntosh
b: 1750 in Scotland
m: Abt. 1794 in Moy and Dalarossie, Inverness-shire, Scotland
d: May 1825 in Moy and Dalarossie, Inverness-shire, Scotland

Ann McGillivray
b: 1773 in Scotland
d: 05 Feb 1850

Catherine McIntosh
b: Jan 1838 in Ohio, USA
d: 15 Aug 1923

Alexander Smith McIntosh
b: 08 Jun 1810 in Yellow Creek, Columbiana, Ohio, USA
m: 02 Mar 1837 in Columbiana, Ohio, USA
d: 18 Dec 1893

Daniel McIntosh
b: 1776 in Scotland
m: 1799 in Scotland
d: 23 Jul 1853 in Columbiana, Ohio, USA

Catherine Smith
b: 1779 in Daviot & Dunlichity, Invernesshire, Scotland
d: 18 Nov 1826

Ellen Noble
b: 19 Aug 1813 in Tombeg, Moy & Dalarossie Parish, Invernesshire, Scotland
d: 26 Feb 1895 in Columbiana, Ohio, USA

Lachlan Noble
b: Jan 1773 in Moy, Inverness-shire, Scotland
m: Abt. 1795 in Moy, Inverness, Scotland
d: 10 Feb 1834 in Yellow Creek, Columbiana, Ohio, USA

Janet Noble
b: 1773 in Moy and Dalarossie, Inverness-shire, Scotland
d: 14 Jan 1851 in Yellow Creek, Columbiana, Ohio, USA

Pedigree charts, like the above for Daniel McIntosh and his Scotland-born ancestors, can help you visualize your ancestors' lives and share your research with others in a compact way.

ize your research and identify any gaps or inconsistencies (image **B**). Family trees are also easy to share with other relatives, opening up opportunities to get family members excited about your work and (hopefully) collaborate with you.

Those who are less tech-savvy may prefer the "old-fashioned" way of creating family trees: printing out genealogy forms and filling them in by hand. The two most popular are pedigree charts (one-page forms that include boxes for four to five generations of direct-line ancestors) and family group sheets (which organize ancestors into couples and their children). *Family Tree Magazine* has free downloads for these and other useful forms on its website: pedigree charts at **<www.familytreemagazine.com/freebie/fivegenerationancestorchart>** and family group sheets at **<www.familytreemagazine.com/freebie/familygroupsheet>**. We've also shared a pedigree chart and other forms in appendix D.

Looking for a digital solution? Check out genealogy software programs, which you can use on your desktop or laptop devices. Popular programs include Family Tree Maker **<www.mackiev.com/ftm>**, Legacy **<legacyfamilytree.com>**, and RootsMagic **<www.rootsmagic.com>**. These programs (which are generally inexpensive) allow you to enter data about your ancestors, attach documents and photographs, and create citations. They can also create pedigree charts, family group sheets, and other forms for you, allowing you to visualize and print out your hard-earned research.

Finally, many genealogy researchers create family trees in large online databases. Thanks to online services like Ancestry.com <**www.ancestry.com**>, FamilySearch.org <**www.familysearch.org**>, MyHeritage <**www.myheritage.com**>, and Findmypast <**www. findmypast.com**>, you can create family trees and access your research from any Internet browser. Since these websites also have databases of digitized records, you can easily integrate documents you find into your family tree. You can also quickly share online family trees with others and use them to collaborate with other users. Some services even sync with select genealogy software programs, potentially saving you even more time.

Step 5: Identify Research Goals and Questions

To conduct your research effectively, you need specific research goals, plus tailored questions that will help you reach those goals. To put it another way: Your research goal is your final destination, and the research questions make up the route you will take to reach it. For example, if your goal is to visit your ancestor's parish in Scotland, you will first identify the immigrant ancestor and the parish he came from.

Your research question should be specific enough to be answerable with concrete research. In its simplest form, your primary research question could ask about a known ancestor's parents (e.g., "Who are Mary McAncestor's parents?"). This is not a bad question, but it doesn't help you find the answer. A more useful research question includes additional words like adjectives, dates, family members, friends, and locations (for example: "What are the names and birth dates of Mary McAncestor's parents?"). Find-

RESEARCH TIP

Compare Conflicting Facts

You may find that your research turns up conflicting information, some big (different maiden names or countries of origin) and some small (different spellings of names or hometowns). To resolve these discrepancies, examine your sources and determine which is more reliable. For example, let's say you believe your great-grandmother (whom you never knew) was born in 1915, but her daughter (your great-aunt) said she was born in 1913. Make note of each of these conflicts so you can resolve them while doing your research. Your great-aunt is likely a reliable source since she knew your great-grandmother firsthand, so you might be inclined to believe her—but be sure to follow up with documents.

ing the right words to add will require you to closely examine documents already in your possession.

Let's look at an example. Family legend says your McQueen ancestors were from Scotland, but you don't know when they came to America. You have traced your American ancestors back to Alexander McQueen, who died in Kansas in 1906. The next step would be to learn the names of his parents. In the 1900 US census, you learn that Alexander was born in November 1830 and his parents were born in Scotland—suggesting they were immigrants, and thus your immigrant ancestors. Using this information, create a research question that will help you locate his parents: Which McQueen family (with parents born in Scotland c. 1810 and living in Ohio in 1830) did Alexander belong to? This question keeps the focus on the age of Alexander's parents (concrete information you could find in a record), assuming they would have been about twenty years old when he was born. This question also features two additional clues that provide records to research—Alexander was born in Ohio, but his parents were born in Scotland. With this research question, you have concrete steps to take—for example, looking for McQueen families living in Ohio in the 1840 and 1850 US censuses.

For more on developing actionable research goals and questions, check out Drew Smith's *Organize Your Genealogy* (Family Tree Books, 2016) **<www.familytreemagazine.com/store/ organize-your-genealogy-paperback>**.

Examples of Primary and Secondary Sources

Primary and secondary sources are crucial to a successful research project. Understanding which are which will help you assess record reliability and how you can use records to reach your research goals.

Primary Sources

- autobiographies
- birth certificates
- death certificates
- diaries
- estate papers
- letters
- marriage licenses
- passenger lists

Secondary Sources

- abstracted records
- academic histories
- articles
- biographies
- encyclopedias
- indexes
- transcriptions
- translations

KEY GENEALOGICAL PRINCIPLES

Following established research methods will help you trace and document the correct ancestors. As you begin to look for the answers to your research questions and delve into records, keep in mind these core principles of good genealogical research.

Primary and Secondary Sources

All people engaged in historical research use two types of sources: primary and secondary. Primary sources provide contemporary, firsthand knowledge of the event or person being documented. Marriage licenses or baptismal records are good examples of primary sources, as the person creating these records witnessed the event for himself and recorded it, either in real time or shortly after. Other documents that are not contemporary but still contain firsthand knowledge (such as eyewitness accounts, autobiographies, and memoirs) also are primary sources.

Secondary sources are documents created without firsthand or contemporary knowledge of an event or person. To put it another way: Secondary sources are records created from primary sources or significantly after the fact. These include family genealogies (including other individuals' research), family lore, record abstracts (which excerpt certain information from primary sources), and indexes (which identify the subject[s] of a record and point to the record's location). Note that record transcripts (which re-create the text from a source word-for-word) are considered secondary sources. See the Examples of Primary and Secondary Sources sidebar for more information.

In general, you should always look at the original, primary source if possible, and validate all information from secondary sources by using primary sources. Primary sources tend to be more reliable than secondary sources, but keep in mind that even primary sources were created by humans and thus could have mistakes.

We also need to make one further distinction: original versus derivative records. Genealogists access many primary documents through derivative sources—i.e., sources that are created from other sources. A primary source like a census record that is viewed online or on microfilm is technically a derivative of the original, but one that seeks to recreate the original exactly. In this case, the distinction isn't worth worrying about. Likewise, secondary sources like databases, indexes, abstracts, or transcriptions are derivative (or interpreted) works based on primary sources. Marriage, birth, and death records (as well as obituaries and wills) are often indexed, abstracted, or transcribed.

So what does all that mean? Transcripts copy an original record as faithfully as possible, while an abstract pulls out information pertinent to genealogical research. An index identifies the subject and points to the original source. A database, designed for rapid

Timeline Report for Daniel McDonald

Yr/Age	Event	Date/Place/Description
1804	Birth (Sister) Elizabeth McDonald	May 1804 Coignafinternach, Moy & Dalarossie, Invernesshire, Scotland
1808	Birth (Sister) Mary E. McDonald	1808 Columbiana, Ohio, USA; calculated date
1810	Birth	25 Dec 1810
1813 2	Birth (Sister) Nancy McDonald	31 Oct 1813 Ohio, USA; calculated date
1830 19	Marriage (Sister) Elizabeth McDonald	03 May 1830 Columbiana, Ohio, USA
1852 41	Death (Father) Angus McDonald	15 May 1852 Columbiana, Ohio, USA
1854 43	Death (Mother) Elizabeth Smith	21 Aug 1854 Columbiana, Ohio, USA
1855 44	Emigration	1855 Richland, Wisconsin, USA; had visited in 1852, his aunt & sister were already in Richland County
1868 57	Death (Sister) Mary E. McDonald	03 Aug 1868
1880 69	Residence	1880 Rockbridge, Richland, Wisconsin, USA; also 1870
1890 79	Death (Sister) Elizabeth McDonald	21 Sep 1890 Marshall, Richland, Wisconsin, USA
1894 83	Death	24 Dec 1894 Marshall, Richland, Wisconsin, USA
1896 85	Probate	1896 Richland, Wisconsin, USA
	Burial	Fancy Creek Cemetery, Marshall, Richland County, Wisconsin

Timelines list the major events of your ancestor's life and help you identify gaps and inconsistencies in your research.

record retrieval, is similar to an index but includes much more information about the individual found in the record. Searching online databases at Ancestry.com or FamilySearch.org usually yields the information contained in the database and a link to the original document, allowing you to compare the two.

Create a Timeline

Timelines (image) are useful tools for organizing your genealogical research and tracking your ancestor's major life events. You can use these visualizations to sort out people with the same name, make sure individuals don't appear two places at once, identify gaps or patterns in an ancestor's life, and determine which historic events she might have experienced firsthand.

Create Source Citation Information for David Hood

Enter the specifics that can help to verify a fact/event for David Hood

1. Source - Where does this information or evidence come from?

Select a source ▾

or create a new source

Easily add sources from Ancestry.com

When you search our **4 billion historical records** online and find a source for **David Hood**, the source information for records you attach to this person will automatically be added.

Search for records now

2. Citation - What are the specifics of the information or evidence provided by this source?

Detail (required)

Enter the title, or the film number, volume, etc.

Date

Enter the publication date of the document or material.

Transcription of text

Transcribe or cut-and-paste exact wording from the source.

Other information

Enter any other pertinent information related to this citation.

Web Address

If the source was found on the Internet, enter the URL here.

What is a Source Citation?

A Citation is a reference to specific information, or evidence about a fact or event in your tree. It should help other researchers retrace your steps to find the same information you found.

Learn more

3. Facts or Events - What fact(s) or event(s) is this source citation related to?

Marriage: 13 Mar 1841 in Kilmaurs,Ayr,Scotland

Name: David Hood

Gender: Male

Ancestry.com and other online family tree services allow you to add citations for documents that you upload to your tree.

At its simplest, a timeline can be a table with columns for the event, date, location, age, source, and comments. Or you can create your table in a spreadsheet, word processing document, or template available online **<www.cyndislist.com/timelines/templates>**. You can also take advantage of features on genealogy websites like Ancestry.com that have a built-in timeline.

Cite Your Sources

A careful researcher always cites her sources, for several good reasons. For starters, citing sources helps you remember where you found data on an ancestor. Having this data can be useful if you later find conflicting evidence and want to revisit a source. And if you share your genealogical research with others, citing your sources will give people confidence in your conclusions. With your citations, they can check your work and look at the same sources.

If you're building your family tree and adding records to it on online services such as Ancestry.com or FamilySearch.org, you'll automatically have one form of source citations in your research. And if you're uploading offline sources to your tree, you can create your own citations within these sites (image **D**). Genealogical software programs like Family Tree Maker and RootsMagic also incorporate citation tools, giving you even more options for documenting your sources.

If you're considering writing a family history or other historical work, stand-alone citation software like EasyBib <www.easybib.com> or EndNote <endnote.com> can help you cite a wide variety of sources in different formats. For more on how to cite your sources, check out the Genealogy Source Citation Cheat Sheet <www.familytreemagazine. com/store/genealogy-source-citation-cheat-sheet>, which will help you create consistent, thorough citations for all your genealogy resources.

Maintain a Research Log

Worried about repeating your research? Not sure where to pick up your research after taking a break? Create a research log: a list of where you looked for records, why you looked there, and what you found. This will hopefully keep you from looking for the same information at the same book or online records collection several times.

Like timelines, your research log can be simple. You can create your own table, photocopy one from a book, or download a template from a resource like *Family Tree Magazine* <www.familytreemagazine.com/freeforms/researchforms> or the FamilySearch Wiki <www.familysearch.org/wiki/en/Research_Logs>.

Networks, or Six Degrees of Great-Grandpa

Most genealogists want to trace their direct ancestors back as far as possible, so they spend most of their time researching these individuals. And while that's a noble goal, you'll limit yourself by looking only at records of these direct-line ancestors. For example, you would normally make the connection between your father and great-grandfather through your grandfather (your father's father). But if your grandfather left no clues, about his ancestry, you might have to turn to his network to find information about him.

At their root, all networks are about communication. In the real world, networks can help you land a new job or find a great restaurant. In the genealogical world, a document for a family member, neighbor, or associate, may provide information about your direct ancestor. All the people who knew your grandfather—his siblings, other relatives, neighbors, or even his grocer—might have left behind some information about him and his ancestors. Perhaps one of his father's siblings left a clue about their shared parents in an obituary or death certificate, or a newspaper article about a neighbor's wedding mentions that your grandfather's family attended the ceremony or reception. Genealogist Elizabeth Shown Mills named this network the "F.A.N." (family, associates, and neighbors) Club, and F.A.N. research can prove invaluable to your ancestry search.

Network research is especially useful for finding the origins of your immigrant ancestors, as many immigrants (including Scots) tended to settle near friends, family, and people from the same parish or locality. Traditionally, community bonds in Scottish communities were long lasting and frequently maintained even after arriving in America. A neighbor in America may also have been a neighbor in Scotland, and perhaps they even witnessed the baptisms of each other's children in either country. Finding a group of people together in America and Scotland will give you confidence that you have found the right people.

KEYS TO SUCCESS

- Start by writing down everything you know about your ancestry, beginning with you. This step is important because the act of writing known information down will help you learn and remember details, plus identify what you still need to learn.

- Expand your knowledge base by searching for home sources and interviewing living relatives. You never know what "low-hanging fruit" you'll find within your family tree.

- Build your family tree by including all known information and augmenting it with records available online. Digital trees, whether online or with genealogy software, are designed to organize genealogical information, create charts, spot mistakes, and figure out relationships.

- Set realistic research goals, which will keep you motivated and on track. You can start by asking yourself concrete research questions.

- Take the time to develop your research skills by mastering the genealogical principles highlighted in this chapter. Read books, take classes, and speak with experienced genealogists to learn more.

3

Identifying Your Immigrant Ancestor

N ow that you've read chapter 2, you should have a strong foundation for your genealogical research. After consulting home sources and interviewing relatives, you should now be ready to broaden the scope of your research to include other important US resources. While you may be itching to research your family in Scotland, you still need to identify your immigrant ancestor. Specifically, you'll need to find his name, vital events dates, and place of birth by learning as much as possible about his life in America. See the Starting Your Search for an Immigrant Ancestor flowchart for a broad outline of how to do this.

In this chapter, we'll discuss how you can use US sources to discover your Scottish immigrant ancestors. With this data, you can finally trace your family line back to Scotland and begin doing research there.

WHAT YOU'LL NEED

Before you jump on the boat back to Scotland, be sure to pick up these three key pieces of information about your ancestor.

Name

Names are crucial to genealogy, but the most important one in your Scottish research is your ancestor's full name, as it would appear in his country of origin. Next, you'll also need to learn the names of your ancestor's family and other relatives, friends, and neighbors. Ideally, you want to be able to create a family group for each Scottish immigrant, as families are easier to find than individuals. Friends and neighbors in America may have lived on the same farm or served as godparents to your ancestor's children, and these connections will help you trace the correct family across the Atlantic.

Dates

Specifically, you'll want to learn the date on which your ancestor arrived in the United States. Knowing this will help set up guidelines for your research: Records of your ancestor before this date will be in Scotland, and records after will be in the United States. Birth and death dates will also help provide a framework for your research.

In addition to adding useful "signposts" for your research, dates will also allow you to identify your ancestor amongst those with similar names. For example, if you know your ancestor Alastair Bowie (born in Scotland in 1825) was in America in 1845, you know that an Alastair Bowie living in Scotland in 1851 probably isn't your ancestor.

Note that, while about 30 percent of immigrants to America at some point returned to their country of origin, a relatively low percentage of Scots (roughly 13 percent) became "birds of passage" that traveled back and forth between Scotland and North America.

Place of Origin

Your ancestor's specific place of origin in Scotland is probably the most important piece of information to obtain. Unfortunately, it may also be the hardest to find. There are several place names that you might find associated with your ancestor: the country (Scotland), a county (Invernesshire), a parish (Kirkhill), a farm (Knockbain), an estate (Lovat), or an address (19 High Street). You'll want to find the most specific of these locales (the farm and the address), as country will have limited usefulness. Scottish records are organized by county, then by parish.

A few quick notes about Scottish places: Within rural parishes, people lived on named farms or in small villages. They rarely owned these farms outright, but rented them from a landlord. Each farm usually included multiple tenants. In larger villages, towns, and cities, an individual's residence may be indicated by house number and street name, or simply by the street name. We'll discuss Scottish geography in more detail in chapter 5.

FINDING YOUR IMMIGRANT ANCESTOR IN US RECORDS

You'll look for your immigrant ancestor's name, dates, and place of origin in US documents, not Scottish documents. These US records—the same ones used by most genealogists—contain all kinds of useful information about your ancestor, bringing his life in the United States into focus. Keep in mind you are looking for not only your ancestor's place of origin, but also the origin of the other Scots he knew since they may have come from the same place.

We'll discuss the most useful records for finding information about your immigrant ancestors in the following sections. You can see a more thorough list of US genealogy resources in a free records checklist from *Family Tree Magazine* <**www. familytreemagazine.com/cheatsheet/recordreferences**>.

Census Records

Few US genealogy records are more valuable than census records. Federal censuses have been taken once a decade by the US government since 1790, making them one of the most consistent record sets. You can use US census records to trace your whole family backward in time, as censuses place your ancestors (and their friends and neighbors) in specific places at specific times. Note: Most of the 1890 federal census was destroyed in a fire and flood, so you'll need to look to other records for information about your ancestors in that year.

The information collected in these documents differs from one census to the next. Censuses taken between 1790 and 1840 only listed the head of household by name, merely tallying information on other household members. The 1820 and 1830 censuses each tallied the number of "foreigners not naturalized" in a household, your first clue that someone in the household was not a naturalized US citizen and therefore of foreign birth. Census records become more useful for tracing your immigrant ancestor in 1850, when census returns questioned place of birth and age (from which you can approximate a birth year). Likewise, all people were asked if their parents were of foreign birth (columns

RESEARCH TIP

Watch for Ireland Immigrants

Keep in mind that a person born in Scotland to *Irish* parents is probably the child of Irish immigrants to Scotland, not of native Scots. Many Irish immigrated to Scotland before coming to the United States, particularly in the nineteenth century when Ireland was ravaged by famine.

Starting Your Search for an Immigrant Ancestor

Once you have identified your immigrant ancestor, you will be eager to dive into records in his homeland. But before you get your ancestor to his Scottish origins, you'll need to take some intermediate steps. You may not need all eight listed here (for example, you may already know your ancestor's place of origin and date of arrival), but these steps can provide a useful guideline.

Confirm the date of your ancestor's arrival in America.

This is crucial, because all records relating to your ancestor before the date of arrival will be in Scotland, and all records afterward will be in the United States.

Confirm your ancestor's name and place of origin.

This chapter focuses on how to find these two crucial pieces of information, along with the date of immigration. In most cases, your ancestor will have the same name in America as he did in Scotland. But be sure that he did not use a nickname in US records. Also be aware of Scots and Gaelic versions of names—see chapter 6 for more on this. Try to identify as specifically as possible your ancestor's place of origin—a street address or farm name is best.

Utilize US-based online resources.

Conglomerate sites like Ancestry.com **<www.ancestry.com>** and FamilySearch.org **<www.familysearch.org>** will provide you with many basics about your ancestor and his life in the United States. Take time learning how to use these sites!

Visit (or write) archives or historical societies.

Not everything is available online, and the crucial clue you might need for locating your ancestor's place of origin may be in an archive or historical society near where he settled in America. If you cannot visit in person, write and ask if an archive's staff can help you find the information you need.

Learn about your ancestor's parish of origin.

Learning about your ancestor's parish of origin will enable you to determine which records exist and which administrative boundaries will impact your search. Chapters 4 and 5 cover Scottish history and geography (including administrative boundaries). Histories may shed light on the conditions in that parish that caused your ancestor to leave. If you are able to determine the name of your ancestor's farm, you might be able to learn which estate that farm was on, then track down those estate records.

Jump into Scottish records online.

You can access the two best Scottish records websites, FamilySearch.org and Scot-landsPeople **<www.scotlandspeople.gov.uk>**, without even leaving home. Take advantage of these resources first. Local genealogy groups also have websites that sell transcriptions of local records, particularly monumental inscription (grave marker) lists of local cemeteries.

Network with other Scottish researchers.

Join a mailing list, make your online family tree available to the public, and connect with genealogists who are researching the same families or have ancestors from the same parish. Due to the commonality of many Scottish surnames, you might want a living male relative to take a Y-DNA test to determine the correct branch of the family. DNA may be the only way to connect your ancestors to their Scottish origins if they came to America by way of Ulster in Ireland.

Visit Scottish archives or hire a local researcher.

If you are unable to find your ancestor in Scottish records online, you may need to visit Scotland to look in records that are not available online. You might also consider hiring someone to do so for you, if you're unable or unwilling to travel.

11 and 12) in 1870, and the 1880 census added a question about each parent's birthplace. The 1900 through 1930 censuses each asked the year a person immigrated. Gaelic was included as a possible foreign language spoken by people enumerated in the 1920 and 1930 censuses. Use these questions (particularly those about immigration and place of birth) to help identify your immigrant ancestor.

You can also use census records in combination with other resources. For example, cross-reference your ancestor's address in census records with contemporary city maps and directories to learn more about the neighborhoods she lived in. You can also use addresses to find tax and land records, or you can use immigration and naturalization information to find passenger lists or naturalization records.

Many US states administered their own censuses in addition to the decennial federal censuses. Use state censuses to fill in the gaps between census years, or to supplement missing information. Check out the United States Census Bureau's list of known state censuses <www.census.gov/history/www/genealogy/other_resources/state_censuses.html>.

Headstones

Headstones can be great sources of genealogical information because of the names and dates inscribed upon them. Depending on your ancestor's circumstances, a headstone may represent the only record your ancestor left behind. In fact, the only record of some women's existence is the names and dates inscribed on a tombstone shared with their husbands. In addition, headstone placement can indicate levels of closeness in life. Proximity in cemeteries, like in census records, counts, as people buried near each other tend

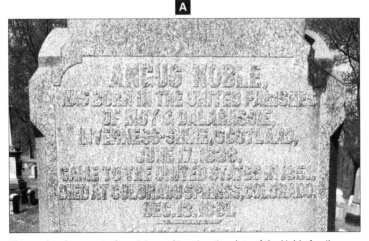

A

This marker documents the origins and immigration date of the Noble family, found in Yellow Creek Presbyterian Church Cemetery, Columbiana County, Ohio.

to be connected either through bonds of blood or friendship. In addition, grave markers for Scots occasionally mention their Scottish origins (image **A**).

Many cemetery inscriptions can be found online. Two of the largest sources of cemetery information are Find A Grave **<www.findagrave.com>** and BillionGraves **<www.billiongraves.com>**. Many genealogical societies have transcribed markers in their local cemeteries and have published them in either book form or online. However, much of this information has been transcribed, and it's always best to see the original marker for yourself. If the site has no image available, you may need to visit the cemetery or see if some kind soul from a local genealogy society would be willing to check for you.

For more on finding and using cemetery records (including tombstones), check out *The Family Tree Cemetery Field Guide* by Joy Neighbors (Family Tree Books, 2017) **<www.familytreemagazine.com/store/family-tree-cemetery-field-guide-r5530>**.

Societies and Fraternal Organizations

The first Scottish association was founded in Boston in 1657. This society, like many other similar groups (such as St. Andrew's Societies, Burns Clubs, Caledonian Societies, and Scottish American societies), provided aid to distressed Scottish immigrants. They also hosted events like Burns Night suppers, which we learned about in chapter 1. These societies limited membership to men, although women frequently formed auxiliary groups for ladies.

These groups' records (if they still exist) may provide useful information about your ancestors, though what information varies by organization and time period. You can find a list of organizations online **<www.rampantscotland.com/features/societies.htm>**, and you'll likely want to contact a group directly about its records. Groups that are no longer in existence may have deposited their records with a local archive. For example, the records of the St. Andrew's Society of Cleveland were deposited at the Western Reserve Historical Society when the society closed in 1962.

Probate Records

Records relating to probate (including minutes of probate courts, will books, and estate files) can be varied and amazing. Though not all estates were probated (and not all records survive), these records can be excellent resources for the family historian. Estate files alone can contain original records like wills, bonds, receipts, inventories, and guardianships, and they can include: property owned; names of wives; and names of children, grandchildren, and other relatives. Witnesses to wills were probably close friends or family members, and therefore part of your ancestor's network. Some estate records may

The last will and testament of Angus McBean of Baltimore names his hometown and his sisters who still resided in Scotland.

mention the Scottish origins of the decedent or (more commonly) named heirs who live in Scotland (image B).

Transcribing and indexing wills was a common project for genealogical societies, and you may be able to search these published volumes in a library. You can also view original estate papers online at either FamilySearch.org <www.familysearch.org> or Ancestry.com <www.ancestry.com>. The collection at Ancestry.com is based upon the images from FamilySearch.org (which, in turn, come from microfilm), but the Ancestry.com collection is indexed and thus easier to use. Note that these collections don't include all probate records, and these collections rarely extend past the 1910s. If you do not find what you need in either of these collections, check with the county courthouse to see if it has additional records.

Newspapers

Newspapers can also be excellent sources for information about your ancestors. You may find obituaries and stories about wedding anniversaries, birthdays, family reunions, and profiles of early pioneers. Obituaries, though rare for all but the wealthy for most of the nineteenth century, become much more common in the late nineteenth and early twen-

RESEARCH TIP

Study Scottish History

Read any history you can find that relates to the area your Scottish ancestor lived in. While no one-volume work can detail all Scottish immigration to the United States, various books cover individual states and communities. Try searching a library catalog for the subjects "Scots—United States" or "Scotland—Emigration and immigration." We also discuss the broad strokes of Scottish history in chapter 4.

tieth centuries. Any or all of these types of articles can provide information about your ancestor's origins and network. Be sure to search for obituaries for all of your ancestor's siblings, as one of them might mention a specific place of origin. Presbyterian magazines and newspapers are particularly worth examining for those with Scottish ancestry. For example, the *Presbyterian Banner* **<chroniclingamerica.loc.gov/lccn/sn88086163>**, published in Pittsburgh from 1860 until 1898, reported deaths and marriages.

Research in newspapers has become an easier enterprise with the advent of digitization and searchable databases. Three main sources for online newspaper collections are GenealogyBank **<www.genealogybank.com>**, Newspapers.com **<www.newspapers.com>**, and NewspaperArchive **<newspaperarchive.com>**. The Library of Congress' Chronicling America program **<chroniclingamerica.loc.gov/newspapers>** also has an impressive collection of free digitized newspapers from around the United States.

Before subscribing to a website, check to see what newspapers it holds for your ancestor's place of residence, as that will determine which will be most useful to you. Also check your local library or genealogical society, as smaller databases might hold newspapers more specific to your area of interest. For example, the Cleveland Public Library provides access to issues of Cleveland's daily newspaper *The Plain Dealer* back to the paper's inception in 1842.

For more on how newspapers can aid your genealogical research, read *The Family Tree Historical Newspapers Guide* by James M. Beidler (Family Tree Books, 2018) **<www.familytreemagazine.com/store/historical-newspapers-guide>**. Inside, you'll learn all about the kinds of records in newspapers (including obituaries, news articles, and marriage announcements), plus how to use and navigate sites like Newspapers.com and GenealogyBank.

Naturalization Records

For most of US history, immigrants took at least five years to become a naturalized citizen. After residing in the United States for a minimum of two years, an immigrant could file

This naturalization document for David Pride in Allegheny, Pennsylvania, in 1802, lists his place of origin as simply "Scotland."

D

UNITED STATES OF AMERICA

ORIG. 150534
BG

No. 150534

PETITION FOR CITIZENSHIP

To the Honorable the US District *Court of* Eastern District of NY *at* Brooklyn, NY

The petition of James Graham , hereby filed, respectfully shows:

(1) My place of residence is 549 - 49th St., Brooklyn, NY (2) My occupation is mechanical engineer

(3) I was born in Glasgow Scotland on September 2, 1897 My race is Scotch

(4) I declared my intention to become a citizen of the United States on September 16, 1925 in the US District

Court of Eastern District at Brooklyn, NY

(5) I am married. The name of my wife is Sarah

we were married on April 8, 1927 at Brooklyn, NY ; she was

born at Glasgow Scotland on November 9, 1902 ; entered the United States

at New York, NY on October 31, 1926 for permanent residence therein, and now

resides at 549 - 49th St., Brooklyn, NY I have 2 children, and the name, date,

and place of birth, and place of residence of each of said children are as follows: William John, Born Dec. 11, 1927; James, Oct.

31, 1929. Both born in Brooklyn, NY and reside at 549 - 49th St., Brooklyn, NY.

(6) My last foreign residence was Glasgow Scotland I emigrated to the United States of

America from Glasgow Scotland My lawful entry for permanent residence in the United States

was at New York, NY , under the name of James Graham

on November 1, 1923 , on the vessel Columbia

as shown by the certificate of my arrival attached hereto.

(7) I am not a disbeliever in or opposed to organized government or a member of or affiliated with any organization or body of persons teaching disbelief in or opposed to organized government. I am not a polygamist nor a believer in the practice of polygamy. I am attached to the principles of the Constitution of the United States and well disposed to the good order and happiness of the United States. It is my intention to become a citizen of the United States and to renounce absolutely and forever all allegiance and fidelity to any foreign prince, potentate, state, or sovereignty, and particularly to

George V, by the Grace of God, of Great Britain,

of whom (which) at this time I am a subject (or citizen). British Dominions beyond the Seas am able to speak the English language.

(9) I have resided continuously in the United States of America for the term of five years at least immediately preceding the date of this petition, to wit, since November King 1923 Defender of and in the County of Kings

this State, continuously next preceding the date of this petition, since October 1, 1925 , being a residence within said county of at least six months next preceding the date of this petition.

(10) I have not heretofore made petition for citizenship: Number on

at and such petition was denied by that Court for the following reasons and causes, to wit:

and the cause of such denial has since been cured or removed.

Attached hereto and made a part of this, my petition for citizenship, are my declaration of intention to become a citizen of the United States, certificate from the Department of Labor of my said arrival, and the affidavits of the two verifying witnesses required by law.

Wherefore, I, your petitioner, pray that I may be admitted a citizen of the United States of America, and that my name be changed to

I, your aforesaid petitioner being duly sworn, depose and say that I have read this petition and know the contents thereof; that the same is true of my own knowledge except as to matters herein stated to be alleged upon information and belief, and that as to those matters I believe it to be true; and that this petition is signed by me with my full, true name.

James Graham
(Complete and true signature of petitioner)

AFFIDAVITS OF WITNESSES

William Graham , occupation supervising foreman

residing at 263 - 60th St., Brooklyn, NY , and

Robert Fraser , occupation millwright

residing at 1242 - 73rd St., Brooklyn, NY

each being severally, duly, and respectively sworn, deposes and says that he is a citizen of the United States of America; that he has personally known and has been acquainted in the United States with

James Graham , the petitioner above mentioned, since October 1, 1925

and that to his personal knowledge the petitioner has resided in the United States continuously preceding the date of filing this petition, of which this affidavit is a part, to wit, since the date last mentioned, and at Brooklyn , in the County of Kings

this State, in which the above-entitled petition is made, continuously since October 1, 1925 , and that he has personal knowledge that the petitioner is and during all such periods has been a person of good moral character, attached to the principles of the Constitution of the United States, and well disposed to the good order and happiness of the United States, and that in his opinion the petitioner is in every way qualified to be admitted a citizen of the United States.

William Graham
(Signature of witness)

Robert Fraser
(Signature of witness)

Subscribed and sworn to before me by the above-named petitioner and witnesses in the office of the Clerk of said Court at Brooklyn, NY

this 3 day of November , Anno Domini 19 30. I hereby certify that certificate of arrival No. 2-90813

from the Department of Labor, showing the lawful entry for permanent residence of the petitioner above named, together with declaration of intention No.

99070 of such petitioner, has been by me filed with, attached to, and made a part of this petition on this date.

By _____ Clerk. (SEAL)

Deputy Clerk.

Naturalization documents from later years include more detail. Here, the naturalization petition for James Graham (filed in the Eastern District Court of New York in 1930) lists his birthplace as Glasgow.

his Declaration of Intent to become a citizen. And after a further three years, he could swear his allegiance to the United States and renounce allegiance to his former country of residence in a Petition for Naturalization (image C). Before 1906, these actions could take place in any court of record, and each could take place in a different court. After 1906, copies of all records were forwarded to the Immigration and Naturalization Service. These valuable documents can provide you with critical information about your ancestor's immigration and early years in the United States.

Many (but not all) naturalization records are available online either as indexes or databases, with images at FamilySearch.org and Ancestry.com. You may have to check with individual state archives, which hold naturalization paperwork for local courts. The National Archives holds records from federal courts <**www.archives.gov/research/naturalization**>.

As we discussed earlier, census records can indicate if and when your immigrant ancestor naturalized. In 1870, men over the age of twenty-one were asked if they were US citizens (column 19), while the 1900 through 1940 censuses ask the citizenship status of the foreign-born.

Early citizenship papers are not very informative, as they do not list a place of birth, just the country of former allegiance. Later records (particularly those after 1906) are increasingly detailed and may include the date and place of birth of the applicant, his wife, and children, as well as the date of arrival in the United States and the ship upon which they traveled (image D).

Passport Applications

Americans, native and naturalized, needed passports to travel abroad. Consequently, any Scot who had naturalized and wished to return to Scotland would need to apply for a passport. Records of these applications usually include place of birth and date of naturalization, and you can find these in the "U.S. Passport Applications, 1795–1925" collection on Ancestry.com and FamilySearch.org. The amount of data included in these records is similar to naturalization records, and the more recent the record the more data will be included (image E).

Passenger Lists

After the passage of the Manifest of Immigrants Act, US officials began regularly creating passenger lists on January 1, 1820. As part of the Act, captains had to submit passenger lists that included a list of all the names of the immigrants on board. These records have obvious utility for those researching immigrant ancestors, though (until the early twentieth century) Scottish immigrants' place of origin is usually just listed as "Scotland," rather

Charles and Christina Cowie submitted this passport application in 1922, giving researchers like me a variety of useful information.

than a specific county. Over time, these lists began to include more information, including an address and name of a relative in the country of origin and the destination in the United States (image **F**).

You can find passenger lists at Ancestry.com and The Statue of Liberty—Ellis Island Foundation, Inc. <www.libertyellisfoundation.org/passenger>. Note that, while the majority of immigrants came to the United States through New York City's Ellis Island (or its predecessor, Castle Garden <www.castlegarden.org>), others may have come through dif-

LIST OR MANIFEST OF ALIEN PASSENGERS FOR THE UNITED

List 25 A.L.SM..

S.S. "COLUMBIA", Passengers sailing from GLASGOW, 20th NOVEMBER, 1922.

The Scots who sailed aboard the *S.S. Columbia* from Glasgow to New York in 1922 had a variety of final destinations in the United States.

ferent port cities. If you're having trouble finding your ancestors in New York passenger lists, also look for passenger lists from Boston, Baltimore, Charleston, and other prominent East Coast cities.

Military Records

Military draft records from the First and Second World Wars may provide information about your male immigrant ancestor of fighting age. These forms required that the indi-

Archibald Hood, my grandfather's eldest brother, not only provided his birth date, but also the name of the small Ayrshire town in which he was born. He also indicated that he had declared his intention to become a US citizen.

vidual list his place of birth. Some men simply listed their country of origin, but others listed the village they were born in (image **G**).

Surviving draft records are available at FamilySearch.org and Ancestry.com. Other military records (particularly pension records) may also include information about place of origin and family members.

Published Sources

If you're lucky, you may find that information about your Scottish immigrant ancestor has already been published in one form or another. For example, *British Aliens in the United States during the War of 1812*, compiled by Kenneth Scott (Genealogical Publishing Company, 1979), is a transcription of the US Marshal's Returns of Enemy Aliens and Prisoners of War, 1812–1815 which is housed at the National Archives (Microfilm R588 rolls 2 and 3). These records document British nationals who complied with the US requirement to register with local authorities at the outbreak of the War of 1812. Different information was collected in different states, but the records generally include the name of the male head of household, how long he had been in the United States, and the names of other members of the household. (These records have also been published on Ancestry.com and its affiliate, Archives.com **<www.archives.com>**.)

Other published sources that list immigrants include the works of David Dobson, plus the *Dictionary of Scottish Emigrants to the U.S.A.* volumes 1 (1973) and 2 (1986), published by the Genealogical Publishing Company and edited by Donald Whyte. Whyte and Dobson abstracted records in United States and United Kingdom to identify Scots in the American Colonies and the United States. Their use of UK records, not readily available to US-based researchers, is especially informative. However, these resources can sometimes give only a name and a date, making it hard to connect ancestors mentioned here to others. You can find books by both men in various libraries, and some of Dobson's have been digitized by Ancestry.com.

STILL CAN'T GET THE DATA YOU NEED?

If you've looked at all of these sources, you will have hopefully found the three pieces of data required to take your search to Scotland. If you are exceptionally lucky, you have also identified your ancestor's specific place of residence—either a farm name or a street address—and have been able to re-create his entire family and identify several members of his network.

But what if you didn't? What can you do now? Since so many Scottish records have been indexed and are searchable online, it is possible to just start looking. First look in places where people in his network came from, then expand your search to neighboring parishes, then to churches separate from the Church of Scotland. It will be slow going, but you may be successful making it worth all the effort in the end.

KEYS TO SUCCESS

- Thoroughly search a wide variety of US sources for information about your ancestor and his network—specifically, your ancestor's name, date of immigration, and place of origin. You never know where you might find a clue.

- Be sure to search a variety of spellings for your ancestor's surname. *Mc, Mac,* and *M'* often have to be searched for separately in databases. Also keep in mind how a surname was pronounced, which may have little bearing on how it was spelled. We'll discuss Scottish names more in chapter 6.

- Keep working on the rest of your family tree, as you may uncover Scottish American ancestors you didn't know about. The more Scottish ancestors you find, the more likely you will be able to find a specific Scottish origin for one of them.

ANCESTOR WORKSHEET

Full Name (maiden name for women): _____

Nicknames and Alternate Names: _____

Surname Spelling Variations: _____

Religion/Church(es) Attended: _____

Birth and Baptism

Birth Date: _____ Birth Place: _____

Baptism Date: _____ Baptism Place: _____

Marriage(s)

Name of Spouse(s)	Marriage Date(s)	Marriage Place(s)

Death

Death Date: _____ Death Place: _____

Burial Date: _____ Burial Church/Place: _____

Obituary Date(s) and Newspaper(s):

Migration

From	To	Departure/Arrival Dates	Companion(s)	Ship (if applicable)

Children

Child's Name	Birth Date	Birthplace	Other Parent

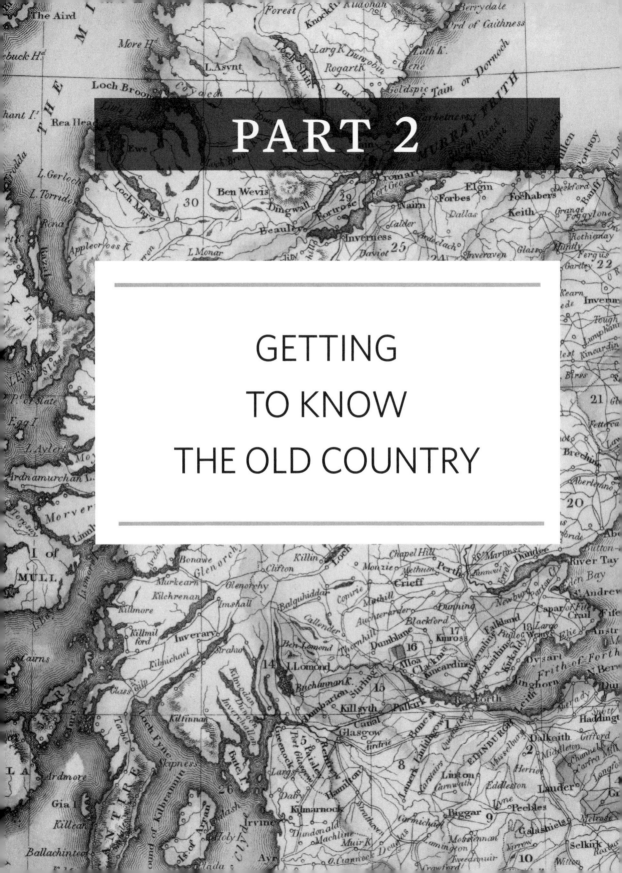

PART 2

GETTING
TO KNOW
THE OLD COUNTRY

4

Understanding Scottish History

Scotland has a long, ancient history, and no one book could cover the whole scope of Scottish history. But learning the basics of the history of Scotland will help you understand your ancestors' time and place. And by putting your ancestors' actions into historical context, you can better imagine their experiences and take a step back in time. This brief introduction to Scottish history discusses how Scotland was created, how it came to join in a political union with England, and some reasons why Scots chose to leave their homeland.

EARLY SCOTLAND

The people of Scotland first entered the historical record when the Romans arrived in Great Britain in the first century. By the end of their conquest, the Romans controlled much of Lowland Scotland between Hadrian's Wall (begun in 122 A.D.) and the Antonine Wall (begun in 142 A.D.; image **A**). The Romans referred to the region as Caledonia and called its native inhabitants "Picts," a Latinate term first used in 297 A.D. to refer to these "painted (or tattooed) people." This seems to have been an umbrella term for the several tribes native to northern Britain whom the Romans saw as uncivilized. (By contrast, Romans referred to natives who adopted their culture as "Britons.")

TIMELINE Scottish History

122 Romans begin building Hadrian's Wall, which eventually forms the boundary between Roman Britain and native-ruled lands.

c.300-500 The Scotti, Gaelic-speakers from Ireland, settle in Scotland.

c.397 Saint Ninian, the first bishop of Galloway, establishes a church at Whithorn. The region becomes Christianized in the centuries that follow.

795 Viking raids in Scotland begin.

843 Kenneth MacAlpine, a Scotti, takes the Pictland throne.

1297 As part of the Wars of Scottish Independence, William Wallace and Scots defeat the English at the Battle of Stirling Bridge.

1306 Robert the Bruce is crowned king of Scots.

1320 Scots assert their independence in the Declaration of Arbroath.

1482 Scotland's modern boundaries are solidified.

1547 In the "Rough Wooing," Henry VIII of England invades Scotland when Mary, Queen of Scots is promised in marriage to the future king of France.

1569 Scotland becomes a Protestant nation under the leadership of John Knox.

1603 King James VI of Scotland is crowned King James I of England, uniting the two crowns under one monarch.

1609 The Statutes of Iona attempt to contain aspects of Highland culture; James VI and I establishes the Ulster Plantation in Northern Ireland.

1639-1651 In the Wars of the Three Kingdoms, the British Isles are thrown into chaos as parliament and the monarchy wrestle for power.

1690s Scotland suffers a massive famine, in which 20 percent of the population dies.

1698 Scots attempt to establish a colony at Darien in Panama.

1707 In the Treaty of Union, Scotland and England merge to become the new nation-state of Great Britain. This new government has just one parliament, based in London.

1759 Robert Burns, the Scottish National Poet, is born.

1769 Scot James Watt patents the steam engine.

1771 Sir Walter Scott, author, is born.

1776 Scottish philosopher and economist Adam Smith publishes *The Wealth of Nations*.

1801 Great Britain and Ireland unify to become the United Kingdom.

1843 In the Great Disruption, about one-third of Church of Scotland ministers leave the church to form the Free Church of Scotland.

1886 The Crofters Act ends predatory practices by Highland landlords, helping to stymie the Highland Clearances.

1920s Economies collapse following the First World War.

1926 Scottish engineer John Logie Baird broadcasts the first television signal.

1999 The Scottish Parliament opens.

2014 A referendum on Scottish independence fails to pass a popular vote. Two years later, the United Kingdom passes a resolution to leave the European Union over significant objection from Scots and Northern Irish.

The Romans controlled Scotland, or Caledonia as they called it, for several decades.

After decades of conflict with these native tribes in Scotland, the Romans fell back from the Antonine Wall in 160, establishing Hadrian's Wall as the Roman Empire's northern border. However, campaigns against the people north of Hadrian's Wall continued until the fourth century.

Altogether, Roman occupation of southern Scotland only lasted about forty-five years in total. However, Roman presence had a profound impact on early Scottish culture. In the areas they occupied, the Romans imposed taxes, altered land ownership, and conscripted men into the Roman Army. They transformed the landscape by constructing forts, watchtowers, roads, and bridges. Most critically, the Romans introduced a new language and new foods, drinks, and dress.

Unlike the peoples of southern Britain, those north of Hadrian's Wall never fully assimilated to Roman culture. Additionally, civilian settlement near a Roman fort did not last after the Romans left, though Christianity was adopted in parts of Scotland before the arrival of St. Ninian.

In unoccupied areas, the presence of the Romans likely contributed to tribal groups uniting into larger kingdoms so that they could better defend their territory, creating an early sense of Scottish nationalism. Drawing on earlier sources, the geography Ptolemy named twelve tribes in northern Scotland in the middle of second century CE. By the end of the second century, two tribes populated the area, and by the fourth century, only one remained: the Picts. There was less transformation in southern Scotland, where Ptolemy identified four tribes before Roman occupation and four tribes remained after the Romans departed (although only three had recognizable pre-Roman origins).

SCOTLAND IN THE MIDDLE AGES

By the early Middle Ages, four cultural groups lived in Scotland:

- the Strathclyde Britons, who spoke a language related to modern Welsh, in the southwest
- the Northumbrians, a kingdom of Germanic Anglo-Saxons who spoke a dialect of English, in the southeast
- the Picts, who spoke a Celtic language, in the northeast (image **B**)
- the Scotti, a Gaelic-speaking people who began to move into western Scotland from northern Ireland in the fourth century, in Argyllshire and the western isles.

Two other invading cultures were added to the mix in the centuries that followed: Vikings who began to raid Scotland in the late eighth century, and the Normans who came north after the Norman Conquest of England in 1066. Scotland was largely Christianized by the time the Vikings arrived, as the noted English scholar the Venerable Bede wrote that all the peoples of the island shared a fifth language, Latin.

B

This stone, known as Aberlemno I, is decorated with elements common in Pictish art.

William Wallace, who led the Scots to victory against the English in the Wars of Scottish Independence, has become a Scottish cultural hero. This statue of him in Aberdeen was erected in 1888.

More forces worked to unite the northern lands of Britain. In 843, a Scotti named Kenneth MacAlpin became king of Pictland. Though the transition of power wasn't noteworthy at the time, this event is now seen as a major turning point in Scotland's national identity. Indeed, the term "Scotland" was first used to describe the region under the reign of Kenneth MacAlpin's grandson. The Scotti expanded their power base outside of western Scotland, bringing with them the Gaelic language and subsuming the other cultural groups. By the eleventh century, the Picts had been fully engulfed by the Scots, and Pictish was apparently no longer spoken.

Throughout its history, the Scots have been at odds with their southern neighbors. This conflict came to a head during the Wars of Scottish Independence in the late 1200s and early 1300s. The English had defeated the Scottish at the Battle of Dunbar in 1296, and Edward I of England began to demand taxes and military service from his new Scottish subjects. This situation displeased most Scots, who rebelled against the new government. The struggle lasted many decades and involved famous figures such as William Wallace (image C), famously depicted in the film *Braveheart*. But the Scots were ultimately successful after substantial victories on the battlefield at Stirling Bridge in 1297 and Bannockburn in 1314. The wars ended with warrior Robert the Bruce, a Scottish king,

"Such a Parce of Rogues in a Nation" by Robert Burns

Fareweel to a' our Scottish fame,
Fareweel our ancient glory;
Fareweel ev'n to the Scottish name,
Sae fam'd in martial story.
Now Sark rins over Solway sands,
An' Tweed rins to the ocean,
To mark where England's province
    stands—
Such a parcel of rogues in a nation!

What force or guile could not sub-
    due,
Thro' many warlike ages,
Is wrought now by a coward few,
For hireling traitor's wages.
The English stell we could disdain,
Secure in valour's station;
But English gold has been our bane—
Such a parcel of rogues in a nation!

O would, or I had seen the day
That Treason thus could sell us,
My auld grey head had lien in clay,
Wi' Bruce and loyal Wallace!
But pith and power, till my last hour,
I'll mak this declaration;
We're bought and sold for English
    gold—
Such a parcel of rogues in a nation!

securely on the throne. The Scots asserted their rights in the Declaration of Arbroath, sent to the pope in 1320:

> ...for, as long as but a hundred of us remain alive, never will we on any conditions be brought under English rule. It is in truth not for glory, nor riches, nor honors that we are fighting, but for freedom—for that alone, which no honest man gives up but with life itself.

Through conquest and consolidation, the Kingdom of Scotland expanded over the next two centuries, reaching its modern boundaries in the late fifteenth century. In 1472, Orkney and Shetland became part of Scotland, previously having been under Norwegian and Danish control. And after changing hands dozens of times between Scotland and England, the border city of Berwick, was captured by the English for the final time in 1482.

UNION WITH ENGLAND

While the boundaries of the nation have not changed since 1482, the political and cultural situation in Scotland changed significantly in the seventeenth and early eighteenth centuries. In 1603, Elizabeth I of England died. Her nearest heir was King James VI of Scotland, and he became James I of England upon Elizabeth's death. He and his court moved south to London, and from that point the King of Scots rarely visited his northern kingdom. James (known as "James VI and I") and his descendants ruled over two separate nations that had two separate governments, often with opposing goals. As England was wealthier and more powerful, the monarch usually sided with the English parliament over the Scottish one.

The seventeenth century, the height of the little ice age, was a difficult time marked by extreme cold, hunger, and social unrest. In the British Isles, these problems were made worse by a political crisis in England when the English parliament executed Charles I (the son and heir of James VI and I) in January 1649. The decade and a half of warfare that followed is known as the Wars of the Three Kingdoms, or the English Civil Wars. The monarchy was restored in 1660, when Charles I's son, Charles II, was crowned. His heir and brother, James II of England (James VII of Scotland), had converted to Catholicism. Enraged that a Catholic ruler was now on the (Protestant) English throne, Parliament deposed James II in 1688 in the Glorious Revolution. The crowns of England and Scotland were then offered to James II's Protestant daughter Mary and her husband, William of Orange (who, himself, was a grandson of Charles I). After William's death in 1702, Mary's sister Anne took the crown.

If all this political instability wasn't enough, Scotland suffered severe famine in the 1690s, during which at least 20 percent of the population died. Further failures followed in 1698, when the Scottish attempt to settle a colony at Darien in Panama failed. Scots (many of whom invested their lifesavings in the project) lost nearly £230,000 in the failed Darien scheme. By 1700, Scotland was in a difficult position. Its population was decimated, it was financially weakened, and its king often acted against the country's best interests.

The English parliament decided to seek a formal union with Scotland. The English were concerned that the Scots might form an alliance with France or with James II's descendants, who lived in exile in Europe. Many Scots were opposed to this suggestion of union. Scots and the English mainly disagreed over whether the union would be federal (e.g., two parliaments, one each for Scotland and England) or incorporating (e.g., one parliament, with representation from all of Great Britain). Scots generally preferred the former, but were given the latter. The Treaty of Union was signed during the reign of Queen Anne, and on May 1, 1707, the independent nation-states of England and Scotland ceased to exist. They merged to form the new nation-state of the Kingdom of Great Britain, led by Queen Anne and her successors. Despite the union of the two parliaments, Scotland maintained its own church and legal system.

Despite the many benefits of Union, many Scots still smarted over the loss of their political independence. These feelings remained, simmering beneath the surface for much of the nineteenth century. The poem "Such a Parcel of Rogues in a Nation," written by the Scottish poet Robert Burns in 1791, encapsulates these feelings. (See the sidebar for the full text of the poem.)

Several decades later, Scotland finally began to reap the benefits of Union. The nation-within-a-state could at long last trade legally with the American Colonies, and Scots took advantage of the opportunities afforded by the growing British Empire. Many joined the British military or became British administrators. The Scottish city of Glasgow dominated the tobacco trade and by the Victorian era was known as the "Second City of Empire."

Popular imagery of Scotland during the nineteenth century highlights kilted Highlanders and beautiful glens, but the reality was probably pretty grim. In the two hundred years between 1700 and 1900, Scotland went from being one of the least urbanized nations on the planet to one of the most urbanized. People from both the Highlands and Lowlands left rural farms (either voluntarily or due to evictions) and moved to the cities where they sought work in the developing industries, exploding urban population. For example, Glasgow had a population of about 77,000 in 1801, and that grew to 762,000 in 1901. The rapid population growth in Glasgow (and all cities in Great Britain) brought overcrowding, poor sanitary conditions, unsafe drinking water, and epidemic disease. Housing conditions for the lower classes were atrocious, with one-third of all families in Glasgow lived in a single-room apartment or structure.

The nature of employment changed for many people. Mechanized mills and factories usurped homemade industries like weaving and spinning. Hand-loom weavers saw their income dwindle and frequently emigrated. Those who came from the countryside to work in the new mills, like the ones in New Lanark, worked long hours in tightly regulated environments.

Men educated in Scotland's universities—future doctors, lawyers, and other professionals—frequently had to leave the country to find suitable employment, much of which was administering the British Empire. Some returned home upon retirement, but many others remained abroad.

Highly successful steel and shipbuilding industries employed a great many people. Prior to the First World War, the shipyards located along the River Clyde produced more ships than Germany and the United States combined, and Scottish mills produced 20 percent of British steel. Both of these industries were reliant on the export market, and part of their success was built on paying workers low wages. Additionally, layoffs came swiftly if there were no orders for ships or steel. The collapse in these industries after the First War led to massive unemployment in Scotland. The decade that followed saw a massive outpouring of emigrants from Scotland who sought their living abroad.

Regions of Scotland

To understand the history and culture of Scotland, you'll need to understand the broad geographical and cultural regions that define it. We'll discuss Scotland's geography in depth in chapter 5, but for now let's examine the two best-known Scottish cultural regions: the Highlands and Lowlands. Though primarily cultural distinctions, the Highlands and the Lowlands are separated by the geographical Highland Boundary Fault.

The Highlands

The Highlands (also known as the Gàidhealtachd) refer to the mountainous northern and western regions of Scotland. Here, Gaelic remained the primary language amongst the people long after the language faded in the Lowlands. Given the Highlands' terrain and climate, farmland was not very productive, and the entire area was less attractive to industrial development. Still, the Highlands were the more populous of the two regions until the nineteenth century.

Scotland has two major geographic and cultural divisions: the Highlands and the Lowlands.

Rents were minimal and often paid in-kind, but clan chiefs also expected military service in return. When landlords decided to rent their lands for financial, not military, gain they raised the rents and dislocated many tenants.

The Highlands were also notable for their clans. Powerful families lived throughout Scotland, but blood kinship (whether real or imagined) took on heightened importance in the Highlands. *Clan* comes from the Gaelic word *clann*, meaning children. And in the Highlands, the clan chief was recognized as being related to (and, therefore, responsible for and loyal to) all of his "clansmen," or people who lived on his estate. The chief's tenants (or tacksmen) paid their chief in either money or military service in exchange for land and security, even if they weren't actually related to the chief by blood (even if they all shared the same name—see chapter 6 for more).

The Lowlands

The Lowlands refer to the southern and eastern regions of Scotland, which (in general) have less extreme changes in elevation. As Gaelic retreated from the Lowlands, the use of Scots and English became more common. Farmland in most of the Lowlands was far superior to that in the Highlands, so agricultural output was better. And since the Lowlands were closer to the major cities of Glasgow and Edinburgh, they attracted migrants during the Industrial Revolution. Indeed, the "Central Belt," the "waist" of Scotland running between Glasgow and Edinburgh, became highly industrialized beginning in the late eighteenth century, leading to job creation and an influx of Highlander migrants.

MODERN SCOTLAND

While the Empire did give the English and Scots an outlet for a shared identity, the two countries (while more similar to each other than they were to, say, France or Russia) still remained distinct and were aware of their differences. The two countries had distinctive religions, education, and legal systems. Scotland was also poorer than England, and since the right to vote depended on property qualifications, many fewer men in Scotland could vote than in England. This was the case until universal male suffrage was enacted in 1918. Not only was Scotland poorer, its people were paid less and many basic commodities such as bread cost more.

Scotland's share of representation returned to the British Parliament was quite a small share of the total number of Members of Parliament. This meant that Scottish calls for reforms of government and society were stymied by a primarily conservative English parliament in the late nineteenth century. People began to call for home rule for Scotland, inspired by a similar movement in Ireland. This movement gained ground and had a positive hearing in Parliament—until the First World War.

Participation in the two world wars helped bind the two nations together. However, the collapse of the Empire and changing politics and economics at home began to change views. For many decades after the Second World War, Scots were not taught Scottish history or literature, and Britain and England were used as synonyms and in textbooks and other media.

Economic hardships worsened the relationship between Scotland and England. Scotland had record unemployment between 1979 and 1981, and Prime Minister Margaret Thatcher began shutting down coal mines in the mid-1980s. The situation impacted those in northern England as much as it did those in Scotland, but Scotland's remedy (a more socialist agenda) was largely rejected south of the border. Scots began to believe that they were being treated differently, and were subject to a Tory (conservative) government they did not vote for. Calls for home rule or devolution began to ring louder. At the same time there was a renaissance in Scottish literature and Scottish history, leading many to reassess Scotland's role in Great Britain, past and present. Parliament held two devolution votes in the 1900s, the second of which resulted in the creation of a Scottish Parliament in 1999.

Scotland's future remains an open question. In 2014, Scotland held a referendum on independence, in which (after a tensely debated campaign) a majority of Scots voted to remain in the Union. But two years later, UK voters passed "Brexit," a referendum removing the United Kingdom from the European Union. Though the referendum passed, a majority of Scots (along with a majority of the Northern Irish) voted to remain in the

Scottish History Resources

You can learn about Scottish history through an assortment of media. Here is a sampling:

Books

- *A Century of the Scottish People: 1830–1950* by T.C. Smout (Yale University Press, 1990)
- *A History of Scotland* by Neil Oliver (Phoenix, 2011)
- *A History of the Scottish People 1560–1830* by T.C. Smout (Harper Collins 1987)
- *In Search of Scotland* edited by Gordon Menzies (Polygon at Edinburgh, 2001)
- *Modern Scotland: 1914–2000* by Richard Finlay (Profile Books, 2004)
- *The Oxford Handbook of Modern Scottish History* by T.M. Devine and Jenny Wormald (Oxford University Press, 2014)
- *Scotland Since 1688: Struggle for a Nation* by Edward J. Cowan and Richard Finlay with William Paul (Cima Books, 2000)
- *Scotland: A Concise Cultural History* edited by Paul H. Scott (Mainstream Publishing, 1993)
- *Scotland: A History* edited by Jenny Wormald (Oxford University Press, 2005)
- *Scotland: A Very Short Introduction* by Rab Houston (Oxford University Press, 2008)
- *Scottish History for Dummies* by William Knox (For Dummies, 2014)
- *The Scottish Nation: A History, 1700–2000* by T.M. Devine (Viking, 1999)

Websites and Video Series

- *A History of Scotland: The Complete 10-Part Series*, presented by Neil Oliver (BBC Home Entertainment, 2010)
- History Scotland **<www.historyscotland.com>**
- Scotland's History **<www.bbc.co.uk/scotland/history>**

European Union. Some have speculated over whether this difference will lead to another Scottish independence referendum, though (at time of publication) there's been no indication that this will be the case.

EMIGRATION

There has probably never been a time when Scotland was not a nation of emigrants. For centuries, Scots journeyed south to England or east to places like Scandinavia and Poland-Lithuania (where Scots peddlers were a common sight). The Protestant Reformation brought close ties with the Netherlands, where Scots Kirks (churches) were founded both in Rotterdam and Amsterdam. Countless Scots served as mercenaries in European

D

Abandoned farmsteads, like this nineteenth-century one in Ross-shire, are a common sight across the Gàidhealtachd thanks to the Highland Clearances.

armies during the religious wars of the seventeenth century. And beginning in 1611, Scots movement turned west—first to Ulster, then to North America. As the British Empire expanded geographically across the globe in the late eighteenth century, so too did settlement options for Scots.

The reasons Scots emigrated were as varied as their destinations. One common need for emigration was limited economic opportunity at home. The Scottish economy hummed along during the American and European wars from 1775 to 1815, and men were able to find work or were drafted into the military. However, with peace came an economic downturn, along with harvest failures in 1816. This led to an increase in emigration from Scotland. Industrial changes also prompted migration, particularly the switch from hand-loom weaving to water-power weaving. This change led to thousands of men losing their livelihood. The mechanization of farm labor led to depopulation of many Lowland parishes. These individuals migrated to industrial centers and many others emigrated.

Some of most dramatic causes for emigration were in the Highlands. Scottish landlords, many of them magnates who spent more time in London or Edinburgh than on their estates, held immense power over their lands, and their tenants had few (if any) rights. Leases were often held at-will, renewed just one year at a time. Landlords began to raise rents or convert in-kind payments to cash payments. Tenants, however, had little or no incentive to increase the productivity of their land, as they were not compensated for these improvements. And if their income improved, their rents would probably be increased. A positive movement to counteract this problem was successful, and many yearly rentals were converted to long leases, usually nineteen years, with provisions for compensation for improvements.

In other cases, landlords consolidated farms and rearranged their estates to make them more economically efficient. This led to what is known as the Highland Clearances, the process by which the Highland estates were cleared of their population. Although the process began in the early eighteenth century, it picked up steam in the 1790s as the price of wool increased. To capitalize on this commodity, landlords began to evict tenants, consolidate their farms, and rent them to single sheep farmers who could afford to pay a vastly inflated rent. Even without the value of the wool, renting to one tenant was more efficient than dozens. A landlord's decisions could impact a few families, an entire parish, or an entire island depending upon the size of their estates.

The traditional way of life in the Highland was fundamentally altered by the Highland Clearances, as people were moved about like pieces on a chessboard. Many ultimately chose to emigrate or move south to the Central Belt or to England, leaving abandoned farms all over Scotland (image **D**). Gaelic-speaking Highlanders faced discrimination nearly everywhere they went, making their lives even more difficult.

Scots agitation, activism, and inspiration from those facing similar situations in Ireland led to the Crofters Act in 1886, which provided security of tenure for tenants, fair rents, and the right to bequeath their tenancies to their children. You can learn more about this whole process in *The Highland Clearances* by Eric Richards (Birlinn Ltd., 2016).

Although an improved Scottish economy usually kept people at home, better financial circumstances often increased emigration. In the 1830s, when agricultural goods commanded high prices, many Scots could afford to leave the country and seek better land and opportunity elsewhere (for example, in the United States, which became an industrial powerhouse at the end of the nineteenth century). As discussed in chapter 3, Scots had the education and skills to command higher wages and better positions than other immigrant groups in America. The cost of living in the United States was higher, but the increased wages more than compensated for it.

Note that those who emigrated were not the poorest, as the truly destitute could not afford to emigrate. Those who wanted to settle in the United States had to pay their own passage, while Scots hoping to emigrate to regions within the British Empire could take advantage of aid programs. Traveling fees could be quite substantial, as government policy enacted in the early nineteenth century made ports in the United States more expensive to reach than those within the British Empire.

As Scots made connections around the world, their networks grew strong, giving them opportunities to learn and live in the world outside even the British Empire's borders. Though many had to leave their homeland to survive, others had enough family and friends outside of Scotland that a move was warranted simply to be near kin.

KEYS TO SUCCESS

(💮) Take the time to learn about the history of Scotland, as it will provide the framework for your ancestor's life. Pay special attention to events that affected emigration, such as famines and the Highland Clearances.

(💮) Study well-researched historical references You can find several one-volume histories that are aimed at the non-specialist, and this chapter has named several.

(💮) Learn about the everyday lives of ordinary Scots, in addition to the wider political and economic trends that affected the country. Historical societies and detailed histories can help.

5

Understanding Scottish Geography

I n order to successfully locate your ancestors in Scottish records, you need to know their parish of origin and their network of associates. But why were Scottish parishes important, and what other administrative units do you need to know? By studying Scottish geography, you'll learn what sort of records might be available—and where you can find them.

In this chapter, we'll dive into Scottish geography and the various administrative units in Scotland: what they are, how they were used, and why they're important to your research. We'll also show you how to use Scottish atlases and gazetteers in your research.

SCOTLAND'S GEOGRAPHY

Scotland is located on the northern part of the island of Great Britain, which also includes the nations of England and Wales (though all three are part of the United Kingdom—see the Making Sense of the United Kingdom sidebar). Scotland itself is split in half by the Highland Boundary Fault (or Highland Fault Line), which runs from Helensburgh near Glasgow to Stonehaven near Aberdeen.

This fault line represents an actual geologic shift in the landscape, and (as we discussed in chapter 4) became a cultural divide in the fourteenth century. The Highland/Lowland

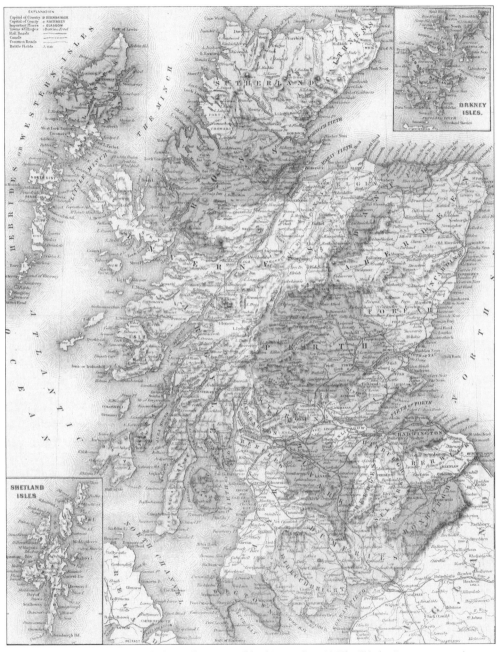

A

Understanding Scotland's geography by studying maps (like this one, from 1865) will help give your research context.

Narrow valleys surrounded by high peaks are common in Scotland.

distinction affects Scottish history and emigration patterns, and can also help you manage your research expectations. For example, parish records in the Highlands were not as regularly kept as they were in the Lowlands.

The craggy coast of Scotland is indented by sea inlets bound by narrow strips of land (image **A**). On the east coast and in the southwest, these are generally known as firths (which has the same origins as the word fjord), such as the Firth of Forth and the Solway Firth. In the western Highlands, similar bodies of water are known as sea lochs, such as Loch Alsh and Loch Linnhe. Nearly eight hundred islands surround Scotland, clustered into four primary groups: Shetland, Orkney, and the Inner and Outer Hebrides.

Inland, Scotland has a great many rivers and lochs (lakes), for example the River Clyde. These bodies of water helped shape Scottish history and trade. The River Tay, for example, was a key component of Glasgow's dominance in the tobacco trade in the eighteenth century and the shipping industry in the nineteenth and twentieth centuries. Others serve as popular tourist destinations. Loch Ness may not have monsters and Loch Lomond may not be bonnie, but both are known to tourists around the world.

The Highlands have more extreme changes in elevation than the Lowlands. Ben Nevis (in the Highlands) is the highest peak in Scotland, and there are so many valleys in the Highlands (image **B**) that they have been divided into two types. Straths are broad and usually created by rivers, while glens are deep and narrow.

Strathnairn (along the River Nairn) and Strathdearn (along the River Findhorn) are located south of Inverness. Glencoe, Glen Lyon, and Glen Nevis (which is popular for film shoots, such as the *Harry Potter* series) have been noted as among the most beautiful in Scotland. The Great Glen (Glen More), home to Loch Ness, is actually a seventy-nine-mile fault boundary that splits Scotland in two. However, straths and glens also exist in the Lowlands with notable examples including Strathclyde and Glen Trool (which is in Dumfries and Galloway).

Making Sense of the United Kingdom

Those of us "across the pond" in the United States can sometimes make the mistake of using "England," "Great Britain," and "United Kingdom" interchangeably. In reality, these three terms have separate meanings, and learning the differences between them can help you better understand your Scottish ancestry:

- **England**: An independent country that's existed since the Middle Ages
- **Great Britain**: The isle upon which modern England, Scotland, and Wales sit; a political union between England (including Wales) and Scotland that began in 1707 and continues today
- **United Kingdom**: A nation-state comprising England, Scotland, Wales, and part of Ireland (all of Ireland from 1801 to 1922, and just Northern Ireland from 1922 to present).

Similarly, the **British Isles** refers to an archipelago in the North Atlantic that contains Ireland, Great Britain, and more than one thousand smaller islands.

To study Scotland's geography, we first have to unpack the difference between "England," "Great Britain," and the "United Kingdom." The United Kingdom refers to Great Britain and Northern Ireland.

UNDERSTANDING ADMINISTRATIVE UNITS

As we discussed in chapter 3, the parish is the most important administrative unit for researching your Scottish ancestors. However, knowing the other administrative divisions in Scotland (and where your ancestors' parish fits within them) will help be helpful to your search. Let's take a look at each in turn.

Counties or Shires

If you've done any Irish or English research, you'll know how important counties are to family history research in the British Isles. The same is true about Scottish counties, which have been around for centuries. Twenty-four of Scotland's thirty-four historical counties were established by 1305, and an additional ten were created over the next three hundred years. The newest Scottish county, Sutherland, was created in 1633 when it split from the county of Inverness. Note that the counties of Orkney and Shetland were treated as a single unit in most records.

Throughout history, several counties had noncontiguous enclaves that existed within other counties, complicating jurisdiction. The government cleared this up in 1890, when some county boundaries and names were altered and enclaves were eliminated. That same year, the four largest cities (Aberdeen, Edinburgh, Glasgow, and Dundee) became counties in their own right, complete with their own local governments whose borders matched the county boundaries. Counties weren't changed again until 1975, when local governments were reorganized into fifty-three district councils and nine regions. This unpopular arrangement was changed in 1996, when the government created thirty-two council areas. (Note: You'll likely only need to know post-1975 government districts if you're researching recent records.)

Most counties are named after the primary town or city, and Scots sometimes include the suffix -*shire* to refer to counties. In fact, counties can be identified in three ways. For

RESEARCH TIP

Set Your Boundaries

Since the earliest surviving Scottish wills and parish records are from 1513 and 1538, respectively, most family historians will only need to be familiar with the present borders of Scotland. Fortunately, these boundaries were finalized in 1482, meaning you won't need to keep track of border changes over time, as you often have to do when researching other countries.

Scotland has thirty-four historical counties, and these are their names as they appeared before 1890. Note that some counties came to be known by different names over time, such as Edinburghshire (now Midlothian), Elginshire (now Moray), and Forfarshire (now Angus).

example, some maps indicate Aberdeenshire (the county containing the city of Aberdeen) as *Aberdeen Shire* or *the County of Aberdeen*, but never *the County of Aberdeenshire*. County names that end in a double *S* either drop an *S* when the suffix *-shire* is added or hyphenate the name (e.g., *Invernesshire* or *Inverness-shire*). Often, the word *county* or suffix *-shire* is left off entirely, especially when the county town has a different name from the county.

See the Historical Counties of Scotland sidebar for a list of counties as they appeared before changes were made in 1890, and image **C** for a map of county boundaries before 1974. Geni.com maintains a page that covers the historic counties of Scotland, providing details such as the county flower and the names of the parishes **<www.geni.com/projects/Counties-of-Scotland-United-Kingdom/14402>**.

Burghs

Burghs, roughly the equivalent of a town or city, held a charter that gave them trading privileges and certain powers of local government. King David I (who reigned from 1123 to 1153) created the first burghs to promote national trade. There were several types of burghs: royal burghs, burghs of regality, burghs of barony, parliamentary burghs, and police burghs. The primary difference between each was how it was formed and how extensive its local powers were, and large burghs could contain multiple parishes.

Royal burghs received their charter directly from the Crown and were usually located at seaports (as they held a monopoly on international trade) or river fords. Peebles, Montrose, Lanark, and Berwick were among the earliest established, and the ancient settlements of Perth and Edinburgh were raised to the status of royal burgh at this time. By the time of the Union in 1707, Scotland had seventy royal burghs.

The Crown granted charters for burghs of barony and burghs of regality to secular and ecclesiastical landowners. Burghs of barony were created mostly to facilitate economic activity, and many of them did not have an administrative structure. In contrast, burghs of regality had rights almost equal to those of the royal burghs, and they were ruled by powerful lords of regality. Between 1450 and 1707, more than three hundred of these two types of burghs were chartered.

Two later administrative distinctions, parliamentary and police burghs, were created in the nineteenth century as part of a program to reform local government. All royal burghs were converted into parliamentary burghs, and they had an elected council and could send a representative to parliament. Meanwhile, a police burgh status permitted populous places to have a police force as well as a commission to oversee maintenance of roads and street lighting and cleaning.

Historical Counties of Scotland

Counties Before 1890	County Seat	Notes
Aberdeenshire	Aberdeen	
Argyllshire	Inveraray (historical) Lochgilphead (administrative, 1890–presentt)	Also known as Argyll, Argyle, Earra-Ghàidheal. Includes the islands of Islay, Jura, and Mull.
Ayrshire	Ayr	
Banffshire	Banff	
Berwickshire	Berwick-upon-Tweed (historical) Greenlaw (1596–1890) Duns (1890–present)	
Bute	Rothesay	Also known as Buteshire. Includes the Isle of Arran.
Caithness	Wick	Also known as Gallaibh.
Clackmannanshire	Clackmannan (historical) Alloa (present)	
Cromartyshire	Cromarty	Merged with Ross-shire in 1890.
Dumfriesshire	Dumfries	
Dunbartonshire	Dumbarton	
Edinburghshire	Edinburgh	Known as Midlothian after 1890.
Elginshire	Elgin	Also known as Morayshire, Moire-abh, Elgin, and Forres. Known as Moray after 1890.
Fife	Cupar	Also known as Fifeshire, Fiobha, Kingdom of Fife.
Forfarshire	Forfar	Known as Angus after 1928.
Haddingtonshire	Haddington	Known as East Lothian after 1890.
Inverness-shire	Inverness	Includes the islands of North Uist, South Uist, Skye, and part of Lewis.

Counties Before 1890	County Seat	Notes
Kincardineshire	Kincardine (historical) Stonehaven (administrative)	Also known as the Mearns, A' Mhaoirne.
Kinross-shire	Kinross	
Kirkcudbrightshire	Kirkcudbright	Also known as the Stewartry.
Lanarkshire	Lanark (historical) Hamilton (administrative)	
Linlithgowshire	Linlithgow	Known as West Lothian after 1890.
Nairnshire	Nairn	
Orkney	Kirkwall	Also known as Arcaibh, Orkneyjar.
Peeblesshire	Peebles	Also known as Tweeddale.
Perthshire	Perth	
Renfrewshire	Renfrew (historical) Paisley (administrative, 1890–present)	
Ross-shire	Dingwall	Includes part of the Isle of Lewis. Merged with Cromarty in 1890.
Roxburghshire	Roxburgh (historical) Jedburgh (historical) Newtown St. Boswells (administrative, 1890–present)	Also known as Teviotdale.
Selkirkshire	Selkirk	Also known as Ettrick Forest.
Shetland	Lerwick	Also known as Zetland, Sealltainn, or Hjaltland.
Stirlingshire	Stirling	
Sutherland	Dornoch (historical) Golspie (administrative, 1890–present)	
Wigtownshire	Wigtown (historical) Stranraer (administrative, 1890–present)	Also known as the Shire.

The status of burghs could change. For example, the bishop of Glasgow was temporarily granted a burgh of barony so that it could host a market each Thursday. More permanently, Glasgow was "promoted" to a burgh of regality in 1450, then in 1611 to royal burgh. A few burghs, such as Roxburgh, disappeared over time, while others never developed into more than a small village. A few were absorbed into other burghs, such as the burgh of Canongate, which was purchased by Edinburgh in 1636.

In the late nineteenth century, the four largest burghs (Aberdeen, Edinburgh, Dundee, and Glasgow) became known as burgh-counties and were called cities for the purposes of local government. All the burghs (except for the aforementioned four cities) were classified large burghs or small burghs in 1929, and this administrative change affected record-keeping. Prior to 1929, some burghs produced their own valuation rolls, while other burghs were included with the county rolls. Beginning in 1930, only cities and large burghs produced their own valuation rolls, all others were included with their county.

Parishes

Parishes are a crucial component of Scottish genealogy because so many records are organized by parish. Though many in the United States will associate the term with a religious institution and duties, Scotland's parishes actually had both religious and civic responsibilities. As the population grew, many of these responsibilities were devolved to civic bodies. In the sections that follow, we'll discuss the changing responsibilities of parishes.

At the time of the Protestant Reformation in the late sixteenth century, Scotland was divided into nine hundred parishes. Known as *quoad omnia* parishes (from the Latin "for all purposes"), they were used for sacred purposes and secular purposes. Sacred purposes included collecting *teinds* (tithes) to maintain the church fabric, burial grounds, and the minister. Secular purposes included taxation, road building, education, and poor relief.

The men responsible for the ecclesiastical and civic duties of the parish were the kirk session, a group of elders working under the direction of the commissioners of supply or town council (depending upon whether it was a rural or urban parish). The people responsible for coming up with much of the funding for these endeavors were the heritors (the parish landowners). Some parishes had only one heritor, while others had upwards of a dozen. Heritors were responsible, by law, for maintaining the church, paying the minister's stipend and providing him with a manse and a glebe (agricultural land), the school and schoolmaster's stipend, poor relief, and other public works.

Over time, many parishes combined, particularly in 1618. A single minister and kirk session usually served these combined parishes, but the parish might have continued to maintain multiple church buildings and cemeteries. As a result, your records might be found in the archives of either the single parish or the combined parish. For example,

Moy Parish merged with nearby Dalarossie Parish, as did Croy Parish with Dalcross Parish. After the merger, Moy and Dalarossie had one set of church records, but Croy and Dalcross kept separate records for each portion of the parish. These records will have been microfilmed together and may be labelled as separate items by FamilySearch.org. In cases like these (in which multiple churches were part of one parish), most people attended the church that was physically closer to them. So, if you know where your ancestor lived, check to see which church was nearby.

Many parish boundaries were tweaked again in the late nineteenth and early twentieth centuries, but knowing your ancestors' historical parish boundaries should be sufficient.

As the population of Scotland grew, especially in the Central Belt, it became clear that additional parishes were required. At the same time, the duties of the church and state began to diverge, and the state took responsibility for poor relief and education. The Church faced difficulties in creating full-fledged parishes due to the number of stakeholders who had to give their permission.

Instead, the Church of Scotland found a solution by establishing *quoad scara* parishes that were for "sacred purposes" only. These new *quoad scara* parishes would have a minister and a kirk session.

The government created civil parishes and parochial boards to administer poor relief in 1845. Initially, these civil parishes, known as *quoad civilia*, had the same boundaries as ecclesiastical parishes. With time and population growth, the boundaries of some civil parishes were changed. Education and recording of vital statistics also became civil and not ecclesiastical responsibilities. The administrative functions of civil parishes were abolished in 1930, although they are still used for census purposes. There are currently 871 civil parishes in Scotland.

The National Records of Scotland houses all ecclesiastical records pertaining to the Church of Scotland that are available to researchers (including dissenting churches that reunited with it). Civil records pertaining to poor relief and education are kept in various repositories throughout Scotland.

PARISHES FOR OTHER DENOMINATIONS

As you might expect, religious traditions other than the Church of Scotland didn't use the Church of Scotland's parish boundaries. Instead, parishes of other faiths (including the Catholic Church, the Society of Friends, the Episcopal Church, and the Free Church) were defined by where the congregation lived, not by any geographical boundary. If you have ancestors who were members of these other faiths, you're probably better off searching for these records by county, as that should include all parishes associated with a particular non-Church-of-Scotland church.

Standardizing Gaelic Place Names

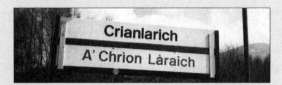

Today, place names in Scotland are listed in both English and Gaelic, as is the case on this railway sign in Crianlarich.

For most of Scotland's history, about half the population spoke Gaelic. As a result, many Scottish place names have Gaelic origins. However, most recordkeepers (many of whom were English) didn't speak Gaelic, leading to inconsistencies in place name spelling, particularly when rendering Gaelic words in English. In Gaelic, the final G in a word is a bit like the English K, so those letters were occasionally interchanged. Likewise, the Gaelic combination cn is pronounced like the English cr, which can cause confusion.

Recordkeepers occasionally wrote farm names in English as opposed to Gaelic. Thus, Corrybroughbegg can be Little Corrybrough, and Balnagordonach can be Gordonstown. In other cases, long farm names were written in Gaelic but abbreviated in records. For example, Tynrich, the modern name for a farm in Daviot and Dunlichity, is a shortened form of the original place name, Taigh na Fraoich.

You don't need to learn Gaelic to read parish registers from the Scottish Highlands, but knowing how letters are pronounced and what the general building blocks of typical farm names mean can be invaluable. We'll discuss the Gaelic language in more detail in chapter 6, but here are a few Gaelic terms that frequently appear in place names, plus their English translations.

Gaelic (as commonly rendered)	Actual Gaelic	Meaning
Beg, Begg	Beag	Small, Little
Ben, Bin	Beinn	Mountain
Dhu, Du	Dubh	Dark
Dun	Dùn	Fort
Mor, More	Mòr	Big
Ty	Taigh	House

You can read detailed meanings and components of places names in Scotland online. Two free resources are Etymology of British Place-names **<www.pbenyon.plus.com/Misc/Etymology.html>** (which takes its data from a gazetteer published in 1900) and Scots Words and Place-names **<swap.nesc.gla.ac.uk/database>** (which is compiled by a professor of Scottish languages and maintained by the Scottish Language Dictionaries and the University of Glasgow). Ainmean-Àite na h-Alba **<www.ainmean-aite.scot>** also maintains a searchable database of Gaelic place names.

Registration Districts

Scotland, like the rest of the modern United Kingdom, had a robust civil registration system, beginning in the 1850s. As part of the program, the government recorded the births, marriages, and deaths of all of its inhabitants. (See chapter 7 for more information on civil registration records.)

To facilitate civil registration, Scotland was divided into 1,027 registration districts in 1855. Most of these districts were based on existing civil parishes, but some parishes and burghs were combined (or divided) for registration purposes. The government created additional districts as the population increased. Each registration district was given a number, and you can find a list at the National Records of Scotland <www.nrscotland.gov.uk/files//research/statutory-registers/registration-district-guide.pdf>.

Estates

Most Scots rented land from a landlord. Some of these landlords owned modest estates, like the McBeans of Tomatin whose estate in Moy and Dalarossie parish included just a handful of farms. At the other extreme, the Dukes of Sutherland owned an estate that, by the mid-nineteenth century, totaled 1.1 million acres and included most of the county of Sutherland. Most estates were somewhere in between, and these can be valuable divisions when looking for records of your ancestors.

The estate owner's fortunes and policies often had a great impact on the tenants and their quality of life. Evictions, estate sales, and farm consolidations could cause your ancestor to be relocated on the same estate, move to a neighboring estate or parish, or emigrate from Scotland.

Many tenants were mentioned in the estate papers of their landlord (known as muniments). Some estate papers have been deposited in public archives, while others are private and maintained by the families. Tenants may have also been listed in Rentals (also called rent rolls), which were yearly lists of tenants that included the name of the person, the name of the farm, and the amount of rent. Check out the guide created by the National Records of Scotland to discover what is available <www.nrscotland.gov.uk/research/guides/estate-records>.

Farms

The smallest rural division of land was the farm or settlement, called a *baile* in Gaelic or a *toun* in Scots. Many farms were joint tenancies, and these tenants often left smaller plots to the poor of the parish. Families often intermarried and otherwise interacted with other families who lived on the same farm.

Statistical Accounts of Scotland

The Statistical Accounts of Scotland <edina.ac.uk/stat-acc-scot> are a great contemporary resource for learning about an ancestor's parish of origin. The first Statistical Account was created by Sir John Sinclair of Ulbster, who sent out questionnaires to every parish minister in Scotland. The ministers were then badgered into completing the forms, and Sinclair's volumes were published between 1791 and 1799. A second series was compiled between 1834 and 1845. These reports, which vary in depth and detail, offer a snapshot of Scotland during their respective time periods and offer insight into a variety of topics, including housing, agriculture, religion, and local customs. An individual can subscribe to the Statistical Accounts for fifteen pounds for two months <stataccscot.edina.ac.uk/static/statacc/dist/support/subscription>, which provides access to more search features and additional materials. However, as you probably already know which parish or parishes you are interested in, simply browsing the scanned images for free is a good option.

Since most farms don't exist today, look for your ancestors' farms on nineteenth-century Ordnance Survey (OS) maps. At ScotlandsPlaces <scotlandsplaces.gov.uk/digital-volumes/ordnance-survey-name-books>, you can view the original OS Name books. These include notes gathered in the field, usually by OS employees who consulted local historians and authorities (often the minister or schoolmaster) in order to fix the spelling of every "object" in the vicinity. (To the OS, the word *object* had a broad meaning and included natural features and man-made structures.)

USING MAPS AND GAZETTEERS

Maps can be very helpful for researching your ancestor. If you can pinpoint your ancestor's farm or street address, you will be able to see where he lived in relation to the church, the market, and neighbors.

Ordnance Survey Maps

OS maps, in particular, contain useful information, including farm names, allowing you to see your ancestor's farm as it was when the surveyors first came to Scotland in the 1850s. If you know where the members of his network lived, you should find those on maps as well.

The surveys (image **D**) generally recorded every feature (whether natural or manmade) they encountered in the landscape, including farms, antiquities, forests, roads of all shapes and sizes, hedgerows, and letter boxes (mailboxes).

This OS map of Kilmarnock, created in 1860, shows a lot of detail about the town and its surrounding areas.

Civil parish, burgh, and county boundaries are clearly marked. In the mid-nineteenth century, most civil parish boundaries were the same as those of the ecclesiastical parish.

Modern OS maps are made for, among other things, outdoor enthusiasts. These topographic maps can tell you much about the modern landscape, but it is best to use historical OS maps for family history research because the depopulation of rural Scotland led to many farms being abandoned. As such, many communities no longer appear on modern maps. By viewing historical maps, you will be able to answer questions like how far your ancestors were from the nearest church or village.

The first edition of these maps in Scotland began in 1843 and was completed in 1882, and a second survey of (with a scale of one inch to one mile) was done at the turn of the twentieth century. Learn more about the history of the OS in Scotland here **<maps.nls. uk/os/6inch/os_info1.html>**. Modern OS maps use a national grid reference system, and these are consistent across all map series **<www.ordnancesurvey.co.uk/resources/maps-and-geographic-resources/the-national-grid.html>**. Historical maps are organized by sheet number, but these do not correspond with modern OS maps.

The National Library of Scotland holds several series of historical maps **<maps.nls.uk/ os/county-series/index.html>**. You can also find historical OS maps at A Vision of Britain Through Time **<www.visionofbritain.org.uk/maps>**, while modern OS maps are available on the OS' website **<www.ordnancesurvey.co.uk>**.

To examine the maps of your ancestor's parish, first visit the main page of the six-inch map series **<maps.nls.uk/os/6inch/index.html>**. You can access the maps in many ways, but I prefer the county text lists **<maps.nls.uk/os/6inch/county_list.html>** since I find the zoomable map too complicated. From the text list, click on the county of interest. At the top of this page is a link to a graphic index of sheets for the county, and below are links to the sheet numbers, the date the area was surveyed, and the date of publication. Since the list of sheet numbers does not provide any named references (like parish, notable feature, or village), the best way to find the sheet you need is to click on the graphic index link. This will take you to a map of the entire county with a grid laid over it, with each square corresponding to a sheet number. Once you've identified the sheet number(s) required, go back to the listing of sheets and click on the one needed. If your ancestor's neighborhood is spread over one or more sheets, then it might help to print them out (you can download them to a PDF file) and tape them together.

You can also view maps that were surveyed at twenty-five inches to the mile **<maps. nls.uk/os/25inch/index.html>** and **<search.ancestry.com/search/db.aspx?dbid=5127>**. The process for viewing these maps at the National Library of Scotland is the same as for the six-inch series. However, the links to the actual sheets include more detail such as the name of the parish. The links also give the primary sheet number, which is the same as it was for the six-inch maps. For example, the village of Riccarton is on Ayrshire sheet XXIII in the six-inch maps, but Ayrshire Sheet XXIII.1 in the twenty-five inch series. At Ancestry.com, select the county (or partial county), then the town. Viewing the legend for the 1/2500 maps **<maps.nls.uk/view/128076891>** and for the six-inch maps **<maps.nls. uk/view/128076894>** will help you figure out if your ancestor's farm was next to a mixed wood or a marsh.

RESEARCH TIP

View Different Scales

OS maps were created at varying scales throughout history, giving you different levels of detail to view your ancestor's community. Maps at lower resolutions (such as the one-inch-to-one-mile map) provide a broad view of an area, while maps at higher resolutions (such as the twenty-five-inches-to-one-mile) show much more detail. Use both to see your ancestor's town in different contexts.

The Topographical,

Statistical, and Historical

GAZETTEER OF SCOTLAND.

ABB

ABBEY, a name frequently given in Scottish topography to a village or hamlet which has been founded upon or near the site of some ancient monastic establishment. Thus we have a village called THE ABBEY in the neighbourhood of the abbey of Cambuskenneth; and another of the same name upon the banks of the Tyne, about a mile below the town of Haddington, marking the site of a once flourishing abbey, but of which scarcely a trace now remains. The palace of Holyrood is also known throughout Scotland, and most significantly in Scottish law, as THE ABBEY, *par excellence* : having been reared within the precincts of a famous monastery, the liberty or sanctuary of which, being recognised by law, affords a retreat for insolvent debtors within which they cannot be arrested.

ABBEY PARISH. See PAISLEY.

ABBEY ST BATHAN'S, a parish in the northern part of Berwickshire; bounded on the north by Innerwick, and Oldhamstocks, in Haddingtonshire, and Cockburnspath in Berwickshire; on the east by that detached portion of Oldhamstocks which lies in Berwickshire, and by Coldingham; on the south by Buncle, a detached portion of Longformacus parish, and Dunse; and on the west by Longformacus. The Ey Water, from its rise on the skirts of Haddingtonshire to near its junction with the Whiteadder, divides it from the parishes of Cockburnspath, Oldhamstocks, Coldingham, and Buncle. It is of a very irregular outline; and measures nearly 6 miles in its greatest length from north-west to south-east; and 4 miles in its greatest length from north-east to south-west. It contains about 5,000 acres, of which nearly 2,000 are arable; the remainder is covered with barren heath or the coarse moorland pasture common to the Lammermoor district within which this parish lies. The best soil is that of the haugh-ground stretching along both sides of the Whiteadder, which flows through the southern part of this parish from west to east, passing to the north of the kirk-town, which is about 7 miles north by west of Dunse. Population, in 1801, 138; in 1831, 122, of whom

ABB

1170, for nuns of the Cistercian order; and soon acquired large revenues. About two furlongs east from the church, and on the same side of the river, in a field called the Chapel-field, were the now obliterated remains of a small chapel; and about a mile to the north-west were the remains, now likewise obliterated, of the parish-church of Strafontane—probably a corruption of Trois Fontaines—united at the Reformation to St Bathan's, and originally an hospital founded by David I.—A little to the north-west of Strafontane, near the banks of the Monynut, a tributary of the Whiteadder, is Gadscroft, once the demesne of David Hume, the friend of Melville, who died in 1620.—The Earl of Wemyss has a hunting-box about a mile south of the kirk-town.

ABBEY-CRAIG, a hill in the parish of Logie, in the vicinity of Cambuskenneth abbey, on which the Scottish army was posted under Wallace, when the Earl of Surrey and Hugh Cressingham advanced to the battle of Stirling, on 12th September, 1297.

ABBEY-GREEN. See LESMAHAGO.

ABBOTSRULE, formerly a parish in Roxburghshire, now divided between Hobkirk and Southdean parishes. It stretched about 3 miles along the eastern side of the upper part of the Rule, from Blackcleugh Mouth to Fultonhaugh.

ABBOTSFORD, the far-famed country-seat of our great national Novelist. It is situated in the south-western part of the parish of Melrose, in the county of Roxburgh, on the southern bank of the Tweed, a little above the junction of the Gala Water; 2 miles south-east of the town of Galashiels, 34½ south of Edinburgh. The road from Melrose to Selkirk passes close to it. With the exception of the site itself, which looks out upon the river flowing immediately beneath, and a beautiful haugh on the opposite bank backed with the green hills of Ettrick forest, Abbotsford owes its name and all its attractions to its late illustrious proprietor. Before his genius began to transform the place to what it now is—a fairy scene, 'a romance in stone and lime' —a mean farm-stead called Cartley-Hole occupied

Gazetteers give great detail about places, such as local landmarks, distance from other localities, and remarks about history. This opening page of the 1847 Gazetteer of Scotland details place names beginning with *ABB*.

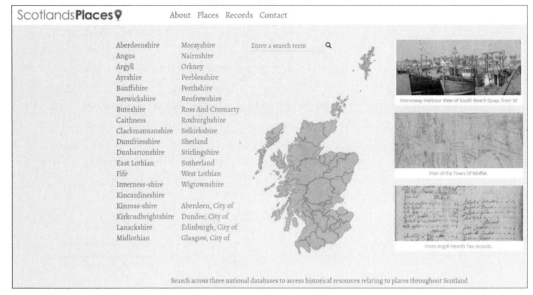

ScotlandsPlaces shows you which records in its database are available by geographic location.

Gazetteers

Gazetteers are specialized dictionaries for place names. When used in conjunction with a map or atlas (which, due to their scale, often leave out local landmarks and smaller towns), gazetteers can help you learn more about where your ancestors lived. The entries, which are listed alphabetically, may include data about former names, distances from other towns, the local economy, heritors, population size, and relevant jurisdictions.

There are many gazetteers for Scotland available online. The Gazetteer for Scotland <www.scottish-places.info> (image **E**) is perhaps the most useful. This is an online geographical encyclopedia with over twenty-five thousand entries, sponsored by the School of GeoSciences, the University of Edinburgh, and the Royal Scottish Geographical Society. You can search the database by map, timeline, or words. The map search allows you to search by Old Counties or Modern Council areas. The database includes information on settlements, parishes, bodies of water, bridges, distilleries, mountains, valleys, moors, and castles. Entries for parishes include a list of features and settlements.

You can also find digitized versions of published versions of nineteenth-century gazetteers. The National Library of Scotland has a collection spanning the nineteenth century, with twelve titles spanning twenty searchable volumes <digital.nls.uk/gazetteers-of-scotland-1803-1901/archive/97491608>. A facsimile edition of the 1882 gazetteer of Scotland <www.gazetteerofscotland.org.uk> is also available.

An 1847 gazetteer of Scotland is available at Ancestry.com **<search.ancestry.com/ search/db.aspx?dbid=7310>**, though it's set up primarily to search for people. The best way to approach this geographic source is to do a keyword search for the location in which you are interested, or simply to browse the volumes. Volume One includes place names beginning Ab–Hy, and Volume Two includes those beginning Ic–Yt.

While not strictly speaking a gazetteer, ScotlandsPlaces **<scotlandsplaces.gov.uk>** (image **F**) has a searchable database that includes various records of Historic Environment Scotland, the National Records of Scotland, and the National Library of Scotland. The results are organized by geographic location and include everything from tax rolls to archaeological records. You may search the database by place name or postal code.

KEYS TO SUCCESS

Understand the administrative units that impacted your ancestors' lives (and the records they left behind).

Learn the building blocks of Gaelic place names and the fundamentals of Gaelic pronunciation, particularly if your ancestors were from the Highlands.

Find your ancestors' place of residence on a map or gazetteer. Look to see if their network lived nearby, which church was closest, and what other geographic or man-made feature may have impacted their daily lives.

6

Deciphering Scottish Names and Handwriting

Being on a first-name basis with someone implies intimacy—you know him well enough to use his first name. In our more casual modern society, we call almost everyone by their first names—and some pop stars (Madonna, Adele, Bono, etc.) only go by one name.

However, no matter how connected we feel to our ancestors, we have to learn their first *and* last names. In Western cultures, children receive both a given name (first name) and a surname (last name) that connects them with their families. Surnames were usually passed down from a father to his children, providing information about family relationships. And studying first and last names (as well as middle names) can help us distinguish our ancestors from others with similar names.

This chapter will provide an overview to Scottish names, both first and last. We'll also address another language-related roadblock you may face in your research: Scottish handwriting.

SCOTTISH FIRST NAMES

Until about 1830, most of your Scottish ancestors will have had only one name (for example: Charles, Donald, Anna, or Grace). Ancestors with what we would recognize as last names likely came from prominent families and had high social status. And even after 1830, the two names you may find associated with an ancestor are likely a first and middle name. The middle name(s), in particular, might be a clue to his family history and relationships, as it might honor another family member or be the mother's maiden name. Note that even people with more than one name usually went by only one.

Families frequently reused names of children who died at birth or at a young age. In most cases, a second child was given the same name after the first child died. However, it was also possible for two living children to bear the same name, particularly if the parents wanted to strictly maintain the traditional Scottish naming pattern (which we'll discuss shortly). For example, if a husband and wife both had a father named *William*, they might have named two sons William, one after each respective father.

Alternative Forms and Nicknames

Scots were fond of nicknames and tended to use them interchangeably with full given names. Many of these will be familiar—*Katie* or *Kathy* for Katherine or *Jamie* or *Jimmy* for James. Some will likely be unfamiliar to you, like *Dod* for George or *Sandy* or *Eck* for Alexander. The formal name might be entered in the baptismal register, but the nickname might be used in other records, especially those made by local clerks and registrars who knew the family. Keep an eye out for nicknames in the records and search for them as well. A book like *Scottish Forenames* by Donald Whyte (Birlinn Ltd., 2005) will help iden- tify nicknames and alternative spellings.

In addition, clerks, ministers, and registrars were fond of abbreviations. You will have seen many of these in US records, like *Wm* for William, *Alexr* for Alexander, or *Mgt* for Margaret. Through trial and error, you'll discover whether the search engine you're using looks for abbreviations. If it doesn't, you'll want to search separately for the abbreviation.

Throughout Scotland, some names were interchangeable: Agnes and Nancy; Jane, Jean, and Jeanne; Donald and Daniel. Additionally, Gaelic names will have been trans- lated or transliterated into English when being documented in church records (which were always in English). Sometimes, the English or Latinized versions of a Gaelic name were used interchangeably. For example, *Aeneas* is used for Angus, *Frederick* for Farquhar or Fearcher, and *Archibald* for Gillespick.

Keep Anglicization in mind as your research takes you back and forth across the Atlantic. Men named *Dòmhnall* from one Highland community I studied were referred to as Donald in Scottish records and as either Donald or Daniel in American records. *Anna* in Gaelic became Ann or Nancy in the United States, while Helen, Ellen, Nelly, and Eleanor were presumably all used interchangeably for the Gaelic name *Eilidh*. So, if you cannot find Daniel McIntosh or his sister Eleanor in the parish records, look for Donald and Helen.

Naming Patterns

Like many peoples of Europe, the Scots had a traditional naming pattern that suggested how couples should name their children. This has obvious uses for genealogists, because you can deduce the names of children's parents based on their own names.

The primary naming pattern for Scots was:

- First son named for the paternal grandfather
- Second son named for the maternal grandfather
- Third son named for the father
- First daughter named for the maternal grandmother
- Second daughter named for the paternal grandmother
- Third daughter for the mother.

Note: There does not appear to have been any settled pattern for the naming of children beyond the third of each gender (e.g., a fourth son or daughter).

Many events or variations could throw the pattern off. For example, a couple might have given primacy to the paternal grandparents, naming the first-born child or children (regardless of gender) after the paternal grandparents. In other cases, parents may have avoided giving their children the same names. For example, as previously discussed, a couple's fathers could have had the same first name, meaning that (following the pattern) their first two sons would have had the same name. Parents may have chosen alternative names to avoid confusion. It was also customary in some areas to name a child after a minister performing his first baptism or a doctor attending his first birth.

Many Scots families also used androgynous names—for example, *Christian* was used as a version of Christina, and *Crawford* has been used as a girl's name in some Ayrshire families. Be sure to keep an open mind about which gender is associated with which

RESEARCH TIP

Don't Make Assumptions Based on Names

Though your ancestor may have a "Scottish sounding" first or last name, he might not have been born in Scotland. He could be the child of Scottish immigrants, or perhaps he was Scots-Irish. For example, there is no way to tell if James Hamilton, for example, was from County Antrim in Northern Ireland or Ayrshire in Scotland, just by looking at his name in US records. You'll need to research other sources to determine where he's from.

names. Often, boys' names were transformed into girls' names by adding the suffix -ina. For example, Robert would be *Robina* and Thomas would become *Thomasina*. And any of these women might be known by the nickname *Ina*.

SCOTTISH LAST NAMES

The languages spoken in Scotland over the centuries have significantly influenced the variety and prevalence of Scottish last names. Of the one thousand surnames included in *Scottish Surnames* by David Dorward (Mercat Press, 2003), 35 percent are Anglo-Saxon or Scots in origin, 21 percent are Scottish Gaelic, 11 percent are Irish Gaelic (mostly from Irish immigrants who arrived in Scotland in the nineteenth century), 7 percent are Norman-French, and 4 percent are Norse. This created a wide variety of last names that can be considered Scottish.

Scots began adopting surnames during the reign of David I (1124–1153). Many of the first surnames to appear were used by Anglo-Norman families who came into Scotland in the twelfth century, and most surnames were taken from the names of the lands these families occupied. Some of the most recognizable Scottish surnames like Bruce, Fraser, Graham, and Menzies belong to these families.

Over time, more families began adopting surnames, all with different origins. We'll discuss the most common of these in the sections that follow.

Patronymics

Patronymic surnames, taken from the father's given name, are perhaps the most cumbersome surname origin. Since they are derived from the father's given name, they would change every generation. So, James (the son of William) would be *James Williamson*, and his son Robert would be *Robert Jamesson* (or Jameson). Likewise, for females, Robert's daughter Ann would be *Anne Robertsdaughter*. Patronymic surnames could also appear with just the letter "s" as a representative for son: *Williams* instead of Williamson. Sometimes pet or diminutive forms would be used. In Scots, these were created by adding the suffix -ie to the name. This would give you *Robie* instead of Robertson and *Dickie* instead of Dickson.

In the Lowlands, Scots stopped using patronymic surnames after the fifteenth century, when patronymics became permanent family surnames. In Shetland, however, patronymics were common until the nineteenth century.

MAC/MC SURNAMES

Mac/Mc surnames, associated with the Scottish Highlands, are also patronymics. Some are associated with the father's given name, while others are associated with his occupation. *MacChormaig* (MacCormack in English) means "son of Cormac." *Mac an t-Saoir* (MacIntrye or any of its spelling variants in English) was the son of the carpenter. The feminine version of *Mac* was *Nc* or *N'*, an abbreviation of *nighean mhic* ("daughter of Mac"). In the previous examples, the surnames for the sisters of these men would be NcCormack and NcIntyre, respectively. These names would also have changed with each generation, a tradition that lasted in some parts of the Highlands until the eighteenth century.

The spellings *Mc*, *Mac*, *Mhic*, *M'* and *Mack* were used interchangeably. The spelling was not fixed, and a person could appear as *Mc* in one record and *Mac* in another. Sometimes two different spellings were used in the same record to refer to the same person. Therefore, when searching databases, you must search for all the various spellings. Alternatively, you can do a wildcard search. For example, searching for *M*cPherson* would find McPherson and MacPherson. In indexes and directories, especially in the United States, *Mc* surnames are often separated from *M* surnames.

In some documents, people were not only identified by the name of their father, but also the name of their grandfather. *Vc* means grandson or granddaughter, and was used in the same way as *Mc* or *Nc*. The melding of cultures in the Northern Isles can also be seen in the surnames like *MacIomhair* (MacIver in English), which has a Gaelic prefix attached to a Norse personal name, Ivarr.

Mac/Mc surnames account for about 20 percent of the surnames currently in use in Scotland today. However, these are only a fraction of those that had been used historically. This loss is due to the names of smaller families being subsumed by larger ones, or (as described later) the names being Anglicized or otherwise being made less Gaelic.

CLAN NAMES

In chapter 4, we discussed Scottish clans. As you'll recall, not all members of a clan may be related by blood—and not all clan members had the same surname. Likewise, not all individuals who carry a common clan surname (like McDonald, McIntosh, or McLeod) are genealogically descended from a common ancestor. It was common for families to take the surname of a more powerful clan if they needed protection, as a powerful clan chief gave them no option but to adopt his surname—or because they moved from one territory to another. If a family did adopt a new surname, the original surname might be preserved as an alias in the parish records for a generation or two.

Occupation Names

Surnames that originated with occupations or professions tend to be found in the burghs or cities of Scotland. The most common surname in Scotland is Smith, the Gaelic version of which is Gow. Other occupations surnames include Baxter ("baker"), Walker ("a fuller of cloth"), and Webster ("weaver").

Locality Names

The great families of Scotland were the first to take their surnames from places. For example, the aforementioned Bruce family takes its name from *de Bois*, a town in Normandy, France. Other families adopted the names of their homes in Scotland: Murray (from Morayshire), Ross (from Ross-shire), and Forbes (from a neighborhood in Aberdeenshire).

Eventually, common people took their names from locations as well. *Fleming* indicates one who came from Flanders, and *Norrie* from Norway. *Douglas* comes from the Gaelic *dubh glais*, or "black water," indicating a loch or ocean.

Nicknames

Scots may also have identified themselves by nicknames, for example to tell apart two men or women with the same name. These nicknames were usually a one-word adjective—a color, size, or age. Some of these nicknames eventually became surnames in their own right, such as Long, Short, and Young.

Another specific type of nickname are Tee-Names (also T-names or To-names). These are used in communities with few surnames to distinguish the people who have the same first and last names, most commonly in fishing villages on the east coast. Tee-Names can come from almost anywhere: the name of a person's boat, a Gaelic name, or other nickname. They were written in two common ways: *James (Deacon) Cowie* or *James Cowie "Deacon."* What makes tee-names different from other nicknames is that they could be used by other family members and passed down from one generation to the next.

The name MacGregor was outlawed for many decades due to the extreme lawlessness of the clan, and so people with this surname commonly used aliases like Neil Robertson (alias McGrigore), whose child was baptized in Kenmore Parish in 1749.

Aliases

Aliases were common features of Highland surnames, as Scots sought to distinguish themselves from others with similar names or to skirt rules about allowed surnames (image). They are usually written in records and represent how a person was known in the community. A man named Gow at birth might have an alias of Smith, or Grant might have the alias Bowie. If a person used an alias as described here, he could use just one or the other in a record, or both. For example, John McPherson (alias Kealoch) of Croy Parish is listed as such in the parish register, but in most entries he is simply John Kealoch. To know for sure, look for other details, such as his residence or his wife's name.

ANGLICIZATION OF GAELIC SURNAMES

To non-native speakers, Gaelic surnames can be unwieldy and challenging to pronounce. Also, Gaelic culture was derided for much of Scottish history. Thus, when Highlanders migrated to the Lowlands or to America, they frequently changed their surnames. Often these changes were minimal—using an Anglicized spelling that sounded the same when pronounced, or using the English equivalent of the name (for example, *Thomson* instead of *Mac Tómais*). Or perhaps they took the name of the primary clan or landowner with

RESEARCH TIP

Read About Surnames

Consult books to learn more about Scottish surnames. *The Surnames of Scotland: Their Origin, Meaning, and History* by George F. Black with Mary Elder Black (Churchill & Dunn, 2015), first published in 1946, is the most comprehensive book on the subject. Two other titles are *Scottish Surnames* by David Dorward (Mercat Press, 2003) and *Scottish Surnames* by Donald Whyte (Birlinn Ltd., 2000). Each volume explains the origins, meanings, variants, and Gaelic versions of surnames used in Scotland. Black's book is best if your surname is unusual, though its nine hundred pages might be intimidating for some.

which they were associated. Alexander McAndrew (alias McIntosh) of Cawdor Parish and Alexander Tory (alias McIntosh) of Croy Parish, for example, both used the surname McIntosh when they settled in Ohio.

Additionally, families might alternate between the Gaelic and English versions of their surnames. For example, MacKay (rhymes with *high*) is the phonetic spelling of MacDhài. MacDhài, in turn, has the same meaning as Davidson, and all three might be used interchangeably. This fluidity of surname use in the Highlands means you will need to look (or at least keep an eye out for) an ancestor who used more than one surname.

HANDWRITING

Many of the records you will be consulting at the beginning of your genealogy journey in Scotland will be handwritten in something approaching modern handwriting. You may have to contend with a minister or clerk with bad penmanship, but (if you know what information you expect from the record) you can probably decipher what it says. If you do need to know more or find records written in an older style of penmanship, you'll need a quick overview of Scottish handwriting practices.

Two handwriting styles were widely in use in Scotland prior to 1750: Italic and Secretary. Many documents include mixtures of these styles in addition to others that the writer might have learned or made up. Italic is fairly easy to decipher, as the

Language in Scotland

Most modern Scots speak English with a Scottish accent. But some still speak their native languages, and you might encounter some of them as you research Scottish ancestors and history. Here are the other historically prevalent languages in Scotland:

- **Scots**: A descendant of Middle English that evolved in parallel with modern English. Scots is spoken by a large minority in Scotland today, and other residents of Scotland still use some Scots words and expressions in conversation.
- **Scottish Gaelic**: The Celtic language spoken in Scotland. also known as simply Gaelic (or, incorrectly, as Erse).
- **Irish**: The Celtic language spoken in Ireland. Though no longer mutually intelligible with Scots Gaelic (the two having different pronunciations), Irish can maybe be read by a Scottish Gaelic speaker.

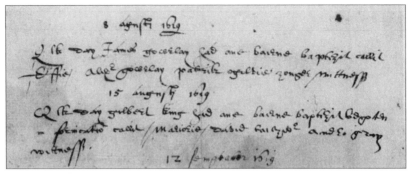

B

This excerpt from Inchture Parish, Perthshire, written in Secretary hand, shows the baptism of Effie Gowrlay, daughter of James, on August 8, 1619, and the baptism of Majorie King, the daughter of Gilbert, on August 15, 1619.

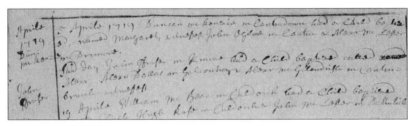

C

This excerpt from the first page of the Croy Parish Register in 1719 shows how much handwriting changed in one hundred years.

Interpreting Unfamiliar Words in Records

Once you have a basic knowledge of the various handwriting styles of Scotland, you may recognize the letters in a record, but the word itself makes no sense to you. Generally, these unfamiliar terms will be legal or archaic words, or Scots vocabulary.

ScotlandsPeople has a glossary of terms <www.scotlandspeople.gov.uk/glossary> that allows you to browse for words in categories such as legal terminology, occupations, and abbreviations. Many of the guides include images of the terms under discussion, including ones for dates, numbers, and currency <**www.scotlandspeople.gov.uk/guides/dates-numbers-and-sums-money**> and agriculture <**www.scotlandspeople.gov.uk/guides/agricultural-produce-and-livestock**>.

The Scottish Archive Network has also made a glossary of terms commonly found in Scottish documents <**www.scan.org.uk/researchrtools/glossary.htm**>. You may also wish to consult the Dictionary of the Scots Language <**www.dsl.ac.uk**>, an electronic edition of *Dictionary of the Older Scottish Tongue* and *Scottish National Dictionary*.

letters are similar to modern handwriting styles. However, Secretary hand, developed in the sixteenth century for administrative and business documents, has different letter-forms than we use today. The National Records of Scotland offers an online tutorial at Scottish Handwriting <www.scottishhandwriting.com>, where you can learn the basics of Secretary hand.

Learning Secretary hand will be especially important if you need to read seventeenth-century parish records (image **B**). These old parish records have been indexed and are included in searchable databases at FamilySearch.org <www.familysearch.org> and ScotlandsPeople <www.scotlandspeople.gov.uk>. Match up the index with the printed page to help you decipher any handwriting you cannot read. Fortunately, most parish records kept after 1700 will be in more recognizable handwriting styles (image **C**).

Kenneth Veitch has written a comprehensive study of common Scottish handwriting styles after 1750, including Copperplate and (later) the "Civil Service Hand." Both of these are similar to modern handwriting styles, but on occasion can stump the modern reader. The seventy-eight-page guide is available from "Dumfries and Galloway: A Regional Ethnology," a project of the European Ethnological Research Centre via PDF <www. dumfriesandgalloway.hss.ed.ac.uk/wp-content/uploads/2016/08/Scottish-Handwriting-A-Concise-Guide.pdf>.

KEYS TO SUCCESS

 Search for many spelling variations for your ancestors' names, especially in databases. Spelling was not fixed in Scotland, and those recordkeepers in America recreated how the name sounded, not how it "should be" spelled.

 Keep location in mind. If your ancestor was from the Highlands, be sure to learn the Gaelic version and any alternatives for his first and last names. Then search the records for each of them.

 Study old handwriting styles, particularly if your ancestor lived in the seventeenth century. These records (though written in English) were written in the difficult-to-read Secretary style. Use record database indexes as your guide, and learn the basics to help you read each record.

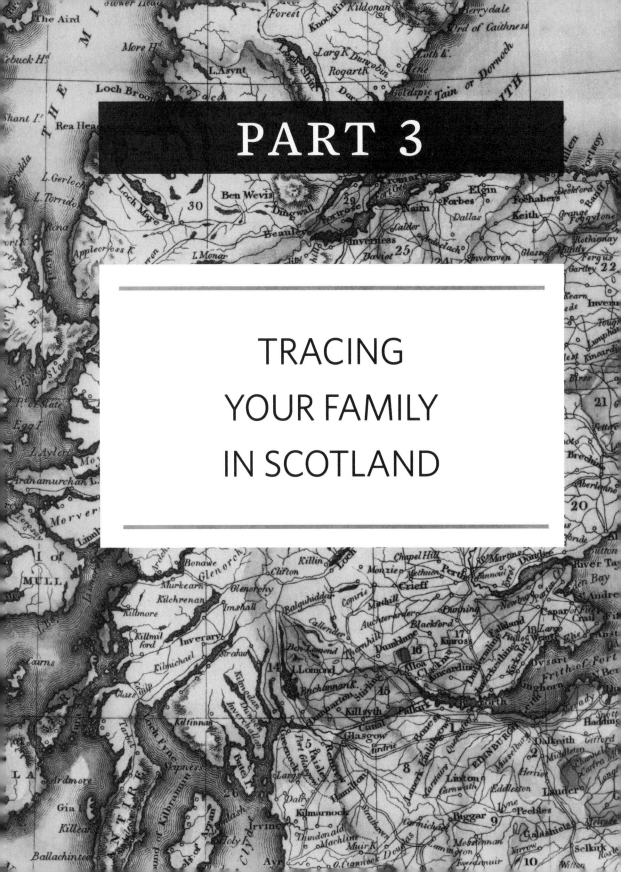

PART 3

TRACING
YOUR FAMILY
IN SCOTLAND

7

Civil Registration

O nce you've identified your immigrant ancestor and his network in US records (plus an immigration date and his Scottish hometown), you can turn your search to records in the home country. This is where you'll discover the important people, places, and events that marked your ancestor's life in Scotland.

If your ancestor was in Scotland after 1855, the first record group to examine is statutory (or civil) records. This chapter will explore the information contained in these records, plus how you can acquire them from places like the ScotlandsPeople Centre.

STATUTORY REGISTRATION

In the nineteenth century, Scotland's lack of consistent birth records became problematic, and it was difficult for lawyers to prove inheritance cases and for factories to prove they were not hiring underage employees. To remedy this, Parliament passed the Registration of Births, Deaths, and Marriages (Scotland) Act in 1854. The act, which took effect on January 1, 1855, made registration of these three vital events (births, marriages, and deaths) free and compulsory, leveling fines for those who registered these events late. Consequently, rates of compliance with the Act were quite high.

These civil records supplemented the records that parishes were already keeping. The first registrars in each district (whose boundaries, as we discussed in chapter 5,

1855: The Special Year

The year 1855 was significant in Scottish history for a few reasons. Most notably, it was the first year that civil registration of births, marriages, and deaths was mandatory. But 1855 was notable for another, related reason: detailed statutory records.

When statutory records were first taken, the government's forms for each vital event requested significantly more information than they did in the years that followed. However, registrars found it too burdensome to collect all of this data, so the government scaled back the forms' details beginning in 1856. In fact, the government overcorrected for a few years, requiring fewer details between 1856 and 1860, when they settled on the formats described in this chapter.

For example, birth records in 1855 included all the information discussed, plus details about other children born to the same couple (e.g., the infant's older siblings) and the parents' birthplaces and ages. Likewise, marriage entries for 1855 included information about former spouses, and death records noted the deceased's place of birth, details about her marriage, the location of the burial, and a list of all children (plus whether or not those children still lived).

were usually the same as the parish's) were the session clerks who worked under the town council. Each registration district was assigned a number, which was also tied to the parent parish. Having this clerk embedded in the community helped the government ensure all events were recorded. After all, a registrar in a small community would have been aware of most births, deaths, and marriages, meaning his records had a better chance of being complete.

BIRTHS

By law, parents were required to register the births of their children in the district where the birth occurred within twenty-one days.

The birth register (image **A**) contains a host of valuable information for researchers: the name of the child; the place, date, and time of birth; the names of the parents; the father's occupation; the mother's maiden name; and even the place, month, and year of the parents' marriage (pointing you to marriage records and registers). In addition, the informant was required to sign the registration form, adding another potential member of your ancestor's network you can research.

Children with unmarried parents are marked as illegitimate until 1919. These entries have only the name of the mother, though the father could be included provided both he and the mother appeared at the same time to register the child.

No.	Name and Surname.	When and Where Born.	Sex.	Name, Surname, & Rank or Profession of Father. Name, and Maiden Surname of Mother. Date and Place of Marriage.	Signature and Qualification of Informant, and Residence, if out of the House in which the Birth occurred.	When and Where Registered, and Signature of Registrar.
19	Andrew Walkinshaw	1868 January Twenty-fifth 7 H. o. m. P.M. Riccarton	M	George Walkinshaw Engine Keeper Sarah Walkinshaw M. S. Smellie 1855. December St. Quivox	George Walkinshaw Father Present	1868 February 1st Riccarton James McClure Registrar
20	Margaret Black	1868 January Twenty-third 3 H. o m. A. M. Hurlford	F	George Black Coal miner Margaret Black M. S. Richmond 1849. September Hurlford	George Black Father	1868 February 3rd Riccarton James McClure Registrar
21	David Hood (Illegitimate)	1868 January Fourteenth 3 H.o.m. A.M. Hurlford	M	David Hood Coal miner Elizabeth Baird Domestic Servant	Elizabeth Baird Mother David Hood Father	1868 February 3rd Riccarton James McClure Registrar

Page 7.

1868. BIRTHS in the District of Riccarton in the County of Ayr

These 1868 statutory records are from Riccarton Parish in Ayrshire. The first two records show the names of the children and their parents, plus the year and location of their parents' marriage. This information would be particularly useful for people who moved from one parish to another after their marriage. The third record shows the illegitimate birth of David Hood; both his mother and father were present to register his birth.

RESEARCH TIP

Search for Neglected Life Events

Any Scot who was born, married, or died between December 30, 1800, and January 1, 1855, and did not have that event recorded in the Old Parish Registers (the precursor to civil registration; see chapter 8) could have that event recorded in the Register of Neglected Entries. Unfortunately, not many people did this. To have an entry made in this volume, a person had to pay a fee and get a warrant from the county sheriff. You can find this collection (Neglected Entries, Roll No. 103538) on microfilm at the Family History Library, but (as of this book's publication) it has not yet been digitized.

1890. MARRIAGES in the District of Hurford (Page 8) in the County of Ayr

No.	When, Where, and How Married.	Signatures of Parties. Rank or Profession, Whether Single or Widowed, and Relationship (if any).	Age.	Usual Residence.	Name, Surname, and Rank or Profession of Father. Name, and Maiden Surname of Mother.	If a regular Marriage, Signatures of officiating Minister and Witnesses. If Irregular, Date of Conviction, Decree of Declarator, or Sheriff's Warrant.	When & Where Registered, and Signature of Registrar.
16	1890. on the sixth day of June at Wallace's Hall, Galston Road, Hurford. After Banns according to the Forms of the Established Church of Scotland.	(Signed.) David Hood, Coal-miner, (Bachelor) (Signed.) Elizabeth Hodge Angus, Domestic Servant, (Spinster.)	22 17	Riccarton Road, Hurford. 2 Garden Street, Kilmarnock.	David Hood, Coal-miner, Elizabeth Hood, M.S. Baird. James Angus, Coal-miner, Catherine Angus, M.S. Hodge.	(Signed.) Alexr Cameron, Minister, of Hurford. (Signed.) G. Hood, Witness. Janet Baillie, Witness.	1890. June 7th at Hurford. John Gourdie Registrar.
16	1890. on the Sixth day of June at 19 D. Block R. Railway Buildings, Hurford. After Banns according to the Forms of the Established Church of Scotland.	(Signed.) William Guthrie, Clerk, (Bachelor) (Signed.) Jeanie Craig, Shop Keeper, (Spinster.)	24 22	10 B. Block Railway-Buildings, Hurford. 19 D. Block Railway-Buildings, Hurford.	William Guthrie, Engine-Driver, Mary Guthrie, M.S. Bowie, (dead) John Craig, General Labourer, Agnes Craig, M.S. Dalziel, (dead)	(Signed.) Emmanuel Morgan, Minister, of Riccarton. (Signed.) Lizzie Craig, Witness. Alexander Guthrie, Witness.	1890. June 9th at Hurford. John Gourdie Registrar.

John Gourdie Registrar.

This 1891 statutory marriage record for David Hood and Elizabeth Hodge Angus holds a wealth of information. The couple were wed at Wallace Hall in Galston Road in Hurford by Alexander Cameron, a Church of Scotland Minister. The record also lists the bride's and groom's places of residence and occupations, plus the names of both their parents and the witnesses.

MARRIAGES

Historically, Scotland recognized two kinds of marriages: regular and irregular. Regular marriages were those that fulfilled the standard requirements for a wedding ceremony: performed by a minister in front of two witnesses after the marriage banns had been read for three consecutive Sundays in the home parishes of the bride and groom.

The second type of marriage (irregular) required neither a minister, nor witnesses, nor banns—a couple simply consented and agreed to be married. However, the couple still had to provide evidence of this agreement, with at least two witnesses if the couple had only oral evidence. After 1855, couples pursuing an irregular marriage had to present their evidence to the sheriff within three months. Over time, this type of marriage became unpopular and was banned in England in 1754, though it remained legal in Scotland until 1939. You can find some surviving registers of irregular marriages at the National Records of Scotland <**www.nrscotland.gov.uk/files// research/irregular-border-and-scottish- runaway-marriages.pdf**>.

The statutory marriage record is quite informative (image **B**). It lists the names, ages, and occupations of the bride and groom; their respective marital statuses (spinster, widowed, etc.); the date and location of the marriage; and the religious rites under which the ceremony was performed. Additionally, you'll find the names of their parents along with the occupa-

Register of Corrected Entries

The statutory registers could not be amended or changed. Consequently, recordkeepers had to create a separate list of additions or corrections: the Register of Corrected Entries. Statutory registers will reference corrected entries (if any) in the left-hand column.

Why would vital event information need to be changed? A child's name may change, or recordkeepers might discover the identity of the child's father in cases of illegitimate births. The latter was a common use of this register—under Scots law, if the parents married after their child was born, that child was legitimized if the parents could have been married at the time of the child's birth. In a similar vein, a person's cause of death may only have been determined after the death was registered, or a marriage record might have a "correction" noting a divorce.

C

This statutory death record for Martha Clark from 1913 reveals a great deal of information: the name of her husband and her occupation; her time, place, cause, and date of death; and the names of her parents. In this case, the informant was a neighbor.

D

This two-page sample record from 1855 is the statutory death record for Ann Mackintosh, nee Smith. The bonus information on this record includes her place of burial and the names of all of her children. This record also highlights one of the difficulties with this form—there often wasn't enough room for all of the information required.

tion of the fathers, the maiden names of the mothers, the minister's name, and the identities of two witnesses.

DEATHS

Like births, deaths were to be registered in the district where the event occurred, preferably by an informant who was present. Deaths were to be registered within eight days, and burial could not take place until a death certificate was received and given to the funeral home.

The death record (images **C** and **D**) will include the deceased's name, gender, age, and occupation. Also recorded are the deceased's marital status and the names of his parents, including the father's occupation and the mother's maiden name. The name of the spouse (if relevant) may also be included, along with a cause of death (helpful if you're compiling a medical family history). For the latter, ScotlandsPeople has compiled a glossary of unfamiliar medical terms to help you better understand these records <www.scotlandspeople.gov.uk/glossary?field_term_type_value%5B%5D=med&=Apply>.

And as with birth records, informants for death records were required to sign and identify their relationship to the deceased. This fact is useful, as it will allow you to gauge the accuracy of the information in the register. For example, the deceased's adult child is more likely to know about the deceased than a landlord.

Vital Records: FamilySearch Versus ScotlandsPeople

You have two primary options for searching for Scottish civil records, but which site is the best? Both sites have their advantages and disadvantages.

In general, the information included in FamilySearch.org's database is more complete and totally free, but you cannot view the images at home. Additionally, the database entry does not link to the images, making it difficult to view the microfilm if/when you get to a Family History Center. At FamilySearch.org or a Family History Center, you can view as many of the pages in the microfilm roll as you want, which may lead to unexpected discoveries.

ScotlandsPeople, on the other hand, links the images with the index, making it easy see the document you are interested in. However, there is a small fee to view each image. This fee is not burdensome if you know it is the image you want, but you may have trouble determining what the correct record is.

> **RESEARCH TIP**
>
> **Search Multiple Spellings in the General Index**
> When using indexes, you may find your ancestor's surname under one of multiple spellings. For example, William Curry (d. 1930) was also indexed as *William Currie*, the more common spelling. However, the indexes used only the most common spelling for given names. So Hellen and Jannet would only be indexed as *Helen* and *Janet*. Tee names were also used in the index and appear in brackets after the given name, to differentiate it from a middle name. For example, *Cowie, James (Weaver)* would appear after Cowie, James and before Cowie, James Thomas. You can learn more about the indexing process by reading the instructions compiled in 1956 **<www.nrscotland.gov.uk/files//research/statutory-registers/index-instructions.pdf>**.

ACCESSING STATUTORY RECORDS

You can find civil registration records at two primary, free-to-search sites: ScotlandsPeople and FamilySearch.org. ScotlandsPeople refers to these as "Statutory Registration in Scotland," while the FamilySearch.org catalog has collected them together as "Civil Registration." ScotlandsPeople has records from 1855 through 2016, but FamilySearch.org has only selected years 1855–1875, 1881, and 1891, as well as indexes for the years 1855 to 1955.

FamilySearch.org

The free FamilySearch.org has two primary records collections for Scottish registrations: "Scottish Births and Baptisms, 1564–1950" **<www.familysearch.org/search/collection/1771030>** and "Scottish Marriages, 1561–1910" **<www.familysearch.org/search/collection/1771074>**. These collections are also available at subscription sites Ancestry.com **<www.ancestry.com>** and Findmypast **<www.findmypast.co.uk>**, and they include Statutory Registration birth and marriage records from 1855 to 1875. FamilySearch.org cautions that the information in these databases may not be 100-percent complete.

FamilySearch.org also microfilmed all the indexes of births from 1855 to 1955, and marriages and deaths from 1855 until 1956. Note that these indexes were handwritten from 1855 to 1865 and printed from 1866 onward (see chapter 6 for tips for reading Scottish handwriting). Recordkeepers also indexed males and females separately (even if bound in the same volume), so you'll need to look in different sections to find the same family and cross-reference the bride and groom in marriage records.

The "Scotland Birth and Baptisms" collection at FamilySearch.org includes the child's name, date and place of birth, and gender, plus the names of his parents. The

"Scotland Marriages" collection shows the name of the couple and the date and place of the marriage.

However, neither collection gives the registration district number or the entry number, nor does it link to the digitized microfilm. These are crucial details for accessing the actual record, which you'll want to request so you can validate the information you find in FamilySearch.org's database. The microfilm number (6035516) shown in many FamilySearch.org citations is actually the *Register of Births, Marriages, and Deaths of Scotland* <www.familysearch.org/search/catalog/593463>, which can help you identify the registration district number for the event location for the years held by FamilySearch.org.

At the time of publication, this useful source is not available digitally. But if you could use the Register, find your parish/registration district on the alphabetical list, then determine what county you need and find a listing of the registration districts and years for that county. Follow this to find out what roll of microfilm is needed, then search for this microfilm number in the FamilySearch.org Catalog.

You can also find a searchable guide to registration districts at the National Records of Scotland as a PDF file <www.nrscotland.gov.uk/files//research/statutory-registers/registration-district-guide.pdf>. This includes an alphabetical listing of all parishes in Scotland, plus the "old" registration district or parish number. (You can also see the number currently used in Scotland, but you'll likely only need the old.) Then visit the Scotland—Civil Registration Page <www.familysearch.org/search/catalog/79310> in the FamilySearch.org Catalog to find the microfilm you need amongst the more than 4,200 rolls. At the top of the page is an alphabetical listing of the parishes or districts and their corresponding numbers. The rolls of microfilm are organized by Birth, then Marriages, then Deaths. Once you find the correct county, year, and parish, you will find the microfilm number. If you are in a Family History Library, click on camera icon to access the records. If you are at home, write down the microfilm number so (when you are at a Family History Center) you can easily search the catalog for it.

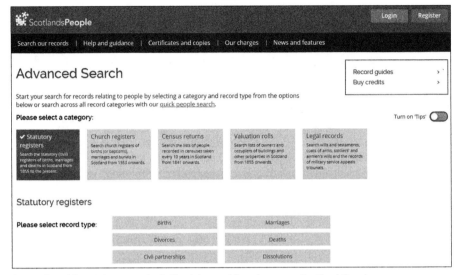

Access Scottish statutory records via the Advanced Search page on ScotlandsPeople.

ScotlandsPeople

Unlike on FamilySearch.org, you'll need to pay to access and download records from Scot-landsPeople. ScotlandsPeople operates on a credit system, in which each record is worth a different amount of credits. Credits cost £0.25 each (about 35 US cents at the time of this publication), or £7.50 (about $10.50) for thirty credits or £10 (about $13.75) for forty credits. The credits expire in two years unless you purchase additional credits; see the charges page <www.scotlandspeople.gov.uk/content/our-charges> for more details. Note you'll need to pay separately for birth, marriage, death, and divorce certificates <www.scotlandspeople.gov.uk/certificate-search>. Helpfully, all images downloaded from Scot-landsPeople will include citation information.

You can access statutory registers on ScotlandsPeople from the Advanced Search page (image) <www.scotlandspeople.gov.uk/advanced-search>. The Birth Index at Scot-landsPeople includes the name of the child, the gender, the year, the RD (or registration district name), and the reference (the district number, plus the entry's number). The Marriage Index shows the names of the couple, the year of marriage, the RD, and the Reference. Note that, at time of publication, ScotlandsPeople is the only resource that makes statutory death records available.

Once you've found the index entry you want, you'll have the option of viewing and downloading the original record. Next to the index entry, you'll see a blue box that will

Step-by-Step: Finding Statutory Records at ScotlandsPeople

Step 1: **Enter your search terms**. For a basic search at ScotlandsPeople, enter the name of the person and (if you want) the dates, then click search. This will return results for all record groups: statutory records, church registers (Old Parish, Catholic, and Other), census returns, valuation rolls, legal records, and more. Your results will be subdivided by record type (birth, death, marriage, etc.).

Step 2: **Review and filter your results**. Click on the record group that interests you to examine the results. My search for the death of John MacDonald returned 5,381 hits—too many results to examine closely. So I used the boxes in the column on the left-hand side to filter results. Depending upon the record type, you can filter by various factors, such as year of death, age, spouse's name, or mother's maiden name. You can filter statutory records by county and/or parish, so I limited this search to John MacDonalds who died in Moy, Inverness-shire, and got three results—much more manageable. You can sort by each column header: Hover over a column header, then click on it when it turns blue. The blue box in the far-right hand column will indicate whether you can view the image for six credits or if you have to order a certificate.

Step 3: Run an advanced search. Alternatively, you can do an advanced search. Using this form, you will first select the record group and type, then you search by name, year range, and location. For example, you can select "Statutory Registration—Births," then enter the details on your ancestor. Your search results will only include birth records. If you get no results, be sure that you have entered the surname in the first box, then the first name in the second box. Most other genealogical sites request the names in the other order (first name first, surname second), so this is an easy mistake to make.

Step 4: **View record images.** If you would prefer to view the image of the statutory record at your local Family History Center or affiliate library, make note of the registration district, year, and reference number. The first number will be the one assigned to the registration district, and the second number will be the entry number for statutory records. For example, John MacDonald died in 1889 in Moy, and this record has the reference number 105/4. You would then look for registration district 105 for the year 1889, and John MacDonald would be the fourth entry. A reference with more numbers indicates that the registration district has been split. For example, Riccarton registration district was 611. In 1887 it was divided into two: Riccarton 611/1 and Hurlford 611/2.

tell you how much it costs to view the image and if it is a "modern record," in which case you will need to purchase a certificate (or extract). Viewing statutory registers costs about six credits, or about three US dollars.

If you need a record that is only available at ScotlandsPeople, make sure you've found the correct name, date, and place. This will limit the possibility of purchasing records for people who are not your ancestors.

Not all images are available to view online due to ScotlandsPeople's privacy regulations. Death records fewer than fifty years old, marriage records fewer than seventy-five years old, and birth records fewer than one hundred years old can't be viewed immediately and require certificate searches to access. If you need certificates (or extracts) of the record, you can order them online for twelve pounds (about $15.53 USD at the time of this publication). In this situation, the blue box will say "order certificate" and when you click on it, the certificate will be added to your shopping cart. Don't worry if you add the wrong certificate to your cart—you can remove the certificate order.

The search results for death records at ScotlandsPeople will show the name, age at death, year of death, registration district, and references. A married woman should be indexed at least twice—once under her married name and once under her maiden name. If a woman married more than once, however, she may or may not be indexed under her other married names. This double (or even more) indexing should help you locate your female ancestors in either the ScotlandsPeople database or the printed indexes at FamilySearch.org. Additionally, some of the entries at ScotlandsPeople include the maiden name of the deceased's mother, helpful if you have an inkling of who your ancestor's parents were. You can then view the image for six credits.

KEYS TO SUCCESS

- Use the information in one statutory record to lead you to additional records. Almost all statutory records will include the names of an individual's parents. Once you have the names of the parents, you can look for their birth, marriage, and death records, which should give you the names of their parents (and so on).

- Decide whether ScotlandsPeople or FamilySearch.org is the better option for your research, then use their search functions and indexes to your advantage. In general: FamilySearch.org is better for thorough research, while ScotlandsPeople is better if you're confident about your research and need records in a hurry.

- Learn where the closest Family History Center or affiliate library is to your house. Many Scottish records are available via FamilySearch.org as digitized microfilm, but you cannot view them from home.

8

Church Records

After exhausting statutory records, turn next to church records. Since religion was a central part of many Scots' lives, records generated by parishes can provide crucial details about your ancestors' lives. Church records pre-date civil records, but the former continued to be created even after the beginning of statutory registration. And since they document people prior to 1855, church records are critical for those researching Scottish ancestors.

This chapter will examine records from the Church of Scotland and other denominations, plus explain how to acquire and use them in your research.

CHURCH OF SCOTLAND PARISH RECORDS

Parish records, collectively known as Old Parish/Parochial Registers (or OPRs), are perhaps the most famous group of Scottish records. Many parishes did not begin keeping regular records until the nineteenth century, and a handful of parishes never kept records at all. The oldest records belong to Errol in Perthshire, beginning in 1553; only twenty parishes have records that began before 1600.

OPRs are an excellent source, as they cover most of the parishes and residents of Scotland over a period of three hundred years. They have also been indexed and (with some exceptions in sixteenth-century registers) are in English, making them more accessible to English-speaking researchers.

However, OPRs vary in detail and completeness. They had no standardized format, so the information available varies from parish to parish. In addition, not all clerks or ministers took their duties to keep the parish records seriously. Some kept them in such a haphazard manner that it can be hard to find what you need. Others didn't make them at all. Generally speaking, registers were better kept in Lowland parishes than in Highland parishes.

In other instances, church records are missing because of parishioners, rather than recordkeepers. For example, many poor families didn't bother having their children's baptisms recorded. Baptismal records were kept (among other reasons) to prove parentage for future inheritance, but those without an estate to pass on didn't feel the need to document baptisms.

Government action also had an impact on parish records. In 1783, the British government imposed a three-pence tax on parish-register entries. Some parishes quit record-keeping until the tax was repealed in 1794, while families in other parishes would pay the tax for their first child's baptism, but not for the second child's baptism. On the other hand, some parishes started keeping records for the first time when the tax was imposed, figuring that, if parish records were important enough to be taxed, they were important enough to be kept.

Birth/Baptismal Records

Baptism registers (image) survive in the greatest quantity, and they contain a great deal of information. Even the least detailed baptism registers contain the name of the child, the father, and the date of baptism. More complete registers will include the name of the child, the names of both parents, the parents' residence, the names of the two or

---

RESEARCH TIP

Look for Record Groupings

Some parishes kept separate volumes or sections for each record type: baptisms, marriages, and deaths. Other parishes mixed all the entries up, so a marriage record for one couple might be followed by the baptisms of several children of the parish. As if to confuse researchers even more, parishes that merged sometimes kept separate books for each constituent parish while others combined them. Be on the lookout for these inconsistencies, and be flexible in your search as a result.

Learning About Your Parish

Once you identify a parish of origin for your ancestor (see chapter 3), your first instinct will be to look for him in one of the many indexes available for the OPRs. But first, you should learn more about the parish itself before diving into records and indexes.

For example, be sure to find your parish on a map. This will put your ancestor's place of worship in geographical context, plus help identify nearby parishes and larger towns where your ancestor may have come from or gone to. On resource, *The Phillimore Atlas and Index of Parish Registers,* is available at Ancestry.com **<search.ancestry.com/search/db.aspx?dbid=8830>**.

All Scottish parishes have been given unique numbers, and the National Records of Scotland has created an index **<www.nrscotland.gov.uk/files//research/list-of-oprs/list-of-oprs-index.pdf>**. These numbers were included in the image frame when the Genealogical Society of Utah microfilmed the records, providing a quick and easy reference. Sometimes, two parishes were put on the same roll of microfilm, so be sure to pay attention to the item numbers in the catalog.

Learning about the history of the parish is also useful. Read the relevant entries in the Statistical Accounts of Scotland from the 1790s and 1840s (see chapter 5), and seek out local histories. To see what is available, check the FamilySearch.org catalog under the heading History for a specific parish. You might also find something of interest in *A List of Works Relating to Scotland,* by George F. Black (New York Public Library, 1916) **<archive.org/details/listofworksrelat00newy>**. Most, if not all, of the works referenced in this volume will be out of copyright, so you may find a copy at the Internet Archive **<archive.org>** or Google Books **<books.google.com>**.

Also determine what records exist for your ancestor's parish. William B. Turnbull prepared an analysis of parish records in 1849, mostly as a way to lobby for statutory registration in Scotland **<dcms.lds.org/delivery/DeliveryManagerServlet?dps_pid=IE10671737>**. Another source for this information is *Key to Parochial Register of Scotland* by V. Ben Bloxham (Brigham Young University Press, 1970). Both volumes are organized by county, so you will need to know what county your parish is in. Two more concise lists are available at the National Records of Scotland **<www.nrscotland.gov.uk/research/guides/old-parish-registers/list-of-old-parish-registers>**. One list was compiled in 1872, and the other is a modern, typed extract that is easier to read.

Some parishes had two churches, but only one set of church records. Pictured is Dalarossie Church in the United Parishes of Moy and Dalarossie, Invernesshire.

This birth register records births in June and July of 1821 in Kilmarnock Parish, Ayrshire. This clerk recorded the name of the child, the name of the parents, the father's occupation, and the child's birth number. This last fact can help you determine how many children the couple had.

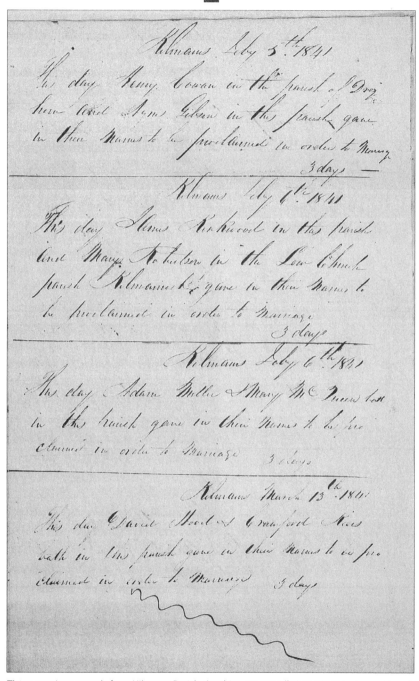

These marriage records from Kilmaurs Parish, Ayrshire, are actually intentions to marry, as each entry includes the names of the couple and that they "gave in their names to be proclaimed in order to marriage."

more witnesses, the residences of the witnesses, the date of birth, and the date of baptism. Witnesses were usually close friends or family members—in other words, part of a family's network. Frustratingly for the genealogist, sometimes the witness was "the congregation."

The language used in the baptism record will provide information about the marital status of the parents. The status of the child would be recorded as legitimate/legal or illegitimate/natural. The abbreviations *l.s.* (legitimate son) or *l.d.* (legitimate daughter) were frequently used. In Scotland, almost all women were known by their maiden names all throughout their lives—including in baptismal records, making it possible for you to find their parents even without marriage records.

Places of residence on baptism registers are especially useful. A place of residence for the child's parents will help you identify the family. And a couple frequently moving addresses indicates they did not have secure access to land. You can plot residences on a map to visualize your ancestors' network and ask questions about it. For example, is the network focused in one part of a parish? Or do they include two different parishes, or people who lived in a city and came home for the baptism?

Marriage Records

Parish marriage records (image **B**) are varied. You might find a record of the actual ceremony, marriage banns, or a marriage contract. Banns were supposed to be posted for three Sundays prior to the marriage in the parish of residence of the bride and groom. The basic marriage record will include the name of the bride and groom and either their residence or occupation and the date of the ceremony or banns. As with US records, you may find the banns or the marriage contract, but not an actual record of the event.

Marriage ceremonies generally occurred in the bride's parish, but might also be recorded in the groom's parish. Be sure to check both. Nonconformist couples frequently had their marriages recorded in the registers of the Church of Scotland, even though they weren't members of that faith tradition. Keep this fact in mind if you find a marriage but no subsequent baptisms of a couple's children.

Death Records

Death and burial records (image **C**) are the rarest among church records. At the most basic, you may find only a name and date of death or burial. You may only find a mortcloth (a cloth that covered a casket at the funeral) rental list. Some parishes even had different quality of mortcloth, the better of which cost more to rent.

If the name is common, it may be impossible to conclusively say that someone in the register is your ancestor.

(C)

1737

Tewsday October 25th

GW	31	Jean Johnstone sp: to Willm Fiddler writter ∘ ∘ ••	24	Decay
GW	32	a Child of Thomas Robertson flesher ∘ ∘ ∘ •	in Pore
GW	40	Susanna Fife re: of Robt neil smith Pensr ∘ ∘ *	85 Old Age

Wednesday 26th

RWBr	46	Margt Carmichael sp: to Wm Ramsay wright ••	50	Palsay
GW	41	an Orphan ∘ ∘ ∘ ∘ ∘ *	1	Decay
GW	42	Elizabeth McDouall Pensr ∘ ∘ ∘ *	60	Suddenly
GW	43	a Child of mr McIllwrath painter ∘ ∘ *	2	Pore

Thursday 27th

RWa	47	a Child of Wm Johnstone smith ∘ ∘ ∘ •	⅔	Teething
RWa	48	a Child of mr Weems ∘ ∘ ∘ ∘ •	2	Decay
RWa	49	a Child of Wm Blake wright ∘ ∘ ∘ •	⅔	Fever
RWa	50	a Child of George Duncan Indwr ∘ ∘ ∘ •	3	Decay
RWa	51	a Child of John Scot Drummer ∘ ∘ ∘ *	1½	Pore
GW	44	Isobel Anderson Indwr ∘ ∘ ∘ ∘ *	40	Decay
GWT	45	Widow Henderson alias Margt Hume ...	72	Old Age

Friday 28th

RWa	52	a Child of John Baveradge wright ∘ ∘ ∘ •	½	Fever
RWa	53	a Child of David Mitchel Chairman ∘ ∘ *	6	Pox
RWa	54	a Child of Henry Gibson Dyster ∘ ∘ ∘ •	½	Teeth
RWa	55	a Child of James Lauder Taylor ∘ ∘ ∘ •	3	Pox
GW	46	a poor Fad	*	20	Decay

Saturday 29th

GWa	33	Magdalan Kinloch re: of mr Bouith Gentleman ••	45	Fever
RWa	56	a Child of John Muir Indwr ∘ ∘ ∘ *	¾	Pox
GWa	57	a Child of John Robertson Prinler ∘ ∘ •	2¼	Pox

The mortality rolls of 1737 for Edinburgh Parish show the name of adults, age, and cause of death. The children are not identified by their name, only the name of their father.

Watch for the Julian-Gregorian Split

For millennia, Europe used the Julian calendar. In this system, the New Year started on March 25. But because this calendar had fallen out of sync with the solar year, a new calendar called the Gregorian (in which ten days were dropped and the year started on January 1) was established in 1582. Scotland first adopted this in 1600, in which December 31, 1599, was followed by January 1, 1600. Scotland didn't adopt the rest of the Gregorian calendar until 1752, when Parliament took eleven days out of the year and jumped straight from September 2 to September 14. Be wary of this disconnect, as documents in England and Scotland were often double dated to indicate both Julian and Gregorian calendars—for example: *2 February 1648/1649*. However, if one date appears in a Scottish parish record (e.g., *5 March 1700*), you can take comfort in knowing it refers to the Gregorian calendar date. You may also see the Julian calendar referred to as "Old Style" (O.S.) and the Gregorian calendar as "New Style" (N.S.).

Finding OPRs

You have several ways of accessing the Old Parish Registers. Searchable databases are available at ScotlandsPeople **<scotlandspeople.gov.uk>** and FamilySearch.org **<www.familysearch.org>**. Both ScotlandsPeople and FamilySearch.org are free to search, but you must register first—and ScotlandsPeople requires a fee to view pages. From the search results page at ScotlandsPeople, you may click on the blue box and pay six credits to see the desired image. Each image downloaded from ScotlandsPeople will include citation details, while the images from FamilySearch.org will generally only include the parish reference number.

The baptism databases at both ScotlandsPeople and FamilySearch.org include the name of the child, the parish where the child was baptized, the date of baptism, and the names of the parents. At FamilySearch.org, you will also see the date of birth (if available) and the corresponding microfilm roll number. At ScotlandsPeople, the baptism database includes the parish number and a page number.

The marriage database at FamilySearch.org shares the name of the couple, the date of the "event," the location, and the corresponding microfilm roll number. ScotlandsPeople has the same data, but also the parish number and a reference number.

The relevant collections at FamilySearch.org are "Scotland Births and Baptisms, 1564–1950" <www.familysearch.org/search/collection/1771030> and "Scotland Marriages, 1561–1910" <www.familysearch.org/search/collection/1771074>. The FamilySearch.org collections are also available at Ancestry.com, MyHeritage <www.myheritage.com>, and Findmypast, all three of which are behind a paywall.

OPR microfilm rolls have been digitized by FamilySearch.org, and you can view them at Family History Centers and affiliate libraries <www.familysearch.org/locations>. However, the digitized microfilm is not linked to the database results page. You must find the roll of microfilm in the card catalog, then click on the icon of the camera. Then start browsing through the digital microfilm as if you were looking at it on a microfilm reader. This may not be as easy as it sounds, as events were occasionally recorded several years after they took place. The clerk may have used blank pages in the front of the book to record later events (forcing you to flip through blank images to find what you want), and the seventeenth-century records will be difficult to read. If you are having difficulty finding the record you need, it may be easier to acquire the record from ScotlandsPeople.

KIRK SESSION RECORDS

While parish records are probably the most useful kind of church records available to Scottish researchers, records from the Church of Scotland's administrative side can also provide insight into your ancestors' lives.

Before we dive into these records, we first need to review how the Church of Scotland is organized. The Church is governed by a series of courts, listed here from lowest to highest:

- kirk sessions at the local level
- presbytery at the district level
- the General Assembly, the highest court

RESEARCH TIP

Find Language Connections

The Gaelic language became part of the religious experience for Presbyterians from the Highlands. This custom was maintained in the United States as much as possible. If you have ancestors from the Highlands, look to see if any of the Presbyterian churches near them were associated with the Gaelic language in any way, then look for your ancestors and their network at that church.

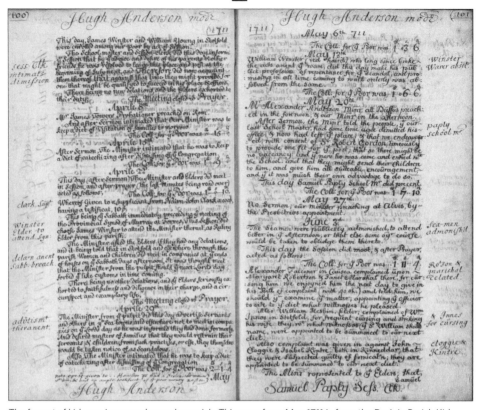

The format of kirk session records vary by parish. This page from May 1711 is from the Drainie Parish Kirk Session in Morayshire.

Each of these courts created records that may include a reference to your ancestor. Notably, kirk sessions created records (image **D**) as they handled church administration and recorded infractions against church law (such as adultery and blasphemy). Individuals charged would be named and called to an account for their actions, then would often be required to do penance for their actions. Your ancestors may be among the accused or the accusers. In addition to the court cases, kirk sessions may list communicants, the names of people receiving poor relief, topics of a minister's sermons, or miscellaneous birth, death, and marriage records.

The National Records of Scotland and a handful of local archives hold nearly twenty thousand volumes of kirk session records. The vast majority of these records were digitized by 2007, available to browse online at the National Records of Scotland in Edinburgh and select local archives throughout Scotland <www.nrscotland.gov.uk/research/guides/

church-court-records-online>. At the time of this book's publication, ScotlandsPeople is developing a project to give international researchers access to these records over the next few years. Once the kirk session records go online, researchers will be able to look up a parish to see what types of records are available in them and browse the records for a mention of their ancestors. (Due to the sheer number of the kirk session records, they likely will not be indexed.)

The Genealogical Society of Utah has also microfilmed some kirk session records. You may find some of them under the heading "Blotter Register" (basically a copy of the original) or "Parish Records." This material is generally not indexed, but much of it has been digitized and is available to view at a Family History Center or affiliate library. However, some extractions of birth, marriage, and death records were included in kirk session records and have been indexed in database called "Scotland Church Records and Kirk Session Records, 1658–1919" <www.familysearch.org/search/collection/2390848>. Some of these index entries are linked to a kirk session volume, but not to the exact page where the entry can be found. Findmypast has a similar collection: "Scotland Non-Old Parish Registers Vital Records 1647–1875" <search.findmypast.com/search-world-Records/scotland-non-old-parish-registers-vital-records-1647-1875>.

Additionally, some kirk session records have been published, at least in abstracted form. Check the FamilySearch.org catalog to see what is available. If the publication is from the nineteenth century, you might find it online in a publication such as *Inverness Kirk-Session Records, 1661–1880* <archive.org/details/invernesskirkses00inve>.

NONCONFORMIST CHURCH RECORDS

The Church of Scotland experienced many divisions in its history, creating daughter Presbyterian churches that had their own structure and records. Nonconformist, or dissenting, denominations like Baptists and Quakers were also established in Scotland. Episcopalian and Roman Catholic churches were also present, mostly in the east and the north of the country. Non-conformist ministers could not perform legal ceremonies until 1834. So, it is likely that a great many irregular marriages prior to this date were not marriages by consent (see chapter 7), but by non-authorized ministers. However, under Scots law, there appears to have been little difference. If your ancestor disappears from the OPR for a number of years or you can't find him in the first place, it is possible that he attended a nonconformist church during that period.

One way to learn what nonconformist records are available is to consult the *National Index of Parish Registers* by D.J. and A.E.F. Steel, which you can borrow from <archive.org/details/nationalindexofp12stee>.

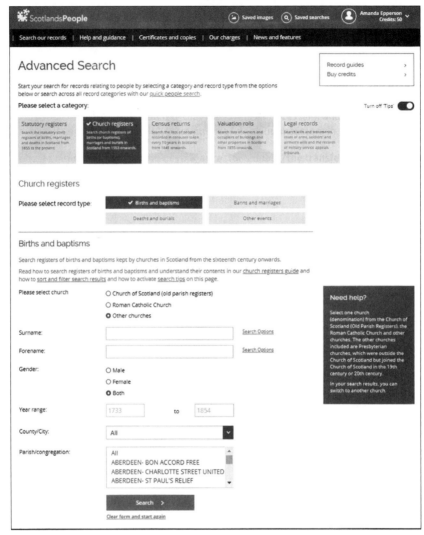

Once you log in at ScotlandsPeople, you can select which types of Church records you wish to search: the OPRs, Catholic records, or other denominations. If you need help, information in the green tip box will provide guidance.

Roman Catholic Church

In the seventeenth century, Scotland had only about fifty thousand Roman Catholics (about 5 percent of the Scottish population), located primarily in Dumfries-shire, Kirkcudbright, Moray, Aberdeen, Inverness-shire, and the Western Isles. After the Reformation, the Church of Scotland assumed the traditional parish structure, and the Catholic Church was organized in large mission territories. The Catholic population of Scotland increased after significant immigration from Ireland in the nineteenth century and Continental Europe after World War II.

The records for most Scottish missions begin in the nineteenth century and primarily include baptisms and marriages, although other records such as of anointing of the sick (or "sick calls") and confessions may be available. You can find a list of available Catholic records at the Scottish Catholic Archive <www.scottishcatholicarchives.org.uk/FamilyHistory/ParishRegisterholdings/tabid/82/Default.aspx>, where they've been digitized and indexed up to 1855. Searchable databases and images are available at both ScotlandsPeople (image **E**) and Findmypast <www.findmypast.co.uk>. Some records may still be with local congregations or kept at diocesan archives.

Other Presbyterian Churches

Over the years (beginning in the seventeenth century), several groups split off from the Church of Scotland to form their own faith communities. The most significant break, known as the Disruption, occurred in 1843 when 451 ministers left to form the Free Church of Scotland. Most of these dissenting branches reunited with the Church of Scotland by 1929. The earliest of these dissenting registers begins in 1716. Records for those churches that rejoined the Church of Scotland are available at ScotlandsPeople: the Reformed Presbyterian Church, the Original Succession Church, the Associate Synods, the Relief Church, the United Secession Church, the United Presbyterian Church, and the Free Church.

The Associate and Reformed branches of Presbyterianism had a strong presence in the United States. If you have an ancestor who was a member of one of these two denominations, she may have attended their counterparts in Scotland. Likewise, a third church was created in the United States when the Associate and Reformed Branches merged in 1782 to form the Associate Reformed Presbyterian Church. It, along with its parent denominations, were seen as being "ethnically Scottish," and held more closely to religious customs of Scotland. In contrast, the mainline Presbyterian Church was seen as being more modern and American. As a result, your ancestor may have been a member of the Church of Scotland and then switched to the Associate, Reformed, or Associate Reformed Church upon settling in America.

Other Denominations

Additional Protestant denominations that had a presence in Scotland include the Episcopalians, the Baptists, the Congregationalists, the Religious Society of Friends (Quakers), the Methodists, and the Unitarians. Some of these churches' records, like those of the Episcopalian Church, are still held locally. Others are held at local authority archives, university archives, the National Records of Scotland, and the Glasgow City Archives.

You can find more details about the specific church records held by the National Records of Scotland by using its online catalog <catalogue.nrscotland.gov.uk/nrsonlinecatalogue/welcome.aspx>. To learn what records local archives hold, you can search the online catalog of the Scottish Archive Network <catalogue.nrscotland.gov.uk/scancatalogue/welcome.aspx>. This is a single catalog for fifty-two archives within Scotland. Each entry provides details about the material and information about where it is held and how to access it.

There was also a small community of Jews in Scotland, and you should check with the Scottish Jewish Archive Centre about how it might be able to help you with your research <www.sjac.org.uk/collections/family-history-genealogy>.

KEYS TO SUCCESS

Learn about your ancestor's parish. Doing so will help you learn what records are available and provide detail and context about your ancestor's life.

Use the residences of your ancestors and other individuals named in the OPR entries to create a map of your ancestor's network. This will visually show not only whom he interacted with, but also other possible contacts who may lead to further clues or records.

Check the records of other denominations if you cannot find your ancestor in the Church of Scotland records.

9

Census Records

Researchers from the United States have come to rely heavily upon federal census records, and for good reason: Census records place your ancestors and their families in a particular place at a particular time, and those kept at regular intervals can be crucial in tracking your ancestors over time.

Fortunately for Scottish researchers, Great Britain also took regular nationwide censuses in the British Isles (including Scotland), beginning in 1801. Inspired by concerns over population and food scarcity, these censuses were not made for genealogists. But they do contain valuable genealogical detail nonetheless. And before 1801, tax records and other documents can provide similar information about your Scottish ancestors.

This chapter will describe Scottish census records and census substitutes, showing you how to obtain and use them.

CENSUS RECORDS

A national census has been taken in Scotland every decade since 1801 (except for 1941, during World War II). The first censuses were taken by schoolmasters, who knew their communities well. But district registrars and other enumerators took over this duty in 1861, the first census after civil registration was first implemented (see chapter 7).

Census-takers created enumeration districts to administer this task, and these districts included only the number of dwellings an enumerator could reasonably visit in one day.

A week before the census, the enumerator took a census schedule to each family in his assigned enumeration district. The heads of household were to fill out the schedule according to the instructions printed on it. Most importantly, they were only to list those who were actually present in the household on census night. The next day, the enumerator would collect all the schedules. If someone had not filled out the form (either because they were illiterate or because they were obstinate), the enumerator would do it for them. Then the enumerator would copy these forms into his official register. All of the originals were destroyed; only the official registers survive.

Because only those present on census night were to be included, people you might expect to find with the family may not be there. In theory, these missing family members should be enumerated where they were on census night—perhaps at a relative's house, or at an inn if they were travelling. However, note that family members who worked what would today be called a "graveyard shift" were to be included on the schedule at their homes.

Scottish census records are, by law, closed for one hundred years after the date of the census. As of this book's publication, the 1911 census is the most recent census available, with the 1921 census slotted for release in 2021.

Let's take a look at the census records from 1801 to 1911. As you'll see, the census asked different questions as time went on. See appendix D for a chart displaying Scottish census questions at a glance.

1801–1831

The earliest census records, 1801, 1811, 1821, and 1831, were merely head counts or tallies of individuals, and they didn't require personal, genealogically useful information. In order to create the official tallies, officials often made a detailed list of all the inhabitants of a parish first, and these documents can be incredibly useful in providing details omitted by the census registers. Only a handful of these complete lists survive (image **A**), and the National Records of Scotland has details on each year's census and where they can be found <www.nrscotland.gov.uk/research/guides/census-records/pre-1841-census-records>.

1841

The 1841 census is the first in which the members of each household were listed individually, along with facts about them and the household's address (image **B**). This census, along with the one for 1851, are particularly useful in Scottish genealogy, as they occurred before statutory registration began and may list people who weren't in the OPRs

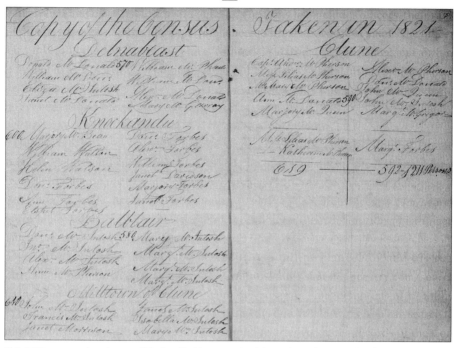

This 1821 census return is one of the few that have survived throughout the centuries. As you can see, the information here is sparse and handwritten. This community, Moy and Dalarossie Parish, also has a surviving 1831 census record.

(e.g., those who died prior to 1855). In fact, these census records may be the only records in which some individuals appear.

While this census doesn't record the relationship between household members, you can usually infer the relationship between them. For example, you can reasonably assume that a household of five made up of a couple in their thirties and three toddlers that all have the same surname are parents and their three children. You'll want to consult other records to confirm your theory, but the census can still provide a useful starting point.

Census Dates

Year	Census Date
1841	June 6
1851	March 30
1861	April 7
1871	April 2
1881	April 3
1891	April 5
1901	March 31
1911	April 2

Parish of _Dunbar_

1			2			3	4	
PLACE	HOUSES		NAME and SURNAME, SEX and AGE, of each Person who abode in each House on the Night of 6th June.			OCCUPATION	WHERE BORN	
Here insert Name of Village, Street, Square, Close, Court, &c.	Uninhabited or Building	Inhabited	NAME and SURNAME	AGE		Of what Profession, Trade, Employment, or whether of Independent Means.	If Born in Scotland, state whether in County or otherwise.	Whether Foreign ct., or whether Born in England or Ireland.
				Male	Female			
High street			Janet Kellie		35			I.
			Susan Do		14			I
			James Do	7				I.
			Ann Do		4			I
			Margt Davidson		25		n.	
			James Do	7			u.	
Do.		1	George Dawson	85		Tailor	g.	
			Margaret Do		60		g.	
Do.	1	1	Catherine Aitchell		75	Ind	g.	
Do.		1	Daniel Moore	35		Meat dealer		E.
			Ann Do		25		g.	
			Margt Do		6		g.	
			Sarah Do		5		g.	
			John Do	3			g.	
			David Do	10mo			g.	
			Christinia Penraith		10	F.S.	g.	
			John Blackley	15			n.	
Do.		1	John Finlay	70		Sh. dealer	g.	

The 1841 census is the first to consistently list individual household members. As we can see halfway down this page, thirty-five-year-old Daniel Muir (Moore) and his family of six lived in Dunbar parish in 1841. Among his children are three-year-old John Muir, who later co-founded the Sierra Club.

C

Robert L. B. Stevenson (line 4) was born just in time to be included with his parents in the 1851 census for Scotland. He later wrote the famous novels *Kidnapped* and *Treasure Island*.

Note that, for some reason, ages were not accurately recorded in the 1841 census for individuals over the age of fifteen. Age was often rounded down to the nearest multiple of five. Thus, someone who was twenty-one would be recorded as twenty, and someone who was forty-nine would be recorded as forty-five. This mandate was often overlooked, so you should view ages in the 1841 census skeptically.

The 1841 census also recorded an occupation for each individual, but not a specific birthplace. Rather, the census only indicated whether or not a person was born in Scotland and (if they weren't native) what country they were born in: *I* for Ireland, *E* for England, and *F* for foreign (all other countries).

The 1841 census records for some parishes, mostly in Fife, are missing. See the National Records of Scotland for a list <www.nrscotland.gov.uk/research/guides/census-records/1841-census#Missing>.

1851

From a genealogical perspective, the 1851 census (image **C**) is a vast improvement over the 1841 census. Ages were recorded accurately (well, as accurately as ages ever are in census records), as are the relationships between each household member and the "condition" of each person (whether they were singled, married, or widowed). The 1851

Two-year-old John Logie Baird, who would go on to invent the television, lived in Helensburgh, Dunbartonshire, in the 1891 census. Thanks to the detail in this census record, we know his father was born in Glasgow and served as a clergyman in 1891.

census also gives a place of birth—often the specific parish—as well as the current address and occupation. The parish of birth is an especially helpful detail if you have not yet found your ancestor in the OPRs. This census also asks if a person was disabled—that is, blind, deaf and/or unable to speak.

1861–1911

The censuses from 1861 to 1911 are all essentially the same. They feature the same information from the 1841 and 1851 censuses, plus some new questions that were added such as if children were home-schooled or if a person spoke Gaelic (image D). In fact, so many questions and detail had been added by 1911 that the census schedule was two pages instead of one. Some responses for the questions regarding unemployment and the disabled were altered. Notably, questions regarding fertility were added in 1911: how long had a couple been married, how many children had been born to the marriage, and how many were still living on census night. This information might help verify any civil registration records found for a couple and their children.

HOW TO ACQUIRE CENSUS RECORDS

Many websites host indexes for the Scottish census: FamilySearch.org <www.familysearch.org>, Ancestry.com <www.ancestry.com>, Findmypast <www.findmypast.co.uk>, and ScotlandsPeople <www.scotlandspeople.gov.uk>. The indexes are free at FamilySearch.org and ScotlandsPeople, but the indexes are behind a paywall at Ancestry.com and Findmypast.

FamilySearch.org has indexes for the census records from 1841 to 1891. Each index entry is for an individual person only—*not* for the entire household in which they resided. The index entry includes the person's name, age, parish, and estimated birth year. Within the citation will be the page number and the microfilm roll number. You can search the catalog for the microfilm number, then click on the camera icon to be taken to the digital microfilm if you're in a Family History Center or affiliate library. (If you're researching from elsewhere, note the microfilm number for your next visit.) Each parish was divided into several enumeration districts, but there does not seem to be anything in the citation to note the enumeration district, just the page. If your ancestor is supposed to be on page 2, you may have to look at the second page of several enumeration districts before you find him.

Ancestry.com has a searchable collection for the 1841 to 1901 Scottish censuses. The collection extracted much more information than the one at FamilySearch.org and includes everyone in a household, plus their ages, estimated birth years, occupations, addresses, registration districts, enumeration districts, household schedule numbers, and page numbers. You'll see a microfilm number here as well, but it's not the same one used by FamilySearch.org. Unfortunately, the Ancestry.com collection doesn't have images.

ScotlandsPeople has indexes for every census from 1841 to 1911. The search results will include the person's name, gender, age, registration district (or parish), and county, plus the year of the census and a reference that indicates the district, enumeration district, and page number. Results are not displayed as complete households, but two individuals in the same enumeration district and on the same page might be living in the same

RESEARCH TIP

Research the Whole Neighborhood

Looking at the other pages in your ancestor's enumeration district will give you a feel for his neighborhood, plus the opportunity to find members of his network. As you dive into census records, be sure to search more broadly so you can explore your ancestor's community and discover those important to his life. These individuals may have served as godparents for his children, or traveled with him to the New World.

household or on the same street. ScotlandsPeople has digital images of all census records, and you can view each for six credits.

ScotlandsPeople also has a search feature that allows you to add the first name of another person on the census page as your primary search term. For example, I searched the 1861 census for David Hood and got fifty-one results. When I added the name of his wife, Elizabeth, I narrowed it down to just six. From there, it was easy to identify the David Hood who lived in Riccarton Parish.

You can use these databases in combination with each other. Ancestry.com shows information for entire households, plus the household number, the enumeration district number, and the page number, while ScotlandsPeople shows only one person at a time but does provide a detailed reference number. You could search these two sites for your ancestor in a census, then go to the FamilySearch.org catalog and search for the registration district (usually the same as the parish) and make note of the microfilm number. During a trip to a Family History Center or affiliate library, you could use that microfilm number to view an actual image of the census record. (Though if you're researching the 1901 or 1911 censuses, you have to go back to ScotlandsPeople to view the images.)

Each site has its pros and cons, so you'll need to be aware of these as you begin your research. For example, ScotlandsPeople shows only one page at a time and charges per image, but FamilySearch.org allows you to view as many pages as you like for the 1841 to the 1891 censuses. But if your ancestor lived in a large metropolis like Glasgow or Edinburgh in the late nineteenth century, it may be easier to obtain an image of his census record from ScotlandsPeople. Scrolling through many enumeration districts on FamilySearch.org's digitized microfilm roll is quite cumbersome, and you may miss the one you need or simply get fed up with the process.

Findmypast <www.findmypast.com> also holds collections of the 1841–1901 Scottish censuses. If you are not sure what county your ancestor lived in, be sure to enter Scotland as the country when searching this collection, since it includes records for England, Scotland, and Wales. Your search results will take you to transcriptions of the census schedule, but it will not link to the image. (Findmypast does, however, have images of the English and Welsh censuses.)

CENSUS SUBSTITUTES: TAX RECORDS

They say that the only certainties in life are death and taxes. And, fortunately for genealogists, our ancestors also often had to pay taxes, and the records created by taxation can serve as useful substitutes in areas in which census records were lost or in times before census-taking began.

Before the seventeenth century, taxes on the general population were quite rare, as most of the tax burden fell on land and was paid by landowners, the burghs, and the church. Wider taxation was usually only collected for a specific purpose, such as defending Scotland in times of war. The tax base broadened in the seventeenth century with the Hearth Tax (on fireplaces) and the Poll Tax (on individuals).

Additional taxes were imposed in the eighteenth century. Some of these were Scottish versions of taxes that had been paid in England before the Union, while others were unique to Scotland. Prime Minister William Pitt (the younger), influenced by the noted Scottish economist Adam Smith, introduced several new taxes in the late eighteenth century, partially to help ease the debt created by trying to maintain the American colonies during the War of Independence. While these taxes were unpopular, Pitt coupled them with a campaign to reduce revenue fraud and the cost of administering the government. Additionally, although the new taxes were nominally levied on all households, they were in actuality paid primarily by the wealthy. When war with France began in 1793, additional taxes were imposed and other taxes were raised. Great Britain levied the first income tax in 1799.

These taxes generated lists of taxpayers, many of whom may be your ancestors. However (unlike the census records they can substitute for), tax lists do not always survive for each county, and many of the

Scottish Currency

Scotland, like the rest of the United Kingdom, uses the pound sterling as its currency today. But before the Union of 1707, Scotland had its own currency, known as the pound Scots. Under this system, a pound Scots comprised twenty shillings, and each shilling was equal to twelve pennies (or pence). Over the centuries, the pound Scots lost value when compared with the pound sterling used in England. In 1603, the exchange of pound Scots to sterling was fixed at a rate of 12:1. Scottish currency was officially withdrawn in 1707, but wages, rents, and the value of agricultural produce was expressed in Scots money for many years afterward.

taxes only record the names of the elite. On the plus side, many of these tax records have been digitized and are available at ScotlandsPlaces <scotlandsplaces.gov.uk/digital-volumes/historical-tax-rolls> free of charge. Additionally, volunteers have transcribed many of these records. ScotlandsPlaces anticipates that additional tax volumes will be uploaded in the future, so be sure to check for additions to their collection. The records are not searchable, but you can look at them line by line since most parishes don't have too many entries.

Let's take a look at each kind of tax levied on Scotland throughout the centuries—and how each can help you fill in information from census records.

Carriage and Cart Tax Rolls

The Carriage Tax <scotlandsplaces.gov.uk/digital-volumes/historical-tax-rolls/carriage-tax-rolls-1785-1798> was levied between 1785 and 1798 on owners of two- or four-wheeled carriages. A tax on more modest carts <scotlandsplaces.gov.uk/digital-volumes/historical-tax-rolls/cart-tax-rolls-1785-1798> was levied in those same years on owners of two-, three-, or four-wheeled carts (typically farmers and landowners in rural Scotland).

These tax rolls include the names of the owners, the type of cart or carriage owned, and the amount of duty paid. The county and burgh records are bound in separate volumes, and each volume contains one year—for example, volume 3 has the counties for 1786 to 1787, while volume 4 has the burghs for the same year. Note that some volumes do not survive for all years, and records from certain counties may be missing from certain volumes.

Clock and Watch Tax Rolls

The Clock and Watch Tax <scotlandsplaces.gov.uk/digital-volumes/historical-tax-rolls/clock-and-watch-tax-rolls-1797-1798>, introduced in 1797, was a duty charged on all time pieces. This tax proved completely unworkable, as people easily lied about their number of clocks and watches, hiding them from inspectors when they visited. Additionally, demand for new clocks and watches dropped so quickly that many timepiece manufacturers found themselves unemployed. The tax was repealed just a year later in 1798, and only two volumes of Clock and Watch Tax Rolls survive for Scotland. Each roll lists the names of the owners, the number of timepieces owned, and the duty owed.

Consolidated Schedules of Assessed Taxes

Beginning in 1787, tax collectors consolidated the schedules recording the many taxes being administered, including: houses and windows, inhabited houses, servants, carriages, horses, and dogs. These can serve as useful substitutes if you're missing individual tax records, though only schedules for 1798 and 1799 in counties that start with the letters A–M survive **<scotlandsplaces.gov.uk/digital-volumes/historical-tax-rolls/consolidated-schedules-assessed-taxes-1798-1799>**.

The surviving records offer a more comprehensive record of the residents of many parishes, as even modest houses were liable to a tax of two schillings and six pence in 1798. Volumes 1–22 contain the surviving consolidated tax rolls for the counties. Most rolls have only one county; Aberdeenshire, Fife, and Invernesshire have been divided in half (so one-half county per roll). A few rolls include more than one county, and another few only contain partial counties. Volumes 23–32 include the surviving consolidated tax rolls for the burghs.

Dog Tax

This two-volume collection showcases a tax on non-working dogs **<scotlandsplaces.gov.uk/digital-volumes/historical-tax-rolls/dog-tax-rolls-1797-1798>** levied in 1797 and 1798. Volume 1 includes records for counties with last names starting with A–K, and Volume 2 includes records for counties with last names starting with L–W. The tax lists include the name of the owners and the number of non-working dogs they owned.

Hearth Tax

The Scottish parliament authorized the Hearth Tax in 1690, and the funds raised were to be used to repay debt. This tax placed a levy of fourteen schillings each on all hearths and kilns, whether they were in the house of a landowner or tenant. Only people living on charity and in hospitals were exempt.

The tax was due on Candlemas February 2, 1690. However, the tax was difficult to collect, especially in remote areas like the Highlands. By 1694, the tax was only collected in some areas. The collectors of the Hearth Tax were required to make lists of those hearths that were taxable as well as that were exempt. A large tax implies several hearths and (by implication) a large house.

Only about half of the counties list the name of the householder, while the remainder only list the number of hearths. ScotlandsPlaces notes whether or not the records contain householders. The Hearth Tax Rolls are difficult to read, but the Scottish Handwriting website has a useful tutorial available specifically for learning to read these documents **<www.scottishhandwriting.com/hearthtax/Introduction.asp>**.

The Hearth Tax Rolls that are part of the Exchequer Papers held at the National Records of Scotland. These are available online, with transcriptions, at ScotlandsPeople (image **E**). These same records have been microfilmed by FamilySearch.org, along with

ScotlandsPlaces

About   Places   Records   Contact

Hearth tax records for Roxburghshire

Records / Historical Tax Rolls / Hearth tax records 1691-1695 / Hearth tax records for Roxburghshire

Contents | **Transcription**

Page	Hearth tax transcription	Transcriber's notes
E69/21/1/1	Hearth money deponed upon Thomas Turnbull of Know his Booke For Roxburgh shire [Page] 1	
E69/21/1/1		Reference No. 21/1
E69/21/1/1	An Just double of the List of Ednim Parioch According as is was Given up to me -- hearths The Laird of Ednim -- 16 Robert Merschall Ednim -- 1 John Turnbull Ednim -- 1 Margaret Hermispoune Ednim -- 1 John Akie Ednim -- 1 Robbel Aitchisone Ednim -- 1 Jean Miller Ednim -- 1 Jennett Dods Ednim -- 1 Robert Sands Ednim -- 1 william Merschall Ednim -- 1 John Robisone -- 1 Margaret Trotter -- 1 George Gillie -- 1 Jean Gibe -- 1 James Couan -- 1 James young wt [with] an Smiddy -- 2 Margaret Lausone -- 1 Patrick Thomsone -- 1 John yeeman -- 1 Robert Lidgaie -- 1 James Thomsone -- 1 Androw Burne -- 1 william Robisone -- 1 william Burne -- 1 Androw Blaire -- 1 James Lausone -- 1 Archbald Dicksone -- 1 Nicholl Akie -- 1 George Aitchisone wt [with] an Smiddy -- 2 Bessie wilsone -- 1 Jennet Blaithe -- 1 william Dickman -- 1 Espith Poncoune -- 1 Alexander Thomsone -- 1 Androw Trotter -- 1 Adam Mewris -- 1 John Hunter -- 1 Androw Brissone -- 1 Agnes Brunfeild -- 1 Christian yeeman -- 1 Alexander Cosser -- 1 James Fairbairne -- 1 [Total] -- 59 [Page] 2 Espith Kennidy -- 1 Thomas Wood -- 1 John Dicksone -- 1 Rodger Dicksone -- 1 John Fairbairne -- 1 Thomas Davidsone -- 1 Robert Dicksone -- 1 Robert Measson -- 1 Androw Graye -- 1 Patrick Shell -- 1 John Burne -- 1 John Trotter -- 1 william Gibe -- 1 John Smith -- 1 Agnes Aitchisone wt [with] an Smiddy -- 2 John Coocke -- 1 John Hudde -- 1 Robert Burne -- 1 George Handisyde -- 1 John Jephray -- 1 John Murry -- 1 John Carbrainne -- 1 John Boyde -- 1 Robert Dicksone -- 1 John Maine -- 1 Katharine Akie -- 1 Thomas Hunter -- 1 David Dods -- 1 William Piller -- 1 Thomas Persone -- 1 George Bosualie -- 1 John Smithe -- 1 Alexander Linsaye -- 1 william Broune -- 1 william Dicksone -- 1 Frederick LilBurne wt [with] an kilne -- 2 James Thomsone -- 1 John Murrise -- 1 Benny Meine -- 1 John Stevinsone -- 1 John Dickman -- 1 Agnes Burne -- 1 Sr. James Done his Interest in the Parioch of Ednim William Measone -- 2 Andow walker -- 1 [Total] -- 47 [Page] 3	
E69/21/1/3		Pages numbered 2 and 3 in modern hand

This screenshot shows the transcription details for the Hearth Tax for Roxburghshire. The transcriptions also accompany each image of the original document. This should enable you to decipher the seventeenth-century handwriting.

the Hearth Tax records that are in the Leven and Melville Papers (image **F**). Additionally, many Hearth Tax rolls have been transcribed and published in books, journals, or online.

The rolls at ScotlandsPeople **<scotlandsplaces.gov.uk/digital-volumes/historical-tax-rolls/hearth-tax-records-1691-1695>** are generally arranged by county, then by parish or landed estate. Some rolls are more complete than others, as several counties don't have all records for their parishes. In addition, there are no surviving rolls for Orkney, Shetland, Caithness, or Ross and Cromarty.

Horse and Farm Horse Tax

Levies of horses and farm horses were collected in the late eighteenth century. The first levy implemented was the Horse Tax **<scotlandsplaces.gov.uk/digital-volumes/historical-tax-rolls/horse-tax-rolls-1785-1798>**, which taxed carriage and saddle horses between 1785 and 1798. This collection comprises thirty-three volumes and gives the owners' names, plus the number of horses.

The following decade, a second levy, the Farm Horse Tax **<scotlandsplaces.gov.uk/digital-volumes/historical-tax-rolls/farm-horse-tax-rolls-1797-1798>**, was enacted and taxed horses or mules used in farming or trade. This collection comprises thirteen volumes, and the rolls name the owners and provide information on the working horses or mules owned. The tax collectors often returned to a parish to track down non-payers, so a parish may be listed twice.

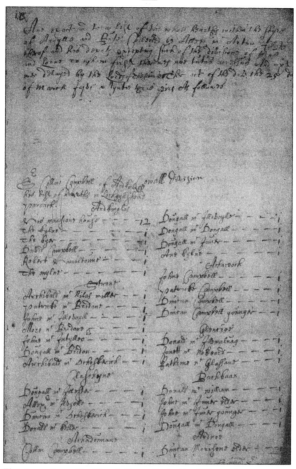

This page shows the Hearth Tax collected by "Allexander McArthur" in part of Argyll and Bute in 1693. Amongst the hearths noted were the mansion house, kiln, and byre belonging to Sir Collline Campbell of Ardkinglas.

Inhabited House Tax

From 1778 to 1798, all inhabited houses that had a rental value of at least five pounds per year were taxed. These records include thousands of pages of householder names and the annual value of their houses. Few rural homes would have reached the threshold value of five pounds, but the rolls would have included many prosperous people living in towns.

The Inhabited House Tax rolls are available at ScotlandsPlaces **<scotlandsplaces.gov. uk/digital-volumes/historical-tax-rolls/inhabited-house-tax-1778-1798>**. Unfortunately,

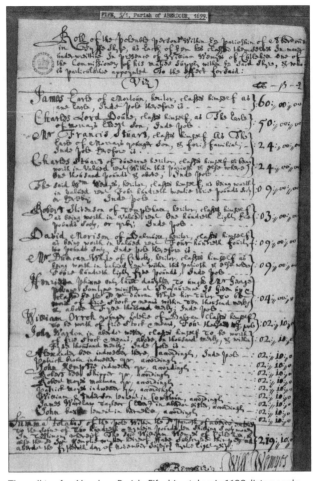

The poll tax for Aberdour Parish, Fifeshire, taken in 1699, lists people by social rank. The first person on the list is James, Earl of Morton who "classes himself as ane Earle [sic]."

many of the rolls are missing: There are no schedules for 1795 to 1797; the only schedules that survive for 1793 to 1794 are those for the county and burgh of Inverness. For most years, the burghs and their parent counties are in the same roll.

Poll Tax

The Poll Tax (image **G**), used to pay the army and navy, was imposed on all Scots four times: once each in 1694 and 1695, and twice in 1698. Each person paid according to their

Culloden House in the parish of Inverness and Bona was completed in 1788. Two years later, owner Arthur Forbes was assessed a duty of seven pounds and six shillings on seventy-eight windows as part of the Windows Tax. His dues were worth well over an equivalent of £1,000 in today's money.

means and rank, so those who were higher in rank paid a higher tax. The basic rate was set at six schillings per head, and only children under the age of sixteen (as well as the poor) were exempt. Despite harsh penalties for non-payment, the Poll Tax was difficult to collect. The records are incomplete and do not survive for all counties for all four instances. Additionally, the information included in the tax records varies.

Despite these limitations, over 1,400 pages of tax records survive for Scots of all walks of life. Surviving Poll Tax rolls are available at ScotlandsPlaces **<scotlandsplaces.gov.uk/ digital-volumes/historical-tax-rolls/poll-tax-rolls-1694-1698>** as well as at FamilySearch.org (where you can view them at a Family History Center or affiliate library).

Window Tax

A tax on windows had been payable in England, Wales, and Ireland since 1696. However, Scots didn't have to pay a comparable tax until 1748 (despite the Union forty years earlier). The tax lasted in the entire United Kingdom until 1851, when mounting protests brought about its repeal. When initially introduced in 1748, the only people liable were those whose houses had more than ten windows (image **H**). Later, the required number of windows was dropped to seven.

The Window Tax rolls for Scotland survive for the fifty-year period from 1748 to 1798, and are available at ScotlandsPlaces **<scotlandsplaces.gov.uk/digital-volumes/historical-tax-rolls/window-tax-1748-1798>**, divided into 218 volumes. The rolls list the name of the householder, the number of windows, and the amount of the tax.

KEYS TO SUCCESS

🏵 Use census records to take your Scottish ancestors back in time, decade by decade. The Scottish census was administered every ten years beginning in 1801, though these earlier censuses don't survive. Genealogically useful details weren't included until 1841.

🏵 Search census databases for every variant of your ancestor's surname, as each one differs in its abilities to recognize different spellings that represent the same surname.

🏵 Turn to tax records if you need to supplement or replace incomplete or missing census records. Some of the most useful are the Consolidated Schedules of Assessed Taxes (for the wide variety of pre-1800 records) and the Hearth and Poll Taxes at ScotlandsPlaces.

10

Wills and Property Records

egal and property records, generally not the most well-known group of records, can provide a detailed snapshot of your ancestors' lives and possessions. Scottish probate and property records notably differ from their American counterparts, so you'll want to take note as you begin researching these documents overseas. Legal parameters constrained to whom a person's goods could be willed, and heirs were often not named in wills because it was not legally necessary. Land transfers were recorded in specialized judicial bodies called sasine courts, with "sasine" referring to either the transfer of land or the documents surrounding a transfer.

Unfortunately, the vast majority of Scots had little or no property to give and so do not appear in these records, and finding those who did can be time-consuming. This chapter will explain the intricacies of Scottish wills and property records, where to find these records, and how to use them.

WILLS AND TESTAMENTS

Scottish testaments (image **A**) are records related to the settling of a person's estate. When a person died testate (i.e., with a will), his will included a testament testamentary, which confirmed the executor appointed by the deceased. If a person died intestate (i.e.,

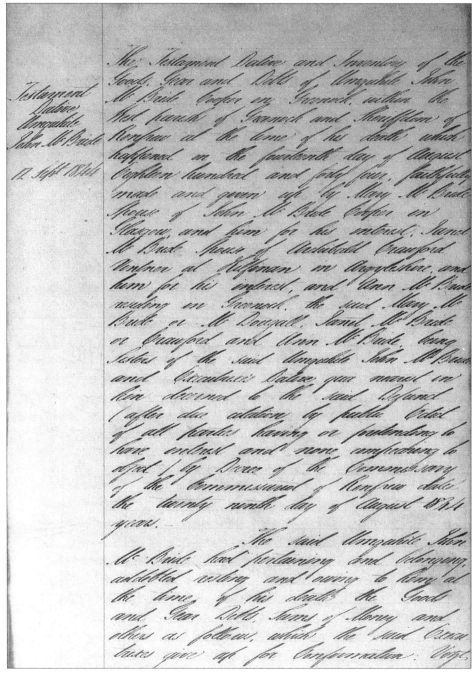

This testament dative for John McBride (a cooper from Greenock) uses the term *umquhile*, which means former or deceased. You might also see the term "the defunct" to refer to the dead.

without a will), the courts created a testament dative that would name a court-appointed executor. All testaments included an inventory of the deceased's possessions and (when applicable) debts. These documents also featured a confirmation, which assured the inventory had been accepted by the court as correct and that the will was valid.

Unfortunately, there was no legal requirement to make a will, so most people did not. And as the Laws of Succession governed most aspects of inheritance, they weren't strictly speaking necessary, even for the wealthy. Most people, especially those of modest means and those who did not own land, simply worked out things on their own. In these cases, courts only became involved when families failed to come to an agreement. Consequently, some testaments may not begin until many years after the death of the ancestor in question. Even if the will is not forthcoming about the testator's family, the inventories (which can be quite detailed) will provide insight into the ancestor's lifestyle, as these were made for people from all social classes.

But before we dive further, we need to understand the two types of property according to Scottish law (image **B**):

- **Heritable** or **immovable property** (collectively referred to as a heritage) included land, buildings, titles, and mineral rights.

- **Moveable property** included anything that could be physically moved (for example, money, jewelry, furniture, cattle, books, crops, and farm equipment).

B

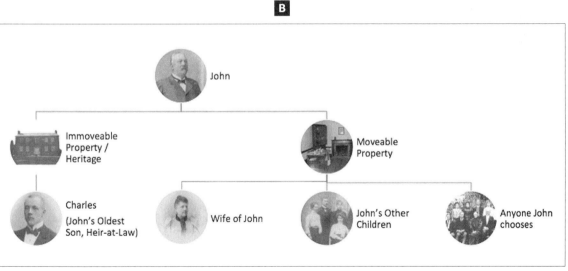

Scottish inheritance law distinguished between "immovable" and "moveable" property, and had set rules for who could inherit each. In this example, John's immoveable property (i.e., his land) went to his oldest son, Charles, while his moveable property (furniture, etc.) was divided amongst his wife, other children, and his person of choice (in this case, other members of the family).

Scottish Legal Terms

As you might expect, Scottish law isn't exactly the same as it is in your home country, and so you may find some unfamiliar legal terms during your research. We've discussed some of them (such as sasine and moveable vs. immovable property) in this chapter, but you'll still want to learn the vocab to better understand your ancestors' records. Several glossaries are available online, including:

- Latin Phrases from the Registers of Scotland **<rosdev.atlassian.net/wiki/spaces/2ARM/pages/58690453/Latin+Phrases>**
- Scottish Land Law Glossary/Dictionary from Scottish Law Online **<www.scottishlaw.org.uk/lawscotland/abscotslawland.html>**
- Glossary from the Judiciary of Scotland **<www.scotland-judiciary.org.uk/29/0/Glossary>**

Occasionally, items usually considered "moveable" (such as furniture or farm equipment) were deemed "immovable" for the sake of inheritance law. This allowed for those items to be inherited along with the farm/land/home so the heir didn't inherit an empty house.

Under Scots law, a person's direct descendants were given precedence when determining inheritance. Specifically, the law of primogeniture decreed that sons received preference over daughters. Therefore, all heritable property such as land and property would first go to the eldest surviving son or his issue, then (if the deceased had no living sons or their issues) to daughters.

Moveable property was a little more complicated. Scots law prohibited a person from disinheriting a spouse or child from movable property, enshrining these relatives' legal rights to an estate. However, any moveable estate was divided into thirds if the deceased had a surviving spouse and children: the widow's part (or *jus relictae*), the children's/bairns' part (or *legitim*), and the dead's (deid's) part. The eldest son, who received the heritable property, was not included in the bairn's part, and the testator (i.e., the deceased) could leave the deid's third of the estate to whomever he wanted. If the deceased had neither a spouse nor children, then the moveable estate was divided in half and his parents (if living) or siblings and their descendants (if any) would inherit it. (More on this later.)

Since inheritance law was absolute and superseded the deceased's wishes, wills often didn't list the individuals involved. After all, the law uniformly entitles the widow to one-third of the moveable estate. So why should documents specifically spell out her claim? Likewise, the eldest son might not be mentioned if he did not receive any additional bequests in the deid's part. This provides obvious challenges for the genealogist.

Accessing Inheritance Records

Until 1823, local commissary courts recorded testaments. These courts only handled the records for a defined region—see the sidebar for a list. However, the commissary court in Edinburgh could handle cases from all over Scotland and was the only place that handled testaments for those who had died outside Scotland. The commissary courts officially ceased to exist in 1824, when the sheriff's court in each county seat began to handle testaments. (See chapter 5 for more on the counties of Scotland.) Note that many commissary courts continued to operate for a few years afterward.

The best way to search for wills and testaments is to use the index at ScotlandsPeople **<www.scotlandspeople. gov.uk>** (image **C**), which you can search for free once you register. This listing includes more than 611,000 entries for testamentary records dating from 1513 to 1925, and search fields include surname and forename of the testator, the year

List of Commissary Courts

- Aberdeen
- Argyll
- Brechin
- Caithness
- Dumfries
- Dunblane
- Dunkeld
- Edinburgh
- Glasgow
- Hamilton and Campsie
- Inverness
- The Isles
- Kirkcudbright
- Lanark
- Lauder
- Moray
- Orkney and Shetland
- Peebles
- Ross
- St. Andrews
- Stirling
- Wigtown

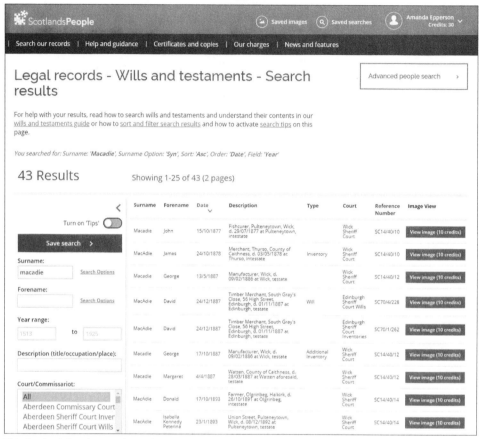

This ScotlandsPeople page shows the results for an all-courts search for the surname Macadie. By clicking on Date, you can sort the results in chronological order. The details, date of registration, and location of court will help you identify the correct individual.

range, the description, and the commissariot or court. Although records before 1560 were technically filed in Church courts (see the Commissary Courts: A History sidebar), they were indexed with the commissariot records. The description field is quite useful as it frequently includes the person's title or status, occupation, residence, and the name of spouse. If you are searching for an ancestor who died around 1823–1824 (when testament recordkeeping switched from commissary courts to sheriff's courts), search the records of both the commissary and sheriff's court.

The search results at ScotlandsPeople will show the name of the deceased, date of the confirmation, description, type of document, court, and reference number. The two most common "types" included in commissary court records are *TD* for testament dative and *TT* for testament testamentor. You may also find a tacked-on inventory, called an "Eik," that provides information about property not mentioned in the original testament. Eiks were only used in commissary courts, and the document type field for testaments from a sheriffs' court is usually empty. You may also find someone listed twice in the index, probably because some sheriff's courts kept separate registers for inventories and wills.

All testaments that have been digitized at ScotlandsPeople can be downloaded from the site. The cost is ten credits each (£2.50, or about $3.50), and the downloads include all pages of the testament. These are usually two or three pages, but can be up to one hundred. These images of the wills and testaments are part of a new digitization process, made directly from the documents rather than microfilms.

Wills dated between 1926 and 1999 have not been digitized at the time of this book's publication, and you can view them by consulting the Historical Search Rooms at the National Records of Scotland archive <www.nrscotland.gov.uk/research/guides/wills-and-testaments>. (For privacy reasons, wills dated after 1999 are not held by the National Records of Scotland.)

FamilySearch.org <www.familysearch.org> also has printed and microfilmed indexes of commissary and sheriff's court records in its holding. Browse the catalog for "Probate records—Indexes" under Scotland or a specific Scottish county. You

Commissary Courts: A History

As with many of Scottish records, consistorial cases (those dealing with testaments, marriage, divorce, and other matters) were originally handled by Church authorities. However, Church courts were dissolved in 1560 during the Protestant Reformation. For several years, confusion reigned, as people took it upon themselves to decide in which of the surviving courts they should present their cases. In 1563, Queen Mary established the commissary court in Edinburgh to handle these cases, and additional, local commissary courts were established over the next several decades. The principal commissary court in Edinburgh had sole jurisdiction over matters concerning marriage and divorce/dissolution of marriage, plus testaments of people who died outside Scotland. These smaller commissary courts had the same boundaries as the Catholic dioceses that existed prior to the Reformation. To see which commissary court had jurisdiction over your ancestor's parish, consult the online Pre-1801 Testament Indexes of Scotland <www.britishislesdna.com/Scotland/SCOT_testndx.htm>.

can view all digitized records at a Family History Center or affiliate library. You can also cross-reference FamilySearch.org holdings with the ScotlandsPeople's index to track down a record, though ScotlandsPeople doesn't provide page numbers. As a result, you may need to browse through digitized FamilySearch.org microfilm page by page until you find the record you're looking for.

Subscription site Ancestry.com <www.ancestry.com> also has several collections of pre-1800 Scottish testaments:

- "Confirmations and Inventories Granted and Given Up in the Several Commissariots of Scotland, 1876" <search.ancestry.com/search/db.aspx?dbid=34565>: This volume includes testaments registered in the whole of Scotland in 1876.

- "The Commissariot Record of Edinburgh, Register of Testaments" <search.ancestry.com/search/db.aspx?dbid=28542>: This volume includes records dating from 1514 to 1600.

- "The Commissariot Record of Inverness: Register of Testaments, 1631–1800" <search.ancestry.com/search/db.aspx?dbid=28545>: The introduction to this publication includes a helpful explanation of Gaelic patronymic terms (see chapter 6).

- "The Commissariot Record of Hamilton and Campsie" <search.ancestry.com/search/db.aspx?dbid=28546>: This publication includes testaments registered between 1564 and 1800.

- "UK, Extracted Probate Records, 1269–1975" <search.ancestry.com/search/db.aspx?dbid=1610>: This collection includes records from the entire United Kingdom from the late 1200s to the late 1900s. The information in this collection was compiled from previously published works, including most commissariot courts in Scotland (though none of them extend past 1800 or 1801).

You can search most of these collections either by keyword or by browsing record images.

One collection at Ancestry.com does include references to some post-1800 testaments: "Scottish-American Wills, 1650–1900" <search.ancestry.com/search/db.aspx?dbid=49335&path=>. This database is drawn from a work of the same title by David Dobson. Here, you'll find the names of two thousands Scots who died in the Americas and had their testaments confirmed in the commissariat or sheriff's court in Edinburgh.

PROPERTY RECORDS

Property records contain information about your ancestor's most valuable asset: his land. However, unlike in some other countries, Scotland's land and property records were influenced by the feudal system for centuries—up to and including the early twenty-first century.

In this feudal system, the king owned the whole country. Since the king could not realistically manage all this land on his own, he delegated power over portions to men throughout the land. These vassals, also known as "subject superiors" or "Crown tenants," further granted portions of their land to their own vassals, and so on. In return for land, vassals owed some kind of service to their superiors (usually military), and this exchange was converted to monetary payment known as a feu duty. The superior retained legal rights to the land they rented out ("feud") to a vassal, and these rights were never extinguished—even if a person owned their property outright. This system takes shape even in recent times: Until 2004, a person owning a house in a subdivision outside Glasgow might owe a feu duty to a feudal superior.

The feudal system of landholding and the laws of primogeniture governed the transfer of land in Scotland and the types of records that were required. As we've already discussed, the heritable portion of an estate could not be left in the will, as the laws of primogeniture governed who would inherit. This then leads to an obvious question: How does one determine the correct heir, especially if there was no living eldest son? And how did the heir, once identified, acquire title to the land?

In the following sections, we'll take a look at these processes, plus how you can find and use the records left behind by them.

Services of Heirs (Retours)

As all property in Scotland was held by the Crown or other feudal superior, a vassal's heir was required to prove his right to inherit. If the feudal superior was the Crown itself, then a jury would formally determine the rightful heir's identity, then make a written return or retours to the Royal Chancery. A "precept furth of Chancery" would then be issued, which simply stated the correct heir had been identified and should be allowed to take possession of the land. If the superior was not the Crown, then the superior took it upon himself to decide the rightful heir. He would then issue a "precept of clare contant" (with *clare contant* meaning "clearly appears" in Latin), and the heir would be granted title to his land. If the superior couldn't determine an heir or the title was contested in some way, the parties involved might turn to the jury system, which would make a return to the Royal Chancery.

Documents regarding vassals of Crown land were known as "special retours" and included a detailed description of the land, while those concerning vassals of superiors who were not the Crown were known as "general retours" and do not describe the land involved (image **D**). All retours are filed in Chancery records and were written in Latin until 1847. The language used is formulaic, and each document includes the date of the inquest, the name of the deceased and their relationship to the heir, the name of the rightful heir, and the names of the jury members and witnesses. After 1868, heritable property could be left to an heir named in a will, and the Service of Heirs system fell into disuse.

You can access the Services of Heirs in several ways. Clerks compiled summaries and indexes for records from 1544 to 1700 and printed them in the early nineteenth century. The three-volume set is organized by county and type or retour, with the third volume containing an index for records in the first two volumes. They are all in Latin, but don't let that put you off—they're easy to understand. FamilySearch.org has these volumes available for free <www.familysearch.org/search/catalog/248869>, as does Google Books <books.google.com> (simply search *Inquisitionum Ad Capellam Domini Regis Retornatarum* to find the text, which has separate listings for each volume). You can also purchase the three volumes on CD-ROM from the Scottish Genealogy Society for thirty-two pounds (about $41 USD) <shop.scotsgenealogy.com/acatalog/Heirs_.html>.

The next series of indexes begin with the year 1700, and each volume includes ten years of records. You can find these on FamilySearch.org <www.familysearch.org/search/catalog/1004156>, where the index and summary is in English and includes the "Name of the Person Served" (i.e., the heir), "Distinguishing Particulars" (including the name of decedent and their relationship to the heir), and the date the retour was recorded. The third set of indexes, spanning the years 1860 to 1929, are available on microfiche at the Family History Library (Fiche No. 6068606). As of this book's publication, these records have not been digitized.

In addition, Services of Heir records from 1547 to 1900, comprising over 280 volumes, are available through FamilySearch.org and can be viewed at a Family History Center or affiliate library <www.familysearch.org/search/catalog/273344>. Generally, there are two volumes per microfilm roll, and each volume is individually indexed. The retours were recorded chronologically, so simply look for the volume that includes the year the retour you seek was recorded.

If you think an ancestor who lived in the Americas might have been an heir to Scottish property, you can check the "Scottish-American Heirs, 1683–1883" collection at Ancestry.com <search.ancestry.com/search/db.aspx?dbid=49334>. The database is taken from a book with the same title by David Dobson, who scoured the Service of Heirs to find the 2,600-plus heirs living in the Americas between 1683 and 1883.

This image shows the general return for John Macadie, son of Peter Macadie. Both were from Pultneytown in Wick, Caithness. Peter died in 1830, but his son wasn't named as heir until 1849.

Sasines

Now that we've studied how heirs were determined, let's look now to the actual transfer of property. Vassals and superiors recorded feudal property transfers using a sasine (pronounced "say-zin"), a term that has the same origins as "seize" (i.e., "to take possession of"). A General Register of Sasines began in 1617 and provided an obligatory, permanent record of property transfers. And since very few Scots owned land outright before the mid-twentieth century, these registers probably don't include many of your Scottish ancestors. You can learn more about the history of the registers at <**www.ros.gov.uk/about-us/our-history**>.

Until 1868, officials maintained two separate kinds of lists: the General Register, and particular registers. The former was based in Edinburgh, where records from all over Scotland could be registered; the latter existed for each of the counties. After 1868, the particular registers were discontinued, and county divisions were added to the General Register. In addition, each of the royal burghs kept their own register from 1681 to 1926. Indexes are rarely available for sasines prior to 1780. However, for this early period,

E

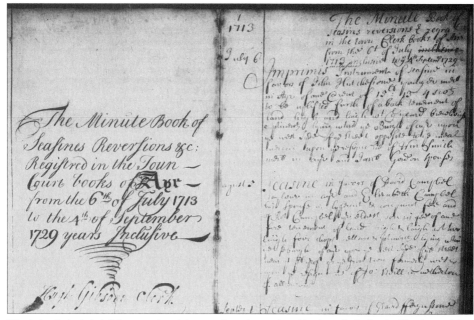

Minute books include brief summaries of documents and are entered in chronological order. They're useful substitutes for indexes, and this one shows the opening pages of minute books for sasines in the Burgh of Ayr, 1713–1729.

F

> (1079)   Nov. 9. 1807.
> ALEXANDER MACGILLIVRAY residing at Daviot, as heir to Archibald MacGillivray late of Charlestown in South Carolina, Merchant, & Lucy Mackintosh, his spouse, his father and mother, *Seised*, Sept. 19. 1807,—in the Town and lands of DAVIOT comp. the MAINS or DAVIOT, Manor place, Town and Fortalice of Daviot, the lands & two Towns called Kirktown of Daviot, the Towns and lands called Belvouny, Easter & Wester Tomlas, Easter & Wester Altgluys & Newlands thereof, Blackcroft, Sandyhill, Tomleavinich, and Miln & Miln croft of Daviot, & Teinds, par. Daviot;—in security of £10,180 Scots, in Con. Wadset between Æneas Mackintosh then of Mackintosh,—and the said Archibald Macgillivray and Lucy Mackintosh, Dec. 19. 1749;—on Pr. Cl. Con. by Æneas Mackintosh of Mackintosh, Dec. 4. 1806.   P. R. 18. 10.

Abridgements, like minute books, contain summarized information from sasines. Here, Alexander MacGillivary acquired "the Town and lands of Daviot" from Aeneas Mackintosh. The entry contains details about the land (listing specific place names) and the transaction, such as the amount of money (10,180 pounds Scot) and the date (Dec. 4, 1806).

you can search the minute books, which are summaries of each entry made in the full register and entered in chronological order (image **E**). One index, *General Register of Sasines 1701–1720*, published in 1915, is available from Archive.org **<archive.org/details/ indexes300scotuoft>**.

Abridgements, or brief summaries, for the General and particular registers, are available from 1781 to 1868. These were printed and are available at FamilySearch.org, where you can find in under "Scotland—Land and Property." Each abridgement references the original source with the abbreviation *G.R.* for General Register or *P.R.* for particular register. Once you've found an entry, you can view an image of the abridgement at a Family History Center or affiliate library. The entries in the abridgments (image **F**) are complete enough that you probably will not need to consult the original records, helpful since the original records are only available at the National Records of Scotland **<www.nrscotland. gov.uk/research/guides/sasines>**. The indexes are organized by person and place, and the numbers referenced in the indexes refer to the number in the abridgement volume itself. You can see a list of abbreviations commonly used in the abridgements from the Scottish Archive Network **<www.scan.org.uk/knowledgebase/topics/sasine_abbs_faq2.htm>**. Note that the Registers of Sasine for royal burghs were not included in the abridgement series.

The next series of records, known as search sheets, begin between 1871 and 1876. Each property in Scotland has its own search sheet, and each contains a summary of all sasines for that property from the 1870s. From these, you can bridge the gap between the beginning of the search sheets (in 1871) and the end of the abridgements (in 1868).

All of the abridgements and associated indexes (as well as most of the minute books) are available on digital microfilm at a Family History Center or affiliate library. The details of their holdings can be found at the following catalog pages:

- "Minute Books of General Registers of Sasines: Abstracts of Registers, 1717–1781" **<www.familysearch.org/search/catalog/259938>**

- "Minute Books of Particular Register of Sasines: 1599–1793" **<www.familysearch. org/search/catalog/259942>**

- "Abridgments of Sasines: 1781–1868" **<www.familysearch.org/search/ catalog/261488>**

- "Index of Persons, to Abridgments of Sasines: 1781–1868" **<www.familysearch.org/ search/catalog/261226>**

- "Index to Places, to Abridgement of Sasines: 1781–1830" **<www.familysearch.org/ search/catalog/261484>**

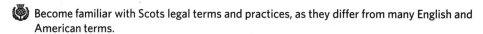

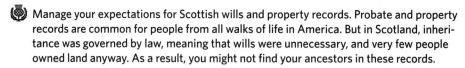

Become familiar with Scots legal terms and practices, as they differ from many English and American terms.

Manage your expectations for Scottish wills and property records. Probate and property records are common for people from all walks of life in America. But in Scotland, inheritance was governed by law, meaning that wills were unnecessary, and very few people owned land anyway. As a result, you might not find your ancestors in these records.

Check the indexes after the date of your ancestor's death/the transfer of property. Many testament and property records were not filed until years after the event.

11

Occupational and Military Records

O ccupation is a crucial characteristic you can discover about your ancestors—especially your male ancestors. Documents related to your ancestor's occupation may provide personal and genealogical data information. Whether farmer, coal miner, or lawyer, occupation will open up additional avenues of research as you investigate your ancestor's life and times, putting your ancestor in the proper social, economic, and historical context. For example, a lawyer living in late eighteenth-century Edinburgh had a very different life experience than a tenant farmer in Invernesshire.

Visit Scotland has a neat page about common occupations in Scotland, including soldiers, domestic servants, crofters, farmers, fishermen, shipbuilders, coal miners, weavers and spinners <www.visitscotland.com/see-do/research-your-ancestry/professions-occupations>. Most practitioners of these occupations would leave few records or be included with business records. But occupational records that do exist can provide great information about your ancestors' lives.

Records of your ancestor's work history are as varied as the occupations they had, especially for ancestors who served in the military. This chapter will help you find and use these valuable records.

MILITARY

Like general Scottish history (see chapter 4), Scottish military history is closely entwined with the country's relationship with England. If you have military ancestry, you'll have to consider Scotland's political history as you investigate records.

Prior to the Union of 1707, many Scots served either for their home country's armed forces when called upon or as mercenaries in other European armies. These records will be scattered about based on where and in what capacity your ancestor served, so you'll need to do some additional legwork to find these records. Steven Murdoch, of the University of St. Andrews <www.st-andrews.ac.uk/history/staff/stevemurdoch.html>, has written extensively about Scots and the military during the seventeenth century. His work likely won't tell you about a specific ancestor, but it will provide context for life during this time period—particularly if you know what branch and regiment your ancestor served in.

As the Scottish government was subsumed into the British state, so too was its military. From 1707, Scots (particularly Highlanders) served in the British armed forces in substantial numbers. The nation's military past was important to Scots, who saw soldiering as an honorable profession. (The English, on the other hand, took more pride in the Royal Navy.) Serving in the military allowed many Scotsmen to send money home to support their families. Conscription didn't exist until the First World War, and the British Army relied on volunteers. However, enlistment in the military was the only viable economic opportunity for many men in the eighteenth and nineteenth centuries. Others didn't choose to serve—the Royal Navy notoriously used forced impressment to take the men it needed, including Scots and US citizens. This fact led some men to leave Scotland during the Napoleonic Wars.

Records of Scots' service are housed at The National Archives at Kew in London. For details about how to search these records, visit The National Archives website <www.nationalarchives.gov.uk/help-with-your-research/research-guides/?research-category=military-and-maritime>, which has more than 140 research guides available to help you trace members of the British armed forces. Many of these guides also allow you to search the records mentioned in the guide, although many can only be viewed after paying a download fee of £3.5 ($4.53 USD at the time of this publication). Other records sets (usually, indexes) can be downloaded as PDF files.

Other military records (such as those for fencible and militia units, which were local forces) are available in Scotland. You can find more information about these record sets from the National Records of Scotland <www.nrscotland.gov.uk/research/guides/military-records>. The War Museum of Scotland <www.nms.ac.uk/collections-research/research-facilities/museum-libraries/national-war-museum-library> also has a library with a significant collection related to the Scottish military, including regimental histories.

To search for ancestors in the Scottish army or navy, you'll need the name of the regiment or ship. Most military resources are organized by these pieces of information, and you often won't have a general index. You can find regiment names next to your ancestor's occupation in a statutory, parish, or census (see chapters 7, 8, and 9, respectively). Many regiments were recruited locally, so you may be able to narrow down your ancestor's regiment by examining local histories to see which regiments were recruited from where. If your ancestor is from the relevant time period, you might also find him by name in one of the searchable military sources, then locate a regiment that way. The name of a seaman's ship is trickier to identify, but (in general) ships were associated with certain ports. If you can discover where your ancestor lived or was stationed, you might be able to narrow down the name of his ship.

You can also discover regiment or ship name by looking at medals sheets. These list the medals and clasps given to those who served in the armed forces. Therefore, these lists function a bit like a service record, as medals were awarded for service in specific wars and theatres of action. Even if the medals sheet featuring your ancestor doesn't mention regiment or ship name, you can research the engagement itself and narrow down which regiments and ships took part in the action.

Many medals lists are available online through various sources:

- "The UK, Military Campaign Medal and Award Rolls, 1793–1949" **<search.ancestry.com/search/db.aspx?dbid=1686>** collection includes information on 2.3 million soldiers who were issued medals in conflicts during this time period (except for World Wars I and II).

- "UK, Naval Medal and Award Rolls, 1793–1972" **<search.ancestry.com/search/db.aspx?dbid=1687>** lists the names of 1.5 million men, officers, and enlisted men who were eligible for medals from the Royal Navy and Royal Marines.

- "UK, Citations of the Distinguished Conduct Medal, 1914–1920" **<search.ancestry.com/search/db.aspx?dbid=1913>**, based on a printed publication of the same name, contains information about those who received the Distinguished Conduct Medal (the second-highest military honor for noncommissioned officers and enlisted men) during World War I.

- "British Army medal index cards, 1914–1920" **<www.nationalarchives.gov.uk/help-with-your-research/research-guides/british-army-medal-index-cards-1914-1920>** are available to download for £3.50 from The National Archives at Kew. You can see images of WWI service medals at the Imperial War Museum **<www.iwm.org.uk/history/first-world-war-service-medals>**.

You can search a database of soldiers' graves from around the world at the Commonwealth War Graves Commission.

- *The London Gazette* **<www.thegazette.co.uk>** has dedicated, searchable archives of its announcements of notices and major military medals from the First World War **<www.thegazette.co.uk/awards-and-accreditation/ww1>**.

- "UK, Silver War Badge Records, 1914–1920" **<search.ancestry.com/search/db.aspx?dbid=2456>** is a listing of almost one million men who were awarded the Silver War Badge during the First World War. This badge was given to those individuals who had been discharged due to wounds or illness. It was a visible reminder to those on the homefront that the men who wore the badge were not shirking their military duty.

For more information on where to search for medal lists, see the British military campaign and service medals guide at The National Archives **<www.nationalarchives.gov.uk/help-with-your-research/research-guides/british-military-campaign-and-service-medals>**. Note that medal lists from the Second World War are not kept at The National Archives. Instead, you must contact the Armed Services Medal Office—visit **<www.gov.uk/guidance/medals-campaigns-descriptions-and-eligibility>** for contact details and images of WWII medals and images of Distinguished Conduct medals like the Victoria Cross.

Army lists and naval lists are also available. The army list includes officers, their ranks, and their regiments, and the navy list (published quarterly since 1814) names the officers, their ranks, and the names of their ships. Military lists from the army, navy, and air force are available as PDFs at the National Library of Scotland <digital.nls.uk/british-military-lists/archive/97343435>. Of the ten sources, however, only one covers the nineteenth century, and the rest are twentieth-century. Navy lists from 1888 to 1879 are available at Ancestry.com <search.ancestry.com/search/db.aspx?dbid=2406>.

Honor rolls can also help you find decorated ancestors. Scottish Rolls of Honour, which are published lists of men who served, are also available at the National Library of Scotland <digital.nls.uk/rolls-of-honour/archive/100261716>. Another database for WWII honors, "UK, Army Roll of Honour, 1939–1945" <search.ancestry.com/search/db.aspx?dbid=1604>, provides the name of the soldiers, their decorations, birthplaces, residences, ranks, and dates of death.

Burial records may also help you identify a military ancestor and his regiment. The Commonwealth War Graves Commission <search.ancestry.com/search/db.aspx?dbid=2706&path=> (image **A**) maintains and cares for memorials of 1.7 million servicemen and women who died in the First and Second World Wars. You can search the database for details on the war dead, and an online archive shares records of the Commission's work. This collection is also available at Ancestry.com <search.ancestry.com/search/db.aspx?dbid=2706&path=>. Likewise, "The UK, Soldiers Died in the Great War, 1914–1919" <search.ancestry.com/search/db.aspx?dbid=1543> is a search-only collection that includes information on more than 700,000 people. In addition to the individual names, the records may also include birthplaces, residences, places of enlistment, ranks, regiments, battalions, types of casualty, and dates and places of death.

Once you have identified the basics of your ancestor's military service, you can search myriad databases and resources at The National Archive, Ancestry.com, Findmypast <www.findmypast.co.uk>, and FamilySearch.org <www.familysearch.org> that can help you uncover more details of your ancestor's period of service.

MERCHANT SEAMEN

Beginning in 1835, official agreements had to be made between masters and crew before they put to sea, and you can find these at various repositories throughout Scotland. FamilySearch.org also has a selection of records and publications for the merchant marine, which you can find by doing a subject search for *Scotland – Merchant Marine*. Among the records are the surviving documents of Trinity House, the guild for merchant seamen based in London that offered charitable assistance to its members and their widows. You can view indexes of the surviving records (1787–1858) from FamilySearch.org and

Who Came to America?

People of all backgrounds left Scotland to seek better fortunes in America, tradesmen and farmers alike. The key was that they had to fund their trip to America, in terms of both the travel expenses and the loss in wages. As a result, the poorest of the poor could not emigrate without assistance. The British government and charities only assisted emigrants reach destinations in the British Empire, which after the 1770s did not include not the United States. As a result, you can expect Scots of all work backgrounds among immigrants to the United States, but the truly destitute were likely stuck in their home country.

Findmypast <search.findmypast.co.uk/search-world-records/british-mariners-trinity-house-calendars-1787-1854>. The originals are held by the Society of Genealogists in London, and the indexes will show you the name of the petitioner, his relationship to the seaman (if not the seaman himself), and further details and circumstances of the petitioner.

A mid-nineteenth-century (1835–1857) list of merchant seamen is available at Findmypast <search.findmypast.co.uk/search-world-Records/britain-merchant-seamen-1835-1857>. These records, provided in association with The National Archives, include several registries of merchant marine. While the information per document type may vary, all documents should at least include the seaman's name and birth year and place.

"The UK and Ireland, Masters and Mates Certificates, 1850–1927" <search.ancestry.com/search/db.aspx?dbid=2271> collection at Ancestry.com includes documents issued to merchant seamen who qualified as masters or mates. These are pre-printed forms that were filled out, but the information requested varied with time. At a minimum, you should find the individual's name, birth date, birth place, port of issue, and history of service. Not everything in the images is indexed, so page forward and backward to be sure that you see all pages of a document. The oldest certificates are dated 1856, but they are listed in Certificate Range 2, range 001–249. (The other Range 1, 001–099, begins with the 1870s, and so the ranges are essentially out of chronological order.) Some records refer to service as early as 1850—hence, that beginning date for the database.

TRADES, BUSINESSES, AND INDUSTRIES

If your ancestor had a specialized skill, you may also find records related to his work in a community. Tradesmen (those who practiced crafts such as carpentry and blacksmithing) usually lived and worked in burghs. People practiced a wide variety of trades in Scottish burghs, among them: bonnet knitters, glovers, tailors, goldsmiths, weavers, and skinners.

To work within a burgh, each individual had to be admitted as a burgess, which gave him the right to vote in local elections. These admissions would be recorded in the burgh records. Through these records, you can follow several generations of a family because trades were usually passed from father to son. And when men were admitted to the burgh, the name of their fathers and addresses may be recorded as well. Burgesses had a higher status than many others in the burgh including servants, apprentices, and dependents. As burgesses often had some say in local government (depending on their charter), they may have had a higher status than farmers in the outlying areas.

In addition to becoming a burgess, a tradesman had to join a guild of incorporated trades to practice in a community. Guilds were essentially medieval unions that provided guidelines for a craft and offered a social safety net for their members. With time, separate guilds developed for the various trades including masons, bonnet makers, fleshers, weavers, and bakers. Guild records, if they survive, can be useful sources of genealogical data, as they frequently include lists of masters, apprentices, and servants and their relationships.

Craftsmen and merchants who were burgesses had a relatively high status within the burgh. However, not all could join a guild (pedlars, for example, were a type of merchant, but they weren't eligible). Many craftsmen maintained journeyman status because they could not afford the fees required to join the guild. Additionally, craftsmen who lived in the suburbs (outside the burgh) could not join burgh guilds and could only legally sell their wares in the burgh on market day. Burgh residents, however, could travel to the suburbs to purchase goods from these merchants.

RESEARCH TIP

Hit the Books

We only cover a handful of historical occupations in this chapter. If your ancestor filled any number of other roles in society, consult other resources such as *Scottish Trade and Professions—A Selected Biography* by D.R. Torrance (Scottish Association of Family History Societies, 1998), which includes many publications regarding trades and occupations in Scotland. Publications such as these (and books reflecting specific historical occupations) will provide more detailed information about your subject.

To see what records might survive for your ancestor's burgh or guild, check with the local repository or search the Scotland Archives Network catalog <catalogue.nrscotland. gov.uk/scancatalogue/welcome.aspx>. This database combines the catalogs of more than fifty archives in Scotland, and each entry provides a summary of the collection and the name of the archive that holds it. Some records for the larger burghs, such as Glasgow and Edinburgh, have been abstracted and published.

In addition, the records of many businesses (such as railways, shipping companies, interior designers, publishers, and chemical manufacturers) have been deposited at archives throughout Scotland. One of the best collections is at the Business Records Centre at the University of Glasgow Archives <www.gla.ac.uk/myglasgow/archives/ collections/business>, which includes guides for a variety of industries including drinks, engineering, and sugar. If you have an ancestor who worked at either the Royal Bank of Scotland <www.rbs.com/heritage.html> or the Bank of Scotland <www.lloydsbankinggroup. com/our-group/our-heritage/our-archives>, you can check company archives for records.

Another collection of business-related records comes from Ancestry.com, which has compiled "Rosyth, Fife, Scotland, Dockyard Employee Books, 1892-1967" <search. ancestry.com/search/db.aspx?dbid=61425>. This collection includes the name of the employee, his date and place of birth, and his employment history, which may include other dockyards prior to 1909. The collection is searchable and includes links to the images of the original documents.

One of the oldest industries in Scotland was coal-mining, and coal accounted for as much as fifty percent of Scotland's exports by 1680. Many Scottish miners brought their expertise to American coal mines in the nineteenth century. The main repository for coal-mining records is the National Records of Scotland, which holds the National Coal Board that includes records of early coal companies nationalized in 1946. Other coal mines were on the property of private landowners, and the records of those mines will be with the family papers. Amongst the papers—no matter the source—you may find lists of employees and their wages. For more information, see <www.nrscotland.gov.uk/research/ guides/coal-mining-records#CB>.

Railways were another important industry in Scottish life. Since the Kilmarnock and Troon Railway was incorporated in 1808, railroads shaped Scottish landscape both literally (carving railways through the Scottish countryside) and figuratively (providing more accessible transportation and new kinds of jobs). The National Archives of Scotland <www.nrscotland.gov.uk/research/guides/railway-records> holds the largest written and pictorial archive of Scottish railway history. Here, you'll find records from many railway companies, plus the private papers of authors, engineers, and officials.

CLERGY

If you have an ancestor who was a Church of Scotland minister, the best source to learn about him is the *Fasti Ecclesaiae Scoticanae: The Succession of Ministers in the Parish Churches of Scotland*. This seven-volume work includes brief biographies of more than two thousand ministers from 1560 to 1866. Within these, you'll find family history data: often the name of the father, the name of his wife and children, and where the minister was born and went to school. Biographies also list the parishes to which the minister was called and the names of any publications he wrote.

Since university education was required, ministers of the Church of Scotland were always university graduates, setting them apart from their less-formally-educated parishioners. Many of them came from noble families, while others descended from long lines of ministers. Some ministers were from more "common families" who were able to send their sons to university.

Once settled in their parishes, these men would have held a respected position in local society—they were educated men of God, and they had care of their parishioners' souls in

B

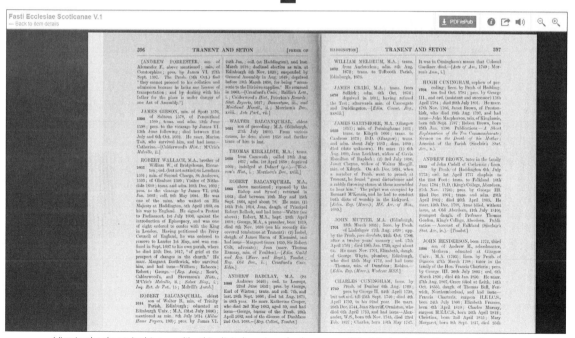

Viewing books at Archive.org, like this digital version of volume one of *Fasti Ecclesaiae Scoticanae*, is almost as good as holding the actual book. Plus, you can do keyword searches and save images of relevant pages to your computer.

their hands. They would have been responsible for the spiritual and religious education of the parishioners and presided over the kirk session. Despite this respected position, ministers' living quarters (called the manse) were often substandard, and their wages were poor.

The *Fasti* is organized by synod, then parish, then each minister in chronological order. Each of the seven volumes covers a different synod:

Volume 1—Synods of Lothian and Tweeddale

Volume 2—Synods of Merse and Teviotdale, Dumfries, and Galloway

Volume 3—Synods of Glasgow and Ayr

Volume 4—Synods of Argyll, Perth, and Stirling

Volume 5—Synods of Fife, Angus, and Mearns

Volume 6—Synods of Aberdeen and Moray

Volume 7—Synods of Ross, Sutherland, Caithness, Glenelg, Orkney (includes the Isles), Shetland, the Church of Scotland in England, and Ireland.

You can access these volumes at Archive.org <www.archive.org> (image **B**). Simply search for *Fasti Ecclesiae Scoticanae*, then select the volume you need. Some volumes have been scanned and uploaded by different organizations, so Archive.org might house two copies of them. Ancestry.com also has a searchable collection of the *Fasti* <search. ancestry.com/search/db.aspx?dbid=1923>.

You can also search for a minister geographically—by presbytery or by congregation. (Congregation and parish names are usually the same in the Church of Scotland.)

Even if you don't have a clergyman among your ancestors, you can search these records to learn more abut your ancestor's community. Find the clergyman who served in your ancestor's parish during his lifetime, and you'll likely find the man who married, baptized, and performed final rites for your ancestors.

Those with ancestors of non-Church of Scotland faiths can search for *Fasti*-like volumes for their ancestors' own denomination:

- Annals and Statistics of the Original Secession Church <archive.org/details/annalsstatistics00scot>

- Annals of the Free Church of Scotland 1843–1900 <ecclegen.com> (short for *ecclesi-astical genealogical*; see image **C**)

- History of the Congregations of the United Presbyterian Church 1733–1900 <archive.org/details/historyofpresbyt01smaluoft>

- Reformed Presbyterian Church in Scotland; its Congregation, Ministers, and Students 1743–1876 <archive.org/details/rschsv02p1couper>

- *Scottish Episcopal Clergy 1689–2000* by David Bertie [not easily available in United States, but it includes biographies of ministers for the period under review]

C

The data at EccleGen, pertaining to the ministers of the Established and Free Churches, is an excellent resource for researching ancestors who were men of the cloth.

MEDICAL AND LEGAL PROFESSIONALS

Like clergymen, medical and legal professionals held special places in communities as highly educated members of society. There were fewer doctors and lawyers as compared to other occupations. In 1851, Scotland had 2,200 legal professions, 500 physicians, and 1,500 surgeons, compared to 3,300 ministers, 48,000 farmers, 32,000 coal miners, and 45,000 in cotton manufacturing. Still, medicine and law served important roles, and records created by these professionals provide insightful context about the community as a whole.

Two directories provide information about doctors: The Medical Register, a mandatory list of practitioners published annually since 1859, and the Medical Directory, a commercial directory published since 1845. The Medical Directory will not include all physicians, but might have more information for those who are included.

Speaking Legal-ese

The US legal system does not distinguish between attorneys-at-law (lawyers who argue cases in court) and those who do not. However, other legal systems, like those of England, Wales, and Scotland, do make a distinction between types of lawyers. In England and Wales, *solicitors* advise and council clients while *barristers* represent clients in court. In Scotland, which has a separate legal system from England and Wales, *writers* advised and counselled clients on legal issues and *advocates* argued cases before the bar. Keep these distinctions in mind as you research your legally minded ancestors.

The Medical Register is available as a collection from Ancestry.com, "UK Medical Registers, 1859–1959" <search.ancestry.com/search/db.aspx?dbid=33538>. Note that, while the registers were published annually, only every fourth year was digitized and indexed. Here, you'll find the person's name, his qualification, his date of registration, and the name of the university he attended (opening the door for matriculation records at that institution).

Likewise, you can find the Medical Directory on Ancestry.com <search.ancestry.com/search/db.aspx?dbid=61053>, Google Books also hosts many issues of the directory. Scots appear in *The Medical Directory of Scotland* from 1852 to 1860, *The London and Medical Directory* from 1861 to 1869, and *The Medical Directory* from 1870 onward.

If you want to research a doctor prior to the printing of the medical directories in 1859, you will need to contact the Royal Colleges of Medicine: the Royal College of Physicians, Edinburgh <www.rcpe.ac.uk>; the Royal College of Surgeon <www.rcsed.ac.uk>; and the Royal College of Physicians and Surgeons, Glasgow <rcpsg.ac.uk>.

The Royal Council on General Practitioners also maintains a page with relevant information for researching a medical ancestor <www.rcgp.org.uk/about-us/the-college/who-we-are/history-heritage-and-archive/researching-a-medical-ancestor.aspx>, which identifies the various specialties and associations of medicine in the United Kingdom. This list will help you decipher the abbreviations in the Medical Register. The Wellcome Library, one of the world's largest collections of materials related to medical history, also maintains a biography and family history page <wellcomelibrary.org/collections/subject-guides/biography-and-family-history>. The lists of sources and publications at this website will allow you to see what types of sources are available and whether they can be obtained from repositories closer to home.

Likewise, if your ancestor was a member of the Scottish legal profession, he will likely appear in specialized records such as local directories (see chapter 12) and university graduate lists. Publications, akin to *Fasti Ecclesiae Scoticanae*, also provide professional and genealogical details for many of these individuals. For advocates (lawyers who represented clients in court), the best source is *The Faculty of Advocates 1532–1943* with Genealogical Notes, published in 1944 <www.familysearch.org/search/catalog/189979>. The biographies in the work include the advocate's birth and death dates and the name of his father. *The Minute Book of the Faculty of Advocates* <www.familysearch.org/search/catalog/118592>, containing records from 1661 to 1798, is another solid resource, including references to member advocates in the seventeenth and eighteenth centuries.

Writers (lawyers who gave clients legal advice but did not represent them in court) are also mentioned in their own publications, frequently called "writers to the signet" such as in *A History of the Society of Writers to Her Majesty's Signet: With a List of the Members of the Society from, 1594 to 1890 and an Abstract of the Minutes* <archive.org/details/historyofsociety00socirich>. This work includes the name of the person he apprenticed to in addition to the name of the writer's father, plus other biographical details.

UNIVERSITY STUDENTS

At the beginning of the eighteenth century, university lectures in Scotland were still given in Latin, and the primary subjects available to study were divinity and law. By the end of the century, universities had transformed themselves by offering new courses, and many taught by towering figures of the Enlightenment like Francis Hutcheson. As Scottish universities had lower fees and social barriers, they became a well-trod path to the professional class and social advancement.

Scotland's four oldest universities (Glasgow, Aberdeen, St. Andrews, and Edinburgh) each provide information about historical alumni. The University of Glasgow has published two volumes: one on matriculation (enrollment) of students from 1728 to 1858, and another for graduates from 1727 to 1897. The matriculation volume tends to have more genealogical information, including the name of the student's father. Likewise, St. Andrew's has published information for the years 1747–1897, which is available as an Ancestry.com collection <search.ancestry.com/search/db.aspx?dbid=34805>. King's and

Charles Scott MacAlpine's fact sheet shows that he earned two degrees at the University of Glasgow. Use the tabs on the left to search for alumni, women, and those who served in the First and Second World Wars.

Marischol Colleges at the University of Aberdeen have published details for students from 1593 to 1860, but the University of Edinburgh has only published the names of graduates in some disciplines.

These same universities also provide online databases for their historical alumni. The Glasgow Story <www.universitystory.gla.ac.uk> (image) provides a list of sources for learning about alumni and students and also hosts databases covering alumni, teachers, women, and WWI and WWII honor (honour) rolls. Likewise, the University of Edinburgh has an incomplete alumni database <collections.ed.ac.uk/alumni>, while the University of Aberdeen maintains separate databases for Kings and Marischal Colleges <www.abdn.ac.uk/special-collections/rolls-of-graduates-212.php>. Finally, St. Andrews has a Biographical Register of Alumni <arts.st-andrews.ac.uk/biographical-register>.

These lists of students may be written in Latin in their earliest years, but you'll likely be able to decipher the names even without any training in Latin (for example, *Jacobus Moneypenny* is "James Moneypenny"). More recent entries likely include more information about the student.

Do you have an ancestor who attended one of the "newer" universities in Scotland? Contact the institution directly to learn what (if any) historical resources are available.

OCCUPATIONAL TAX RECORDS

In the eighteenth century, the government implemented a series of taxes that levied a fee on shops, apprenticeships, and "non-essential" servants. In many cases, these lists will shed light on your ancestor and his employers. The government also kept track of the men who collected these taxes, opening up even more potential avenues of research.

Shopkeepers

Look for records of your shopkeeper or merchant ancestors by searching for shop tax records. Records only survive for the years 1785–1789 in some counties <scotlandsplaces. gov.uk/digital-volumes/historical-tax-rolls/shop-tax-rolls-1785-1789>, and those that survive include the names of shopkeepers plus (sometimes) the nature or names of their businesses. All eight volumes have been transcribed, and note that counties and burghs are in separate volumes.

Servants and Masters

In particular, taxes targeted wealthy individuals who could afford to hire a variety of domestic servants. Farm servants and laborers were not taxed, but "non-essential" servants (such as butlers and cooks) were. The tax on male servants began in 1777 <scotlandsplaces.gov.uk/digital-volumes/historical-tax-rolls/male-servant-tax-rolls-1777-1798> and female servants in 1785 <scotlandsplaces.gov.uk/digital-volumes/historical-tax-rolls/female-servant-tax-rolls-1785-1792>. The twenty-eight volumes are arranged by county or royal burgh, then by parish and household. The name of each householder liable for the tax is listed, along with the name of each servant. These records have also been transcribed.

Apprentices

For a hundred years (from 1710 to 1811), masters were taxed on the fees they received for an apprenticeship indenture, and the tax was not payable until one year after the indenture was completed. (The apprenticeships of youths who were placed by a parish or charity were not taxed.)

This index card for Thomas MacAllen provides information on his marriage to Laing Simpson, his residence in Edinburgh, that he was admitted as a burgess and guild brother, and that his son (Alexander) was admitted to the Faculty of Advocates.

The earliest records (until 1752) are the most useful, as they include the name of the apprentice's father. However, even later records will include the master's name, address, and trade, plus the apprentice's name and the dates of indenture. The complete series is available as a searchable collection (including images) at Ancestry.com <search.ancestry. com/search/db.aspx?dbid=1851>. This record series is also held by FamilySearch.org <www.familysearch.org/search/ catalog/281086> and can be viewed at a Family History Center or affiliate library. Findmypast has the same database <search. findmypast.com/search-world-Records/ britain-country-apprentices-1710-1808>. However, this collection (on both sites) is not searchable, and indexes only exist from 1710 to 1774.

Excisemen

Most of the records of the Excise Office, tasked with collecting duty on whisky, were destroyed in a fire during the nineteenth century. Luckily, historians were able to reconstruct some of the data regarding excisemen (or tax collectors) for the period after 1707. The "List of the members of the Scottish Excise Department, 1707–1830: Card Index" <www. familysearch.org/search/catalog/93326> has one individual per card, and each card references publications in which the individual can be found (image **E**). Note the collection is not searchable, so you'll have to browse.

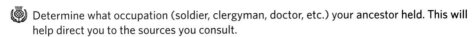

KEYS TO SUCCESS

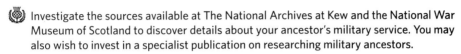

Determine what occupation (soldier, clergyman, doctor, etc.) your ancestor held. This will help direct you to the sources you consult.

Investigate the sources available at The National Archives at Kew and the National War Museum of Scotland to discover details about your ancestor's military service. You may also wish to invest in a specialist publication on researching military ancestors.

Use the sources included in this chapter as a starting point for finding occupational records, and check databases like Ancestry.com, Findmypast, MyHeritage **<www. myheritage.com>**, and FamilySearch.org for additional resources. The National Record of Scotland may hold sources relating to your ancestor's profession.

GLOSSARY OF ARCHAIC OCCUPATIONS

accomptant accountant

aeronaut balloonist or a trapeze artist

alewife woman who keeps an alehouse or tavern

amanuensis secretary or stenographer

axle tree maker maker of axles for coaches and wagons

baxter baker

bluestocking female writer

brewster beer manufacturer

cohen priest

collier coal miner

cooper barrel-maker

costermonger fruit seller

couranteer journalist

crocker potter

gaoler jailer

hind farm laborer

huckster seller of small wares

husbandman tenant farmer

joyner/joiner skilled carpenter

lavender washer woman

leech/sawbones doctor/surgeon

pedascule schoolmaster

perambulator surveyor

peruker wigmaker

ratoner rat catcher

scappler person who roughly shapes stone in preparation for a mason

scutcher person who beats flax to soften the straw

slopseller seller of ready-made clothes

snobscat shoe repairer

tide waiter customs official

tie maker maker of wooden railway ties

tipstaff policeman

vulcan blacksmith

webster weaver

whitewing street sweeper

12

Other Records

The genealogy records available for Scotland are vast—so vast, in fact, that several do not fit neatly into a single category, unlike the census, church, civil, legal, and military/occupational records we've already discussed. In this chapter, we'll cover the miscellaneous records that can contain critical information about your Scottish ancestors: newspapers, directories, gravestones, and more. You never know where you will find the clue you need!

TOMBSTONES

Tombstone inscriptions can be useful tools for genealogical research, and many genealogists feel just as comfortable in a cemetery as they do in a library. In some cases, a gravestone may be the only place where someone's existence (particularly, a woman's existence) is recorded. In Scotland, tombstones are considered supplements to Old Parish Records, and (as a result) volunteers and genealogists have made a great effort to transcribe markers for those who died prior to 1855. Many genealogical societies have published these gravestone transcriptions and made them available to the public.

Tombstones frequently mention more than one family member, and may include several generations. It was not uncommon for a family member who emigrated to erect a

tombstone for their ancestors in the Scottish parish churchyard—even after they had left Scotland (image ). Luckily, the deceased's name and new home was often mentioned on these monuments as well.

The Scottish Association of Family History Societies has a list of all known cemeteries in Scotland <www.safhs.org.uk/burialgrounds.asp>. If you click on the name of a burial ground, you will see a table of information, including coordinates to the cemetery's location and where you can purchase a transcription of the tombstones. In most cases, this is the local Family History Society <www.safhs.org.uk/members.asp> or the Scottish Genealogy Society <shop.scotsgenealogy.com/acatalog/Monumental_inscriptions.html>.

Gravestone database Find A Grave <www.findagrave.com> hosts more than 170 million online memorials that sometimes include gravestone entries, but not many of them are specific to Scotland. If you're researching Scottish graves, you'll probably have more luck browsing by location. This will let you know quickly if your ancestor's county (let alone home parish) has been added to the site. Note that some communities have entries in the locations list, but no cemeteries attached to them. Furthermore, some cemeteries only have one headstone.

BillionGraves <www.billiongraves.com> is another great resource, and it includes thousands of markers in Scotland in its database. BillionGraves' neat map feature allows you to pin a grave's location on a

Tombstones can provide valuable genealogical information (though some stones are in better shape than others). John Smith of North Carolina had this stone erected in his Scottish home parish in memory of his father, David Smith.

map of an area, giving you exact geographic coordinates and helping you determine what cemeteries are near your current location.

Likewise (and more helpfully), Findmypast has a Monumental Inscriptions collection for Scotland <search.findmypast.com/search-world-records/scotland-monumental-inscriptions-index>. This contains records for inscriptions from 209 cemeteries in fourteen counties, and Findmypast has also provided a list of burial grounds the collection includes <www.findmypast.com/articles/scottish-monumental-inscriptions-index-burial-ground-list>. Findmypast also has burial databases for Linlithgowshire <search.findmypast.com/search-world-Records/scotland-linlithgowshire-west-lothian-burials-1860-1975> and Aberdeenshire, Banffshire, and Kincardineshire <search.findmypast.com/search-world-Records/aberdeenshire-banffshire-and-kincardineshire-monumental-inscriptions>. The transcriptions for each of the markers will vary, but will probably include at least a name, location, and date of death.

Deceased Online <www.deceasedonline.com> is another database of burial and cremation registers, this one based in the United Kingdom. Most of these entries are submitted by crematoria and burial authorities. You can search for free, but must register to see more details about a particular entry. You'll need to pay to view full entries, either by subscription or pay-per-view. This database is especially helpful for more modern burials for which no headstone exists. You can check "coverage" to see if the area you are interested in is included in the database.

ELECTORAL REGISTERS

Due to the property qualifications required for voting (and how impoverished Scotland was compared to England), very few people could vote in Scotland before 1832. The franchise expanded after the Reform Act of 1832, and similar acts passed in the nineteenth century. Still, only men who met the property qualifications could vote in parliamentary elections for much of Scottish history. Women could not vote in parliamentary elections until 1918, though they could vote in local elections beginning in the 1880 provided they met the property qualifications. Learn more about expansion of the vote from the BBC <www.bbc.co.uk/bitesize/higher/history/democracy/changes/revision/1>.

As the franchise expanded, the government required a record of who was eligible to vote. These lists were known as electoral registers, or voters' rolls. From 1832 to 1918, they included the person's name, occupation, home-ownership status (e.g., whether they were a landowner, a tenant, or a lodger), and the property that qualified the person to vote. It is possible that a person lived in town, but the property that qualified them to vote was actually a country estate outside of cities.

Unfortunately, electoral registers aren't stored or indexed in one central place, and not all voter rolls have survived. Many of those that have, especially for the period 1832–1870, have been deposited at the National Records of Scotland. Many more remain in local repositories. Luckily, electoral rolls from some localities are available at Ancestry.com:

- "Fife, Scotland, Voters Lists, 1832–1894" <search.ancestry.com/search/db.aspx?dbid=1984&path=>
- "Glasgow, Lanarkshire, Scotland, Electoral Registers, 1857–1962" <search.ancestry.com/search/db.aspx?dbid=61020>
- "Perth and Kinross, Scotland, Electoral Registers, 1832–1961" <search.ancestry.com/search/db.aspx?dbid=60557>
- "Edinburgh, Scotland, Electoral Registers, 1832–1966" <search.ancestry.com/search/db.aspx?dbid=61486>
- "Scotland, Linlithgowshire (West Lothian), Electoral Registers 1864-1931" <search.findmypast.com/search-world-Records/scotland-linlithgowshire-west-lothian-electoral-registers-1864-1931-image-browse>

POOR LAW

Prior to the Poor Law Amendment (Scotland) Act of 1845, heritors and the kirk session in each parish organized assistance to the poor. Heritors would make donations, and the kirk session would collect funds from the poor box and from various fees paid to the church. Records of distributions would be in the heritors' or the kirk session records. Surviving records might include discussions of poor relief and lists of paupers.

The Poor Law (Scotland) Act changed that when it passed in 1845, creating parochial boards that were tasked with administering relief to the poor. People who needed relief had to apply and demonstrate their need via an application; if their claims were rejected, they could appeal to the sheriff's court. Records typically included the name, age, and place of birth of the claimant, plus the names of any dependents. Records for East Lothian, Midlothian, and Wigtownshire are held at the National Records of Scotland, while the remainder are still held in local archives. You can search the Scottish Archive Network <www.scan.org.uk> or check with the local Family History Society. Findmypast also has Poor Law record transcripts from Linlithgowshire (West Lothian) <search.findmypast.com/search-world-Records/scotland-linlithgowshire-west-lothian-poorhouse-records-1859-1912>.

LAND TAXES

In chapter 9, we discussed the variety of taxes levied by the government in the seventeenth and eighteenth centuries. But land records are amongst the most useful of this hodgepodge group of records, though they apply only to wealthier Scots. Very few land tax records from before 1855 survive, with the earliest dating to 1643.

In 1667, the office of Commissioner of Supply was created to help standardize the land-taxing process. This committee, comprising wealthy landowners, was tasked with collecting the land tax from their peers. As most Scots did not own land, few are included in these early tax lists. These early lists were also known as valuation rolls, and include those records that pre-date 1854. ScotlandsPlaces hosts records held by the Scottish Exchequer <scotlandsplaces.gov.uk/digital-volumes/historical-tax-rolls/land-tax-rolls-1645-1831>, including their transcriptions. You may find other tax records in local authority archives.

A more uniform land tax was established in 1854, and the first was collected in 1855. These valuation rolls were created annually in a process that started at Whitsunday, the traditional day for the ending of leases in Scotland. Legally, this day was fixed on May 15, but an assessor resurveyed each property over the next two months and calculated new rates by August 15. People could appeal their new rates before they were fixed on September 15. However, the process did not always work this smoothly, and it may have taken a year or two for a change to be reflected in the rolls.

The printed rolls include the property's location, the name of the proprietor (owner), the names of the tenants or other occupiers, and the taxable value. However, if your ancestor rented land valued at less than four pounds per annum, it wasn't taxed. The only person listed was the head of household—unfortunately no one else was included. Despite the limited information available, the valuation rolls can help you track ancestors in between the census records.

The National Records of Scotland hold a complete set of the valuation rolls (from 1855 to 1989). You can also search and view online the valuation rolls for the years 1855, 1865, 1875, 1885, 1895, 1905, 1915, 1920, 1925, 1930 and 1935 on ScotlandsPeople <www.scotlandspeople.gov.uk/advanced-search/valuation>. Viewing an image costs two credits.

When searching for your ancestor, it is helpful to know where your ancestor lived in the census on either side of the valuation roll you are searching. Access to a map is essential as well—in most cases, a modern map will do, but if the area has greatly changed you might need a historical map (see chapter 5). If your ancestor lived in a large city such as Glasgow or Edinburgh, you will probably also need to know the city ward in which they lived. I searched for my great-grandfather in the valuation rolls for Ayrshire in 1895, five years after he married. For that year, there were six David Hoods in Ayrshire, one in Ayr, three in Riccarton Parish, and one in Mauchline (image **B**). I knew from census records that my David Hood lived in the village of Hurlford in the parish of Riccarton. Since he was a coal miner, he was probably the tenant living in Mauchline Road, the main street through Hurlfurd. Since the David Hood on this page was a miner and lived near three other miners (image **C**), I'd likely found the correct one.

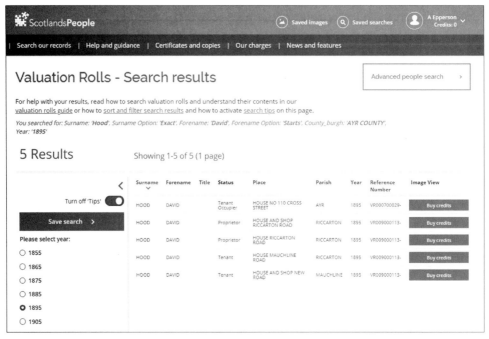

The valuation roll search results show my choices for a David Hood who lived in Ayrshire in 1895.

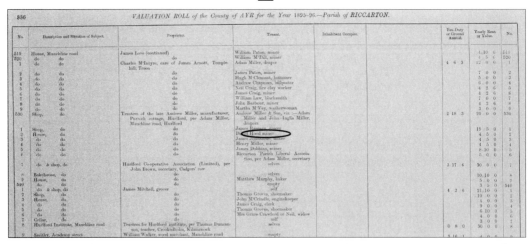

According to this valuation roll, David Hood, a miner, lived in a house on Mauchline Road in Ayrshire that was owned by the Trustees of Andrew Miller. The yearly rent for his home was valued at four pounds, five pence. His near neighbors were miners as well.

NEWSPAPERS

Newspapers are a boon to genealogical research because, even if they don't contain genealogical data for your ancestor, the contents will contain information that will provide context to your ancestor's life. Many Scottish newspapers are available online through subscription services, and many more must be viewed in person in local repositories.

The British Newspaper Archive <www.britishnewspaperarchive.co.uk>, a partnership between the British Library and Findmypast, provides access to more than 25 million pages dating to the 1700s, although most date to after 1800. The archive offers annual, trimonthly, and monthly subscriptions. You can view a list of Scottish titles <www.britishnewspaperarchive.co.uk/titles/countries/scotland> to see if the collection includes any papers relevant to your research.

The Glasgow Herald and *The Scotsman*, the two national newspapers for Scotland, are both part of the British Newspaper Archive. *The Scotsman* also offers its archive from 1817 to 1850 as a standalone subscription site <archive.scotsman.com>, with several packages from as short as two days to a full year. *The Herald* is available at the Google News archive, but I have found this site very difficult to use <news.google.com/newspapers>.

In addition, FamilySearch.org offers a sixty-five-page typescript publication called *Scottish Newspapers held in Scottish libraries* <www.familysearch.org/search/catalog/207535>. Compiled in 1956, this document logs which libraries hold various Scottish publications. Many libraries and publications have probably added newspapers since then, but it's still an excellent starting point for determining where to find newspapers from your ancestor's region of Scotland.

To access other publications, you'll need to visit archives or libraries in person. Another notable paper, *The Caledonian Mercury* (published in Edinburgh from 1720 to 1867), is available online through FamilySearch.org, but you can only view it if you are in the Family History Library in Salt Lake City <www.familysearch.org/search/catalog/1671132>.

The National Library of Scotland maintains a list of Scottish newspapers that have been indexed <www.nls.uk/collections/newspapers/indexes>. To be clear, the 183 titles in this list are not the only newspaper titles in Scotland—just the only ones that have been indexed. The entry includes information on where the indexes and the newspapers can be accessed. And in 2001, the National Library of Scotland (NLS) embarked on an ambitious plan to preserve Scotland's newspapers and make them more accessible. A key component of the plan was to microfilm many newspapers titles. Visit <www.nls.uk/about-us/working-with-others/newsplan-scotland/titles_all.cfm> for a list of newspaper titles now available to view in the library's reading room.

Ancestry.com also has three collections of Scottish newspapers:

- *"Edinburgh Courant* (Edinburgh, Midlothian, Scotland)" <search.ancestry.com/search/db.aspx?dbid=7200> has select issues from 1884.

- "Perth, Scotland Newspaper Index Cards, 1809–1990" <search.ancestry.com/search/db.aspx?dbid=1220> includes abstracted information from the newspaper for the period in question. The index cards typically include the name of the individual, event type and date, and the title and date of the newspaper and page number of the article. This information should be enough to allow access to the original.

- *"Dunfermline Journal*, 1851–1931" <search.ancestry.com/search/db.aspx?dbid=1235>. This was the main newspaper for Dunfermline. The run of issues is not complete, so you'll notice gaps in coverage.

FAMILY HISTORIES

We, in the twenty-first century, are not the only ones interested in family history. Scots of the nineteenth and early twentieth centuries were interested too. As a result, they published a great number of clan and family histories. While most of these relate to the important and landed families (rather than the common folk most of us are descended from), they are often incredibly detailed. The NLS has a collection of 383 memoirs, genealogies, and clan histories available to view as PDF files <digital.nls.uk/93506071>. These works include titles as varied as *Genealogical Memoirs of the Family of Robert Burns and of the Scottish House of Burnes* and *The Earls of Cromartie: Their Kindred, Country, and Correspondence*. Ancestry.com also has a couple family histories among its collections, including *A History of the Douglas Family of Morton in Nithsdale (Dumfriesshire) and Fingland (Kirkcudbrightshire) & Their Descendants* <search.ancestry.com/search/db.aspx?dbid=17779> and *History of the House of Ochiltree of Ayrshire, Scotland: With the Genealogy of the Families of Those Who Came to America and of the Allied Families, 1124–1916* <search.ancestry.com/search/db.aspx?dbid=12168> are available as collections at Ancestry.com.

The "great and the good" are often the easiest to research because they leave behind more records, and people have written about them. Biographical dictionaries are an excellent resource for these individuals, as they include a brief synopsis of the individual's life and accomplishments. These books contain not just contain biographies of the nobility, but also of judges, poets, soldiers, physicians, and noted travelers.

For example, *The Scottish Nation Or, The Surnames, Families, Literature, Honours, and Biographical History of the People of Scotland*, a three-volume set compiled by William Anderson in 1864, is available on Ancestry.com <search.ancestry.com/search/db.aspx?dbid=7331>. Other editions of this alphabetical dictionary are also available at Archive.org and Google Books.

Likewise, the *Biographical Dictionary of Eminent Scotsmen* was compiled by Robert Chambers and published in 1875 **<digital.nls.uk/74458002>** and includes biographies of Scots who lived from the sixteenth to nineteenth centuries. Various editions of volumes of this work are also available at Archive.org.

Burke's Peerage has been publishing the genealogy of the nobility of the United Kingdom since 1826. The entries are alphabetical and include the accomplishments, honors and titles of each individual, plus children and lineage. They have published updates to their genealogy regularly since 1847, with volume 107 published in 2003. *Burke's Peerage* now maintains a website **<www.burkespeerage.com>**, where you can search for names and see snippets for free. To see entire images, you must subscribe to the volume (not the entire site) for a period of time. Two volumes are available at Archive.org: Volume 31 (published in 1869) **<archive.org/details/genealogicalhera00inburk>**, and volume 99 (from 1949) **<archive.org/details/burkesgenealogic1949unse>**.

Another publication of the company, *Burke's Family Records*, includes entries for "cadets," junior members of British noble families. Published in 1897, it is available as a searchable collection on Ancestry.com **<search.ancestry.com/search/db.aspx?dbid=1860>**. You can also view volume 1 as an e-book at Archive.org **<archive.org/details/familyrecords01burk>**, where information is arranged alphabetically by family.

Some other works deal only with the peerage of Scotland. *A Peerage of Scotland*, compiled primarily by Sir Robert Douglas, was published in 1798 **<archive.org/details/peerageofscotlan02douguoft>**, **<quod.lib.umich.edu/e/ecco/004896980.0001.000?view=toc>**. A revised edition was published by John Philip Wood in 1813. A nine-volume work, *Scots Peerage*, was published between 1900 and 1914 by Sir John Balfour, and expands on Sir Robert Douglas'. All nine volumes are available at Archive.org, and you can also find them by searching for *Scots Peerage*.

IMMIGRATION, EMIGRATION, AND NATURALIZATION RECORDS

Americans tend to focus on the immigration story to figure out when and why our ancestors crossed the Atlantic to get to the United States. This is such a significant component of our national story that we tend to forget that people emigrated to places other than the United States. The wise researcher does not overlook migration records in the homeland.

You might also find that an ancestor returned to Scotland for a visit. The United Kingdom kept records of people coming into the country from 1878 to 1960, and these are available to search at Ancestry.com **<search.ancestry.com/search/db.aspx?dbid=1518>**. You'll notice gaps in coverage and the forms and information they collected, but you will at least find the name of the passenger and his arrival date.

The Scots Abroad collections at the National Library of Scotland may lead you to sources that will shed light on your ancestors' emigration experiences.

At least twenty-eight thousand people who were born in Scotland applied for readmission to British citizenship. Most of these individuals likely spent a great many years abroad and were now returning home to Scotland. These records can be found in the "UK, Naturalisation Certificates and Declarations, 1870–1916" collection on Ancestry.com **<search.ancestry.com/search/db.aspx?dbid=9156>**.

The NLS maintains several records collections related to Scots abroad (image). For example, "Scots in North America" **<www.nls.uk/catalogues/online/scots-abroad/sna>** contains accounts that Scots published of their travels in North America. A similar "Emigration from Scotland: Emigrants' Correspondence" collection **<www.nls.uk/catalogues/online/scots-abroad/mss>** includes letters and papers in the NLS collections that contain personal correspondence, while "Emigrants' Guides to North America" **<www.nls.uk/catalogues/online/scots-abroad/egna>** includes guides that helped an emigrant prepare for and settle in North America. The collections do not link to digital versions of the original sources, but they do let you know what is available.

Once you know the name of a published title, you can then see if a work is available online or at a library near you. However (with the exception of historical correspondence), these sources are unlikely to mention your ancestors by name. However, they may help you understand emigrant journeys and experiences, plus how your ancestor learned about their American destination.

DEEDS

In America, deeds are almost always about property. But it Scotland, deeds are legal agreements that their signers wanted recorded for posterity—for example, contracts for marriage, partnership, and apprenticeship. You may also find agreements regarding property, particularly tacks (leases). However, the recording of the *transfer* of property in the Register of Sasines was required by law (see chapter 10). Having said that, wills are also occasionally found in deed registers.

Many more legal agreements were probably written in Scotland than were recorded in the various deed registers, and mining surviving records can prove fruitful for Scottish researchers. The interested parties may not have taken the time (or the expense) to have the agreement recorded unless necessary, such as if one party was worried that the other might renege on the arrangement. For example, a marriage contract may not have been recorded until the death of one of the spouses.

Document Types in Deed Indexes

The following list of documents types was taken from two indexes of seventeenth-century deeds and provides an overview of the range of legal issues that were recorded in deed books:

- Agreement
- Assignation
- Bond
- Bond of Corroboration
- Bond of Provision
- Commission
- Contract
- Contract of Division
- Declaration
- Decree Arbitral
- Discharge
- Disposition
- Grantee
- Granter
- Heritable Bond
- Indenture
- Interdiction
- Marriage Contract
- Minute of Alienation
- Minute of Sale
- Mutual Discharge
- Obligation
- Principal Party
- Procuratory
- Ratification
- Renunciation
- Retrocession
- Reversion
- Revocation
- Submission
- Tack
- Translation
- Victual
- Wadset
- Warrandice

This page from the General Register of Deeds shows the grantor, grantee, type of deed, date of issuance and registration, and reference to where you can find the original record.

Because deeds can detail family relationships and provide other details about your family, they can be quite useful to family history research. The higher your ancestors were on the social scale, the more likely they were to appear in deeds (image **E**).

However, searching the deeds can be inherently tricky and downright impossible unless you are on site in Scotland. The first problem is that the deeds could be recorded in any court, anywhere. After 1809, the courts where deeds could be registered were limited to sheriff's courts, burgh courts, and the Court of Session. Therefore, you need to know where the deed might have been filed before you can start to look for it. The primary court for such registration was the Court of Session in Edinburgh, the highest court in Scotland, where deeds involving important people would be filed in the Books of Council and Session (commonly known as the Register of Deeds) no matter the residence of the parties involved.

Some records of the Register of Deeds of the Court of Session are available at FamilySearch.org. Included are the minute books (summaries of entries made in the register and recorded in chronological order) and indexes from 1542 to 1851 <www.familysearch.org/search/catalog/262868>. For part of that period, deeds were organized by the clerk who recorded them, and since several clerks were working at the court at the same time, you will need to check several minute books to find one deed. Most of the microfilm has been digitized and is available to view at a Family History Center or an affiliate library.

You can also find a few published indexes on Archive.org:

- Index to Register of Deeds 1663 <archive.org/details/indexes100scotuoft>

- Index to Register of Deeds 1664 <archive.org/details/indexes200scotuoft>

- Index to Register of Deeds 1665 <archive.org/details/indexes400scotuoft>

- Index to Register of Deeds 1666 <archive.org/details/indexes500scotuoft>

In addition, Ancestry.com offers a searchable version of the Index to Register of Deeds, 1667 <search.ancestry.com/search/db.aspx?dbid=34579>.

Many records from smaller courts have been deposited with the NRS, but they have not been indexed. Others remain in their original courts (also unindexed), and you'll need to search these records in situ. If you think (or hope) that an ancestor is mentioned in a local court, you will need to search the records on site or find someone to do it for you. In either case, consider contacting a local genealogical society to find out more about the state of local records.

DIRECTORIES

City and town directories may show you what your ancestor did and where he lived, either in between censuses or before civil registration. However, Scottish directories are not as inclusive as their American counterparts. While professionals, tradesmen, and farmers would be included, employees, laborers, miners, and crofters would not. Women were often only included if they were the head of household.

Directories were published for most of the large cities in Scotland beginning in the eighteenth century, although they are most numerous in the 1800s. The earliest directories mostly provide details for the notable people in town—for example, the nobility, business owners, ministers, and physicians. Eventually, they start to include tradesmen, clerks, and other residents in town. You'll find fewer directories for rural areas, though Pigots and Slaters published a few <www.nls.uk/family-history/directories/post-office/?place=Scotland>. Directories are generally organized in at least one of three ways (alphabetically, by street, and by location), and this structure should allow you to identify your ancestors and their neighbors.

F

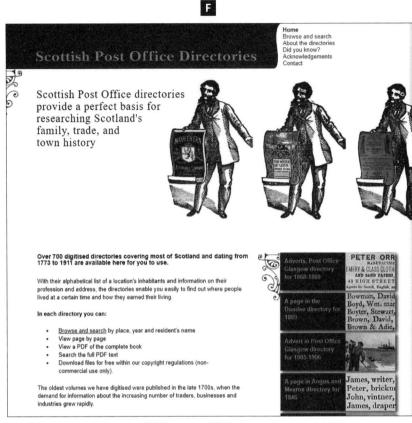

Hundreds of directories are available to search by name or keyword at the National Library of Scotland.

An extensive collection of directories is available at the National Library of Scotland <digital.nls.uk/directories> (image **F**). You can search the seven hundred directories at the NLS by name, place, and year. You can also view each page individually or download an entire PDF copy of the book. The NLS also provides links to each directory at Archive. org <digital.nls.uk/directories/browse>. Likewise, Findmypast has a collection of over 250 volumes including almanacs, trade directories, and county guides <search.findmypast. com/search-world-records/britain-directories-and-almanacs>.

Keep your eye out for "miscellaneous" record groups, such as city directories, published family histories, and newspapers. The records we've covered in this chapter are among the basic kinds of "other" records, but your ancestors might be mentioned in still more kinds of documents.

 Search online first. Many kinds of records can only be accessed in person at Scottish libraries and archives. But before you book your trip to the homeland, make sure you investigate which documents can be accessed online from the comfort of your computer or your local Family History Center.

 Be flexible with your spelling when searching databases. Also experiment to see which spelling variations are recognized by the database and which are not. For example, a search for *Mc* may also return results for Mac, but not Mack.

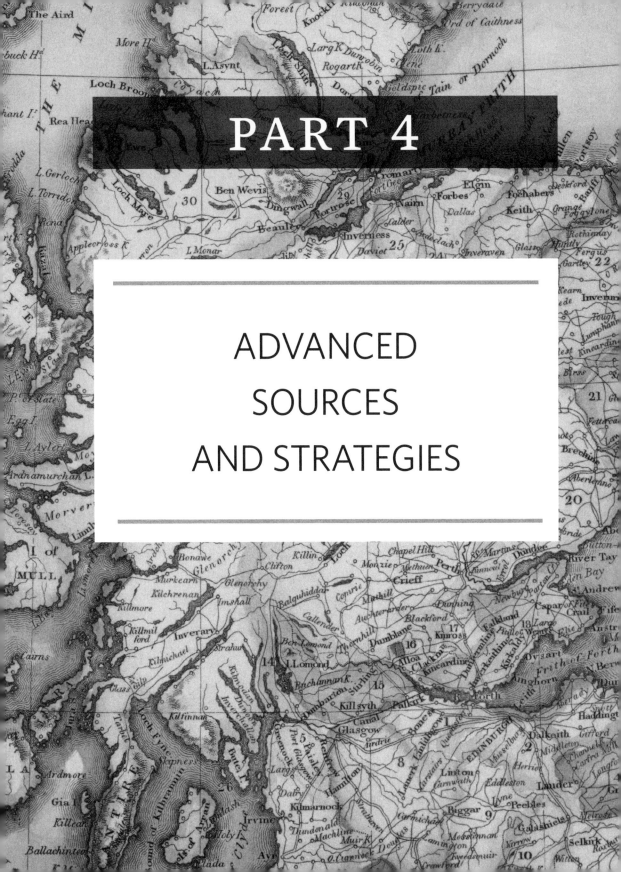

PART 4

ADVANCED SOURCES AND STRATEGIES

13

Putting It All Together

These real-life case studies will help you apply what you've learned throughout this book to your own research.

A BUMPER CROP OF MCINTOSHES

Scottish families often immigrated in groups, which can be both a blessing and a curse for genealogists. That's what I discovered when investigating the McIntosh family, who are well documented in family histories but become difficult to distinguish from each other.

The patriarch, Alexander McIntosh, was among the earliest settlers in his town of Scotch Settlement in Columbiana County, Ohio. Arriving in 1801, Alexander became the first ruling elder of the local Presbyterian church, and the first church services were held at his farm in Yellow Creek Township at the eastern end of Scotch Settlement. Genealogists have taken great interest in Alexander and the several McIntosh families of Scotch Settlement, and so I've been able to find a great deal of information about them that was compiled by local genealogists and historians. But the two family group sheets I had for this Alexander McIntosh had conflicting information: a woman with two different maiden names, plus nineteen(!) different possibilities for children. See the sidebar for a comparison.

McIntosh Research: Beginning

Group Sheet 1		
	Birth info	Death info
Alexander McIntosh	1750	10 Oct 1812
Isabella Smith	1760	22 Apr 1847
William	1773 in Scotland	10 Feb 1851 in Ohio
Margery	1774 in Scotland	16 Aug 1850 in Ohio
James	1780 in Scotland	6 Nov 1854
Angus	1790 in Scotland	24 Jul 1842 in Ohio
Evan	1793 in Scotland	2 Dec 1818 in Ohio
John	1795 in Scotland	24 Nov 1819 in Ohio
Jane	1796 in Scotland	unknown
Mary A.	1798 in Scotland	14 Mar 1876 in Ohio
Alexander	n.d. in Scotland	unknown
Donald	n.d. in Scotland	unknown
Nancy	n.d. in Scotland	unknown

Group Sheet 2		
	Birth info	Death info
Alexander McIntosh	ca. 1750	1812
Isabella Calder	ca. 1760	1847
Donald	1780	1875
Isabella	1787	1859
Evan	1793	1842
Margaret	1794	1875
Jane	1796	unknown
Alexander	1796	1839
Mary A.	1798	1846/1876
James	1801	1854

Unfortunately, neither genealogist provided any documentation for these group sheets. According to the Scotch Settlement records, all the possible children were "real people" in the community, but I couldn't easily determine if they were connected to "my" Alexander and Isabella. US census records from 1850 or later (which listed individuals in a household by name) would not be useful for this family, since most of the people suggested in these lists were dead by 1850. (And if they were still living, they were not with their family of origin.) This meant I had to rely on other records: tax records, probate

Cemetery markers can help provide information about your deceased ancestors and their relatives. These are the tombstones for Alexander McIntosh and his wife, Isabella.

records, cemetery markers (image **A**), property records, county histories, and Scottish parish records.

My first step was to confirm Alexander McIntosh's death date. Estate records indicated that an Alexander McIntosh of Yellow Creek Township died intestate (without a will) in 1812. The items in his estate inventory—a quilling wheel, loom, and gear; spools; linen; yarn; and seventeen acres of wheat—indicate he was a weaver as well as a farmer. The administrators of his estate were Isabella McIntosh (likely his wife) and Andrew Smith. Neither of the witnesses, John McPhail and Andrew McPherson, were obviously related to Alexander McIntosh. The estate papers did not indicate the specific location of his land, nor did they name his heirs-at-law. I believed some of his heirs were still minors, since the estate record mentioned a provision for supporting his widow and children for twelve months.

I then examined property records. An Alexander McIntosh acquired the deed to 156.62 acres in the northeast quarter of section 6 in Yellow Creek Township in 1809 from Angus and Catherine McBean. That same year, he purchased twenty-seven acres that adjoined his primary property, though this land was in section 36 of St. Clair Township. Tax records show McIntosh paid tax on his land in section 6 as early as 1806, and he was still listed as the taxpayer until 1819. The following year (1820), Isabella McIntosh was listed as the taxpayer instead, suggesting this Alexander died in 1819 or early 1820. The

Alexander McIntosh who died in 1819 owned property in Madison Township, so this change in taxpayer cannot refer to his property.

The family didn't hold on to this Alexander's land for long after his apparent death. In 1833, Evan McIntosh, Alexander McIntosh, and Philip Smith and his wife sold 158 acres in section 6 in Yellow Creek Township and twenty-seven acres of land in section 36 of St. Clair Township to a James McIntosh. It's unclear if or how James McIntosh was related to the family (and Isabella isn't mentioned in the deed), but it seems that Isabella and Alexander's children were selling the family farm. Based on this, I believed I was following the right Alexander McIntosh. But the property records still did not provide enough details about his family.

I turned again to probate records, searching for every McIntosh I could find. I also looked for members of the Calder family, since that was one of the options for Isabella McIntosh's maiden name. (I decided to save the Smith probate records for last.) In one such record from 1821, a fifteen-year-old Margaret McIntosh (daughter of Alexander) chose Evan McIntosh as her guardian. An Alexander McIntosh in the area had died in 1819, but he named his children in his will and did not have a daughter Margaret. Therefore, the Alexander referred to in Margaret's 1821 record was probably the one who died in 1812.

This piece of evidence suggests that Alexander (d. 1812) and Isabella had a daughter, Margaret, who was born about 1806 and chose her own guardian—perhaps an elder brother.

In another probate record, an Ann Calder wrote her will in 1817, but it was not probated until 1833. She left her estate to her sister Isabella McIntosh (née Calder). Ann named two executors: Isabella, and her nephew Daniel McIntosh. Another Calder, John, wrote his will in 1830, leaving his wife Betsy as the primary beneficiary. Amongst his many relatives, he named a sister (Isaballa McIntosh), some nephews (Even McIntosh, Daniel McIntosh, Alexander McIntosh, and James McIntosh), and a niece (Peggy McIntosh). In the list of legatees for this estate, Evan McIntosh received $115 as guardian for Margaret (possibly nicknamed "Peggy") McIntosh.

A third Alexander McIntosh of Yellow Creek Township died intestate in 1839, likely the son of the Alexander who died in 1812 (as the other Alexander had no son with that name). Evan McIntosh and James McIntosh were named administrators, but by the time the final report was filed in 1845, James McIntosh was noted as the "surviving administrator," indicating that Evan had died in the intervening years. Indeed, further records indicate Evan McIntosh died intestate and his estate was probated in 1842. The administrator of Evan's estate was Alexander McIntosh, probably Evan's eldest son. James McIntosh and John Falconer stood security for Evan's estate. The fact that these three men (Alex-

Alexander McIntosh's two sons, Alexander and James, are buried next to each other in Scotch Settlement. There markers look very similar to those of their parents.

ander, Evan, and James) appear together in several records associated with each other suggest that I was following the correct family.

As I continued searching, I found a James McIntosh who died intestate in 1854 (image B). The administrator was an Alexander McIntosh, who may have been his nephew. In 1856, legacies were paid to Isabella and Philip Smith, Margaret McIntosh, a "B.C. Hill" of Pittsburgh, Mary Ann McIntosh, Jennett McIntosh, and Alexander McIntosh. Based on previous research, I determined Isabella McIntosh Smith was the sister of James McIntosh, and that most of the other individuals appeared to be the heirs of Evan McIntosh. James had sold the family land to Alexander McBain on 1 May 1854, just a few months before James' death in November of that year.

Following the Isabella McIntosh Smith clue, I found an Isabella McIntosh who married Philip Smith in 1815. She died without issue in 1861. Her will, signed in 1859, divided her estate between the heirs of her brother-in-law (William Smith) and the heirs of her brother, Evan McIntosh. These heirs (named Alexander, Janet, Isabella, Margaret, Elizabeth, Evan, James, and Catherine) received a share of what Isabella had inherited from her brother (James McIntosh, d. 1854).

The wills and property records reveal that Isabella Calder was the wife of Alexander McIntosh, and they had at least six children: Evan, Daniel, Alexander, James, Isabella, and Margaret. Based on the research we've already covered here, we also have death dates

McIntosh Research: The Results

	Birth info	Death info
Alexander McAndrew (McIntosh)	ca. 1750	1812
Isabella Calder	ca. 1760	1847
Jane	1786	unknown
Isabella	1788	1861
Anna	1790	unknown
Evan	1793	1841/1842
Daniel	1794	1839
Alexander	1797	1839
John	1799	unknown
James	1801	1854
Margaret	1806	before 1839

for some of these children: Evan in 1841 or 1842, Alexander in 1839, James in 1854, and Isabella in 1861. Census records can give us some idea of when three of these family members were born: Evan between 1791 and 1800, James about 1801, and Isabella about 1787. The remaining two, Daniel and Margaret, likely died prior to 1839, as they are not mentioned in the probate records of any of their siblings. This is especially compelling, since Daniel and Margaret would have normally been allocated land from their siblings who died according to Ohio intestate law. This information also indicates that Evan married and had children, while Isabella married but had no children. James and Alexander did not marry. If Daniel and Margaret married and had children, they all must have died before 1839, because any of their children would have been considered heirs-at-law and have inherited their parent's portion of the estate. (And even if they were over-looked here, it seems likely that Isabella McIntosh Smith would have included any surviving children of her other siblings in her 1859 will.)

Collateral research provided more evidence to help determine which McIntoshes were part of the family. John Calder's will, which we previously mentioned, noted additional siblings, nieces, and nephews: sisters Nancy Calder, Isabella Ogilvie, and Nelly Rose; nephews John Calder, Alexander Calder, and William Calder; and niece Isabella Calder. The inclusion of these younger relatives who had the surname Calder suggests that John had a male relative who was an heir (likely a brother) and passed the Calder name onto his children. Alexander Calder is a solid candidate, and his will, written in 1828 and probated in 1831, named his wife Ann and the same children mentioned in John's will. I read between the lines to determine the relationship here: John may have disinherited his brother Alexander in favor of his children if Alexander was, himself, on his deathbed.

The records examined show that neither of the family group sheets that I acquired is entirely accurate. Family group sheet 1 includes many people who are actually the children of a different Alexander McIntosh—one who died in 1819. Family group sheet 2 is more like the family I identified in the records, but some of the dates are wrong. For example, family group sheet 2 shows a son Donald (Daniel) who died in 1875. However, the family I've been researching has a Daniel who died before 1839. Perhaps, if I can find this family in Scottish records, I can figure out the correct birth order of the children of Alexander McIntosh and Isabella Calder.

Having exhausted my records in the United States and learned as much as I could about the "true" Alexander McIntosh, I was ready to move abroad. I found a third family group sheet from a genealogist who thought the Scotch Settlement-based Alexander McIntosh family (as established in family group two) strongly resembled the Alexander McAndrew and Isabella Calder family of Ardclach Parish in Nairnshire. The family group sheet he created for the Nairnshire McAndrew family did not include the farm where the family had lived in Scotland, nor did it include the names of the witnesses of the baptisms. Could this family be the McIntoshes that I've researched for so long?

To find out, I began looking for Old Parish Registers for this family (see chapter 8). Alexander McAndrew and Isabella Calder resided at Boath, a farm in Ardclach parish. Boath was part of an agricultural district known as Highland Boath, which in turn was part of the estate of the Earl of Cawdor. The parish registers indicate that Alexander McAndrew and Isabella Calder had seven children at Boath: Jane (b. 1786), Isabella (b. 1788), Anna (b. 1790), Evan (1793), Donald (b. 1794), Alexander (1797), and John (b. 1799). While this did look promising, some of the names didn't quite match up, and I'd need additional evidence.

Fortunately, more data came in the form of baptismal witnesses: An Alexander Calder was witness to the baptism of three of Alexander and Isabella's children, and John Calder was witness to a fourth. I already knew the Calders had a connection to my McIntosh family, so this lent support to the "McIntosh equals McAndrews" theory. A William Forsyth was witness to two of the children, as well—and additional research would show that William Forsyth was Isabella Calder's stepfather.

A continued look at baptismal records revealed that an Alexander Calder and his wife Christina McIntosh had four children: Donald (b. 1785), Margaret (b. 1787), John (b. 1790), and Alexander (b. 1793) at a location described as Boath or Balville, both part of the Highland Boath district. That seemed to line up with the Alexander and John Calder in the McAndrew baptismal witnesses—and Alexander Calder had a daughter, Isabella, with Anne Sinclair at Ballville in 1800. Witnesses at the baptism of these children included Alexander McAndrew, John Calder, and William Forsyth.

Additionally, three of these children "match" people mentioned in John Calder's will: his nephews John and Alexander and his niece Isabella. Alexander's will named his wife (Ann) and these same children.

The connection between the Calder and McAndrew families in Scotland and the Calder and McIntosh families in Ohio strongly suggest that Alexander McIntosh and Isabella Calder of Yellow Creek Township in Columbiana County are the same couple as Alexander McAndrew and Isabella Calder of Boath in Ardclach Parish, Nairnshire, Scotland.

By researching records from both sides of the Atlantic, we were able to sift through all the repeating names and multiple identities to discover the "right" McIntosh/McAndrew family.

FACT-CHECKING THE MANY RELATIONSHIPS
OF CATHERINE HODGE

Sometimes you have to build your family tree from the ground up, and other times you have pieces of it passed down to you through the generations. In either case, you need to cite your sources to ensure your tree has only the best and most accurate data. My research into the Hodge line of my family is a great testament to this, as some family stories seem too wild to be true—until you've proven them.

In the late 1990s, I imported two files that I received from my mother into my genealogy software program. The first was related to my mother's research about her father, William Hood, who was born in Scotland in 1914 and came to America with his parents and several siblings in 1923. The second was a file of new information collected on Catherine Hodge McLay (Angus) Baillie, William Hood's maternal grandmother. The files had no citations or images attached. Rather, the data had been collected by my mother via microfilm at the local Family History Center and through correspondence with her first cousins in America and more distant cousins in Canada and the United Kingdom. But, given the explosion in online genealogy research, I wanted to create a fully sourced genealogy for this branch of my family. I also wondered, despite the apparent "completeness" of the genealogy, if I could learn anything new by looking at original records.

Catherine Hodge McLay (Angus) Baillie is pictured here surrounded by three of her children—Elizabeth, Robert, and Margaret—and three of her grandchildren.

Over the course of the next several weeks, I uncovered all kinds of small details about my ancestors, confirming some that I already knew and slightly adjusting some others. In a research dive that included bonnet-making in Kilmarnock and coal-mining in Stirlingshire, I was able to solve a few family mysteries that only newer records were able to solve. For example, the 1911 Scottish census showed that the Highland "grandmother" that I'd heard stories about as a child was really a great-aunt from Isle of Lewis.

But none of these discoveries were as interesting as the information I found about Catherine Hodge, my great-great-grandmother (image **C**). According to what my mother and I knew, Catherine had an active romantic life. She married twice and had a relationship with a third man in between her marriages. In fact, she had more illegitimate children than legitimate, and some family stories even said she ran a bordello (a brothel). If there ever were an ancestor's history calling out for confirmation with documents, it was hers. It seems no one in the family had traced all her children to help determine if these family tall tales were true.

I started with those two marriage records, which (along with her death record) consistently identified her parents as William Hodge and Ann Finnickam. I found her parent's 1820 marriage record in Kilmarnock, Ayrshire, but I did not find a baptismal record for Catherine. In the 1841 Scottish census, a widowed Ann headed a household with six children, including four-year-old Catherine (born about 1837). Ann married again (this time to a man named John Orr) later that year. While I could not identify Ann and John in the 1851 census, Catherine is probably the same Catherine Hodge, aged fourteen, listed as living with her brother (also called William Hodge) and his wife in 1851 in Kilmarnock.

Having outlined the basics of Catherine's youth, I started to look into her young adulthood. Sometime between 1851 and 1857, Catherine met a man named James McLay. They had two children, Ann in April 1857 and James in June 1859. But there's a twist: The statutory record for their marriage states they were not wed until December 1859, but neither Ann nor James is listed as illegitimate on their birth records. How could this be? Perhaps Catherine and James had an irregular or unsanctioned marriage and (instead of facing fines or tracking down witnesses to confirm it) they decided to just get married again. Or, perhaps, they weren't married in any formal way whatsoever. In any case, the couple likely took advantage of the fact that birth records did not ask for marriage information about the couple—just the names of the father and mother.

Then, tragedy struck. James died in a mining accident in March 1860, and the couple's son (also named James) died at seventeen months old from smallpox. Catherine worked as a bonnet maker to make ends meet, and the family also accepted borders to help bolster income as is shown in Catherine's 1861 census entry.

Catherine didn't remain single for long, however. She soon met James Angus, a miner originally from New Monkland parish in Lanarkshire. Their first child, Margaret Simpson Angus, was born in July 1862. Unlike her half-siblings, Margaret was listed in her birth register as James and Catherine's illegitimate daughter. Another son, James Simpson Angus, also illegitimate, was born in September 1864 and died two months later from an abscess.

In the mid-1860s, the family moved to New Monkland, Lanarkshire—and continued to grow. Robert Cook Angus, a son to James Angus and Catherine Hodge, was born at Meadowfield in 1866. But another piece of intrigue struck in Robert's birth register: It said that he was legitimate, and that his parents had married in Kilmarnock in December 1860. When I first saw the record, I thought it couldn't be "my" James and Catherine, since I was led to believe the couple never married. It seems more likely that Catherine and James (Angus) simply fibbed—they were likely able to get away with this subterfuge, since no one in Lanarkshire would know about their situation in Ayrshire. Another daughter, Jean, was born in 1869 in Kilmarnock, and both parents appeared to register

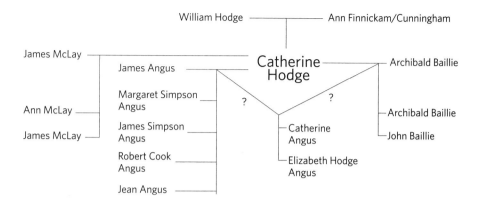

William Hodge ——————— Ann Finnickam/Cunningham

James McLay

James Angus

Margaret Simpson
Angus

Ann McLay

James Simpson
Angus

James McLay

Robert Cook
Angus

Jean Angus

Catherine
Hodge

?   ?

Catherine
Angus

Elizabeth Hodge
Angus

Archibald Baillie

Archibald Baillie

John Baillie

Catherine Hodge McLay (Angus) Baillie had quite the complicated life. Here's the family tree that I discovered throughout my research.

her even though she was listed as illegitimate. She died just two months after being born, and James reported her death.

Catherine gave birth again to a daughter (also named Catherine) the following year, but only the mother's name was on the birth record—potentially indicating that James Angus was not the father. Could that be the case? The family is listed as a whole unit in the 1871 census: James Angus was head of household, with wife Catherine Angus (or McLay), step-daughter Ann McLay, daughters Margaret and Catherine, and son Robert. But when young Catherine died in 1872, James Angus reported the death and declared he was a "friend."

The drama didn't end there (image **D**). Catherine Hodge's final daughter, Elizabeth, was born in 1873. Elizabeth was labeled illegitimate, and (as with Catherine the younger) only her mother's name was listed on the birth record. I have yet to find a document that confirms James Angus was Elizabeth's father, but Elizabeth seemed to think he was. She lists her name as Elizabeth Hodge Angus on her marriage record, and she names James Angus as her father in that document. James' name also appears on her 1935 death certificate filed in Ohio.

Elizabeth's fatherhood gets even more complicated in 1875, when Catherine (noted as the widow of James McLay) married for a second time, this time to a man named Archibald Baillie, in Kilmarnock. They had two sons, Archibald and John. If he were her father, Archibald Baillie (the elder) could have legitimized Elizabeth after his marriage to Catherine, but it doesn't seem that he did. The records and the timing suggest that the

The statutory marriage record of Robert Angus includes the many surnames used by his mother, Catherine Hodge.

relationship between James and Catherine may have become "complicated" in the early 1870s—they likely broke up.

So after Catherine married Archibald, what happened to her other children (Ann McLay, Robert Cook Angus, and Margaret Simpson Angus)? From the 1881 census, we know Elizabeth, Robert, and Margaret were all listed as Archibald Baillie's children, though we know that isn't the case. Statutory records for Kilmarnock help fill in the rest of the story. Ann McLay married in 1874, Margaret Angus married in Kilmarnock in 1879, and Robert Cook Angus married in 1885. The latter registration was particularly useful to the story of Catherine, as Robert's mother was listed Catherine Baillie, formerly Angus, maiden surname Hodge (image **E**).

We don't know much beyond that. Archibald Baillie died suddenly in March 1900. Catherine lived with her grandson (likely Robert Angus' son, also named Robert) at 14 Strand Street in Kilmarnock during the 1901 census. Then, Catherine's occupation was listed as "general dealer." She died in September 1902: Catherine Baillie, the widow of James McLay and Archibald Baillie.

And what became of James Angus? Based on the genealogy my mother shared with me, James was married and had two children with a woman named Mary Maxwell before he showed up in Kilmarnock and had a decade-long relationship with Catherine Hodge. But in the research my mother had, I discovered this James Angus died in November 1881, and the informant for the death record was his widow (Mary Maxwell).

This didn't square up with what I thought I knew about Catherine's James Angus, but my searches in indexes and databases suggests he's the one. ScotlandsPeople <www.scotlandspeople.gov.uk> indicates only six men named James Angus died in Ayrshire between 1873 and 1881, only three of whom were the right age. Of those three, two were listed with their wives and children in the 1871 census index on Ancestry.com, leaving just one: James Angus who died in Kilmarnock in 1881 and was likely Catherine's partner. That also explains why Catherine and James never officially married: James already had a wife, who he apparently abandoned.

Even though I didn't find any new direct ancestors or serious mistakes in my family's genealogy, I did find a whole lot of interesting details as I re-checked my mother's research. Catherine Hodge consistently identifies herself as a bonnet knitter until 1901, when she is employed as a general dealer. Neither of these, so far as I know, has anything to do with a bordello. (Bummer!) Perhaps the grandchildren didn't really understand how she could have so many children and not be married and so came up with that theory as an explanation.

There's always something to learn, especially if you are picking up on decades' old history. I've still got families to trace and questions to answer, but (at least for this branch) I have confidence that what we have is correct and fully documented.

14

What to Do When You Get Stuck

There will come a time when the research stalls and you cannot find answers to your questions. These stopping points are commonly known as "brick walls," a catch-all term in the genealogical world for when you can't identify an ancestor's parish of origin, a woman's maiden name, or anything that keeps you from finding previous generations. When you reach this point, take time to try and figure out why you are stuck.

Specifically, you will likely encounter a problem in at least one of two areas. The first will be failing to identify your immigrant ancestor's Scottish parish of origin. The earlier your ancestor came to America, the harder this information will be to find. The second will be tracing your ancestors in Scottish records prior to 1850. Using statutory records and the 1851 census should be fairly straightforward for most individuals, but earlier records are harder to find and use.

Luckily, certain research strategies can help you solve almost any research problem. In this chapter, we'll discuss some of these solutions for breaking down the brick walls in your Scottish research.

IDENTIFY THE PROBLEM

Perhaps you are following the wrong person who happens to have the same name and is about the same age as your ancestor. Maybe you are looking in the wrong place, whether it be a parish or county. Maybe you have misread or misinterpreted a document. Then again, perhaps you really are at a dead end and didn't notice the "no way out" sign when you turned towards that piece of information.

These different scenarios require different responses. Mistakes and misinterpretations can be righted, allowing you to continue with your research. But in other cases, you might not be able to find an answer to your research question because you cannot find surviving records or evidence that preserved it.

As a result, you need to identify the specific problem as best as you can. This will help you better understand the status of your research and what other work you need to accomplish, plus select a course of action that will best help your research.

RESEARCH YOUR ANCESTOR'S NETWORK

Discovering the names of your ancestors, their family members, and known associates is key to successful network genealogy. As we discussed in chapter 2, all immigrants— including the Scots—tended to settle near people they knew. Because of this, lines of communication between the old community in Scotland and the new one in America can provide valuable information about lives on both sides of the Atlantic. Family members and neighbors in the old community can become valuable sources of information for both members of their town in Scotland and for you as a modern researcher. Even if someone in your ancestor's Old World community had no direct relationship to those already in America, he might have heard useful information about your ancestor's life in the new country and decided to emigrate to the same location. So if you're having trouble finding relatives in Scotland, research the other Scottish-born people in your ancestor's New

RESEARCH TIP

Define Success

Sometimes the problem isn't with your research answers—it's with your questions. If you're not getting the results you expected, change your definition of success. If you can't fulfill your lofty goal of tracing your Scottish ancestors back to the year 1500, for example, settle for learning even more about them in the 1800s and 1900s. Setting more obtainable goals will help you feel better about your research and provide you with more realistic benchmarks.

World neighborhood. Scottish communities in America usually had immigrants from several areas, but narrowing your possibilities to a handful of parishes or even a county or two is better than trying to research the entire country of Scotland.

In addition, try researching your ancestor's siblings in Scottish or American records, as appropriate. Even if these records don't provide information about your direct-line ancestor, the death records or obituaries for a sibling might include the names of their parents or their parish of origin. Siblings may have lived longer and therefore appear in more records. Additionally, siblings may record or tell different stories about the family than each other. For example, my aunt Annie once told me that she could see Bannock-burn from her house when she was young. My mother had never heard that story from either her aunt or father (and so never passed it on to me). By talking to this non-direct-line relative, I gained new perspective on my family's story.

SEEK NEW SOURCES

The information you seek may turn up in unexpected places, so broaden the kinds of documents you're searching for. As we've discussed, research records for members of your ancestor's community, as place of origin is bound to be included in at least one of their records (though, of course, your ancestor may have come from a different place than did a member of their community).

Also consult original records whenever possible. Searching online databases can only get you so far, as indexes have their limitations. Many Scots had the same or similar names, and transcription or indexing errors can complicate your search.

Another option is to investigate sources at American repositories near where your ancestor lived. Check websites for archives and historical societies to see what might be available before you plan a research trip. In the catalogs, keep an eye out for memoirs, diaries, family papers, and correspondence that contain names associated with your ancestor's community. Prominent families are more likely to leave documents, and (even if your ancestor wasn't high-class or well-known) your ancestor may have done business of some sort with them and be mentioned in their documents.

Also be sure to search the library catalogs of Scottish and American universities, plus works that examine the areas and people you are interested in, either in America or in Scotland. Also look specifically for local histories written about communities in Scotland. Local histories, too, can provide detailed contextual information about your ancestors' lives.

TURN TO DNA

DNA testing is an excellent tool for finding distant relatives or proving family connections. Most researchers will want to take an autosomal DNA test. These tests, which can be taken by men and women, can match you (with reasonable accuracy) to fifth cousins and closer, representing about 125 years of family history. The tests can also identify sixth to eighth cousins, though those relationship predictions are much less reliable. At the time of this book's publication, four major companies offer autosomal DNA tests: 23andMe <www.23andme.com>, AncestryDNA <dna.ancestry.com>, Family Tree DNA <www.familytreedna.com>, and MyHeritage DNA <www.myheritage.com/dna>.

You may also want to look into a Y-DNA test if you have questions about your male-line ancestors. The Y-DNA test can only be taken by men, but women can encourage male relatives (such as a father, brother, or paternal uncle) to test. Y-DNA is passed from father to son with few if any mutations, making it a great test to determine shared paternal ancestry. Since surnames are also passed from father to son, many surname projects incorporate Y-DNA results and are able to group men into genetic families. If you decide to take a Y-DNA test, be sure to join a project for your surname or clan name <www.familytreedna.com/scottish-clan-list.aspx>. Consider joining special projects if relevant. For example, Family Tree DNA, the leading and sole provider of Y-DNA tests, has several: Scotland-Flemish Project <www.familytreedna.com/groups/flemish-in-scotland/about>, the Scottish Prisoners Project <www.familytreedna.com/groups/scottish-po-ws/about>, and the Scottish Mapping Project <www.familytreedna.com/groups/scottishmapping/about>.

RECHECK YOUR SOURCES

If you are really stuck (and fed up), put the genealogy problem aside and closely re-examine the data that you've already collected. You never know what information might jump out at you by casting a fresh eye on your research.

Take time to ensure you have saved a digital copy or made photocopies of all documents, and that they are adequately sourced. If you are using genealogy software, be sure you've consistently entered, formatted, and sourced all your data—names, dates, places, and images. Check over your entries for any mistakes.

In a similar vein, write out what you have found and what conclusions you have drawn from that data. This "report" has no audience except you, so don't worry about the format, grammar, or sentence structure. Simply think analytically about your work and carefully examine each document, making sure that you have noticed every detail.

Once you're done with your report, put the entire project aside. When you come back to the project with fresh eyes, you'll likely notice new connections and possibilities. Ideally, your subconscious has been hard at work on your genealogy problem while you've been doing something else, and you will notice a change after taking a break.

Since genealogy is an ongoing project full of spits and spurts, you'll likely go through this "assess and reassess" process several times. Each time, you will have an opportunity to determine if you are at a brick wall or dead end.

TRAVEL TO ARCHIVES

Sometimes, online research and mail correspondence aren't enough, and you'll need to travel to do on-site research. Check with US societies to see what repositories are near them. You can find many genealogical societies in the United Sates at USGenWeb **<www. usgenweb.org>** or the Federation of Genealogical Societies **<www.fgs.org>**. Many archives will have information about visiting and perhaps even a place to send a query. Smaller societies indicate how much they are willing to do for you for free.

Once you have identified a repository you wish to visit, examine its website to see what its hours and rules are. Some local societies will be fairly casual, while major archives may require a reader's ticket or pass that you must apply for in advance. Pay attention to the rules for researchers. For example, you may be required to use only a pencil, especially if you are using original manuscripts. Many places will not allow you to take your things into the reading room with you and will have lockers or cubbies for these items.

Make sure the documents you wish to view are available to the general public. Some items are incredibly fragile and/or valuable, and only academics and other serious researchers can view them. Some libraries set aside designated seating locations for researchers consulting manuscript collections. Also see if everything you want to see is *stored* on site. Many large libraries with extensive collections have off-site storage for rarely used items or those published prior to a certain date. You can usually request these items, but it may take a couple of days for them to reach the reading room. If you're on a tight schedule, ask if you can request materials in advance so they will be waiting for you when you arrive.

All of the above applies to research in both the United States and Scotland—and, of course, visiting your Scottish homeland can be a powerful (in addition to knowledge-filled) experience. You can see your ancestor's hometown firsthand and walk the streets

Hiring Professional Researchers

If you are truly stuck (or it is not practical to travel to a repository to find what you're looking for), it is probably time to hire a professional. A professional genealogist will be able to look at your problem with fresh eyes, local knowledge, and emotional detachment—all three are necessary. Since a professional has never seen your research before, he will probably notice different facts and options for research. Once you send a summary of your research and copies of relevant documents, a professional will examine this prior research and be able to assess its accuracy. Since a professional is not emotionally attached to your ancestors, he will be able to critically examine your evidence through the lens of local history and availability of records. If he believes your project has potential, the professional make take up your case and put his local knowledge of history and records to work, perhaps recommending sources you hadn't thought of.

You can find listings of genealogists who work in Scotland at the Association of Professional Genealogists <**www.apgen.org**>, the Association of Scottish Genealogists and Researchers in Archives <**www.asgra.co.uk**>, and the National Records of Scotland <**www.nrscotland.gov.uk/research/researching-online/paying-for-research**>. Unfortunately, not many people on these lists for genealogists work in Scotland. But if there isn't a professional genealogist who lived near your ancestral hometown, you might ask for recommendations from a local family history society <**www.safhs.org.uk/members.asp**>.

When preparing to approach a genealogist in Scotland, be sure to get your research in order. Write a summary of your research on the Scottish ancestral line you want researched. Prepare copies of pedigrees and family groups sheets, and have copies of documents handy. Finally, write out what exactly you want the research project to accomplish. Do you want to find John McDonald's father (and perhaps grandparents) who you believe was born on the Isle of Skye? That goal gives the researcher wide leeway in approach and kind of records needed. Or do you want them to look only at a certain group of records for one particular ancestor—say the Earl of Cawdor's estate rent lists—for evidence of Donald Rose, who probably was a tenant on his estate? Preparing all of this information will help you figure out what you want and will help the researcher accomplish it for you.

When selecting a researcher overseas, try to learn as much about him as you can. Check out his website to see what types of projects he has done in the past. Some genealogists also describe typical work products and packages and their pricings. Most will charge an hourly rate plus money for transportation, copies of documents, and entrance fees to research facilities (for example, a day's pass to a ScotlandsPeople Center is fifteen pounds).

Most researchers in Scotland will expect at least a partial payment up front, and some accept payments via PayPal. A contract might also be wise, if only because then you and the researcher will know what is expected. The contract should spell out the research to be performed and whether the results will be conveyed in a written report, plus whether you will get transcriptions or copies of documents. If the quoted price gives you sticker shock, ask what work can be done for a price you can afford. Perhaps a research calendar instead of a report would be sufficient.

For more on hiring professional genealogists, check out *Family Tree Magazine*'s article on the subject <**www.familytreemagazine.com/premium/go-with-the-pro**>.

where they did. Maybe you'll even be able to stand at the feet of your ancestors' graves! Consult a listing of several Scottish societies at the Scottish Association of Family History Societies <www.safhs.org.uk/members.asp>.

KEYS TO SUCCESS

Return to each source and analyze the information you have collected. Have you gleaned all possible information from it?

Search more broadly for records. Your ancestors can be mentioned in all kinds of documents and resources. If your research is struggling, make sure you've fanned out to include members of your ancestor's community and even obscure kinds of records.

Ask for help from the genealogy community. Join a surname study or relevant genealogy group for advice, or hire a professional researcher to help you break down a nasty brick wall.

A

Websites, Publications, and Archives

WEBSITES

Records

Ancestry.com
<www.ancestry.com>

FamilySearch.org
<www.familysearch.org>

Findmypast
<www.findmypast.co.uk>

FreeCEN
<www.freecen.org.uk>

ScotlandsPeople
<www.scotlandspeople.gov.uk>

ScotlandsPlaces
<www.scotlandsplaces.gov.uk>

Maps and Places

Ainmean-Àite na h-Alba (AÀA)—Gaelic Place-Names of Scotland
<www.ainmean-aite.scot/gd>

Etymology Of British Place-names
<freepages.genealogy.rootsweb.ancestry.com/~pbtyc/Misc/Etymology.html>

Gazetteer for Scotland
<www.scottish-places.info>

National Library of Scotland—Maps
<maps.nls.uk/index.html>

General Resources

Am Baile Highland History and Culture
<www.ambaile.org.uk>

Association of Scottish Genealogists and Researchers in Archives
<www.asgra.co.uk>

Cyndi's List—Scotland
<www.cyndislist.com/uk/sct>

Dictionary of the Scots Language
<www.dsl.ac.uk>

Electric Scotland
<www.electricscotland.com>

FamilySearch Wiki: Scotland Emigration & Immigration
<www.familysearch.org/wiki/en/Scotland_Emigration_and_Immigration>

GENUKI Scotland
<www.genuki.org.uk/big/sct>

Library of Congress: Sources for Research in Scottish Genealogy
<www.loc.gov/rr/genealogy/bib_guid/scotland.html>

National Register of Archives for Scotland
<www.nrscotland.gov.uk/record-keeping/national-register-of-archives-for-scotland>

Rootschat—Scotland
<www.rootschat.com/forum/scotland>

Scottish Archive Network
<www.scan.org.uk>

Scottish Archives for Schools
<www.scottisharchivesforschools.org>

The Scottish Emigration Database (University of Aberdeen)
<www.abdn.ac.uk/emigration/index.html>

Scottish Handwriting
<www.scottishhandwriting.com>

The Scottish Register of Tartans
<www.tartanregister.gov.uk/index>

Statistical Accounts of Scotland
<stataccscot.edina.ac.uk/static/statacc/dist/home>

Blogs

The GENES Blog
<britishgenes.blogspot.com>

The Scottish Diaspora Blog
<thescottishdiaspora.net>

The Scottish Emigration Blog
<scottishemigration.blogspot.com>

BOOKS

Genealogy

A Genealogist's Guide to Discovering Your Scottish Ancestors by Linda Jonas and Paul Milner (Betterway Books, 2002)

Scottish Ancestry: Research Methods for Family Historians, second edition by Sherry Irvine (Ancestry, 2003)

Scottish Genealogy, fourth edition by Bruce Durie (The History Press, 2018)

Reunion: A Search for Ancestors by Ryan Littrell (Self-published, 2012)

Scottish History

The Highland Clearances, new edition by Eric Richards (Birlinn Ltd., 2016)

To the Ends of the Earth: Scotland's Global Diaspora, 1750–2010 by T.M. Devine (Smithsonian Books, 2011)

Scots in America

Cargoes of Despair and Hope: Scottish Emigration to North America 1603–1803 by Ian Adams and Meredyth Somerville (John Donald, 2001)

Colonists from Scotland: Emigration to North America, 1707–1783, reprint edition by Ian Charles Cargill Graham (Clearfield, 2009)

A Dance Called America: The Scottish Highlands, the United States and Canada by James Hunter (Mainstream Publishing, 1995)

Carolina Scots: An Historical and Genealogical Study of Over 100 Years of Emigration by Douglas F. Kelly and Caroline Switzer Kelly (Seventeen Thirty Nine Publications, 1998)

Scotland and Its First American Colony, 1683–1765 by Ned C. Landsman (Princeton University Press, 1985)

The Highland Scots of North Carolina, 1732–1776 by Duane Meyer (University of North Carolina Press, 1987)

Scottish Highlanders in Colonial Georgia: The Recruitment, Emigration, and Settlement at Darien, 1735–1748, revised edition by Anthony W. Parker (University of Georgia Press, 2002)

ARCHIVES

The National Archives
Kew
Richmond
Surrey
TW9 4DU
UNITED KINGDOM
<www.nationalarchives.gov.uk>

National Records of Scotland
(formerly known as the National Archives of Scotland [NAS] and the Scottish Record Office [SRO])
General Register House
2 Princes Street
Edinburgh
EH1 3YY
UNITED KINGDOM
<www.nrscotland.gov.uk>

National Library of Scotland
George IV Bridge
Edinburgh
EH1 1EW
UNITED KINGDOM
<www.nls.uk>

The Mitchell Library
North Street
Glasgow
G3 7DN
UNITED KINGDOM
<www.glasgowlife.org.uk/libraries/venues/the-mitchell-library>

Burns Monument Centre
Kay Park
Kilmarnock
East Ayrshire
KA3 7RU
UNITED KINGDOM
<www.burnsmonumentcentre.co.uk>

Highland Family History Society
The Highland Archive Centre
Bught Road
Inverness
IV3 5SS
UNITED KINGDOM
<www.highlifehighland.com/archives-service>

County Archives
Note: Due to administrative changes, records from some historical counties are now held by organizations or archives in different (usually neighboring) counties. Other counties have combined their archives.

ABERDEEN

Aberdeen City and Aberdeenshire Archives
Town House
Broad Street
Aberdeen
AB10 1AQ
UNITED KINGDOM
<www.aberdeencity.gov.uk/services/libraries-and-archives/aberdeen-city-and-aberdeenshire-archives>

ANGUS (FORFAR)
Angus Archives
Hunter Library
Restenneth Priory
Forfar
DD8 2SZ
UNITED KINGDOM
<archive.angus.gov.uk/historyaa/
archives/resources/familyhistory.htm>

ARGYLL
Library Headquarters
Highland Avenue
Sandbank
Dunoon
PA23 8PB
UNITED KINGDOM
<www.liveargyll.co.uk/
libraries-and-archives/
local-studies#overlay-context=>

AYR
Ayrshire Archives
Watson Peat Building
SAC Auchincruive
Ayr
KA6 5HW
UNITED KINGDOM
<www.ayrshirearchives.org.uk>

BANFF
Town House
Broad Street
Aberdeen
AB10 1AQ
UNITED KINGDOM
<www.aberdeenshire.gov.uk/registrars/
aberdeenshire-and-moray-records>

BERWICK
Heritage Hub
Kirkstile
Hawick, Roxburghshire
TD9 0AE
UNITED KINGDOM
<www.liveborders.org.uk/localhistory>

BUTE
Library Headquarters
Highland Avenue
Sandbank
Dunoon
PA23 8PB
UNITED KINGDOM
<www.liveargyll.co.uk/
libraries-and-archives/
local-studies#overlay-context=>

CAITHNESS
High Life Highland
12/13 Ardross Street
Inverness
IV3 5NS
UNITED KINGDOM
<www.highlifehighland.com/
nucleus-nuclear-caithness-archives>

CLACKMANNAN
Clackmannanshire Archives
Archives and Records Management Officer
Library Services
Speirs Centre
Primrose Place
Alloa
FK10 1D
UNITED KINGDOM
<www.clacks.gov.uk/culture/
heritageservices>

CROMARTY

Highland Archive Centre

Bught Road

Catherine Street

Inverness

IV3 5SS

UNITED KINGDOM

<www.highlifehighland.com/
highland-archive-centre>

DUNDEE

Local History Centre

Central Library

The Wellgate

Dundee

DD1 1DB

UNITED KINGDOM

<www.leisureandculturedundee.com/
library/localhistory>

DUMFRIES (AND GALLOWAY)

Ewart Library

Catherine Street

Dumfries

DG1 1JB

UNITED KINGDOM

<www.dumgal.gov.uk/article/15308/
Local-archives>

DUNBARTON (EAST)

East Dunbartonshire Archives (EDLC)

William Patrick Library

2–4 West High Street

Kirkintilloch

G66 1AD

UNITED KINGDOM

<www.edlc.co.uk/heritage-arts/archives>

DUNBARTON (WEST)

West Dunbartonshire Council Archives

Dunbarton Heritage Centre

Dumbarton Library

Strathleven Place

Dumbarton

G82 1BD

UNITED KINGDOM

<www.west-dunbarton.gov.uk/
libraries/archives-family-history/
archives-collections>

EDINBURGH (CITY)

Edinburgh City Archives

Level 1

City Chambers

253 High Street

Edinburgh

EH1 1YJ

UNITED KINGDOM

<www.edinburgh.gov.uk/cityarchives>

EDINBURGH (COUNTY)

Local Studies and Archives

Dalkeith Library

White Hart Street

Dalkeith

EH22 1AE

UNITED KINGDOM

<www.midlothian.gov.uk/info/458/
local_and_family_history/30/
midlothian_archives>

ELGIN (MORAY)

Museums Service

Falconer Museum

Tolbooth Street

Forres

IV36 1PH

UNITED KINGDOM

<www.moray.gov.uk/moray_standard/
page_620.html>

FIFE

ON at Fife Collections Centre

Bankhead Central

Bankhead Park

Glenrothes

Fife

KY7 6GH

UNITED KINGDOM

<onfife.com/libraries-archives/archives>

HADDINGTON (EAST LOTHIAN)

John Gray Centre

15 Lodge Street

Haddington

East Lothian

EH41 3DX

UNITED KINGDOM

<www.johngraycentre.org/about/
archives>

INVERNESS

Highland Archive Centre

Bught Road

Catherine Street

Inverness

IV3 5SS

UNITED KINGDOM

<www.highlifehighland.com/
highland-archive-centre>

KINCARDINE

Town House

Broad Street

Aberdeen

AB10 1AQ

UNITED KINGDOM

<www.aberdeenshire.gov.uk/registrars/
aberdeenshire-and-moray-records>

KINROSS

Perth & Kinross Archive

A K Bell Library

York Place

Perth

PH2 8EP

UNITED KINGDOM

<www.culturepk.org.uk/
archive-local-family-history>

KIRKCUDBRIGHT(GALLOWAY)

Ewart Library

Catherine Street

Dumfries

DG1 1JB

UNITED KINGDOM

<www.dumgal.gov.uk/article/15308/
Local-archives>

LANARK (NORTH)

North Lanarkshire Heritage Centre

High Road

Motherwell

ML1 3HU

UNITED KINGDOM

<culturenl.co.uk/museums/archives-
and-local-history-museums/
north-lanarkshire-archives>

LANARK (SOUTH)

South Lanarkshire Council Archives and Records Centre

30 Hawbank Road

East Kilbride

G74 5EX

UNITED KINGDOM

<www.southlanarkshire.gov.uk/
info/200165/local_and_family_history>

LINLITHGOW (WEST LOTHIAN)

West Lothian Local History Library
(Reference library)

Tam Dalyell House

Linlithgow Partnership Centre

High Street

Linlithgow

West Lothian

EH49 7EQ

UNITED KINGDOM

<www.westlothian.gov.uk/article/2055/
Local-History-Library>

NAIRN

Highland Archive Centre

Bught Road

Catherine Street

Inverness

IV3 5SS

UNITED KINGDOM

<www.highlifehighland.com/
highland-archive-centre>

ORKNEY

Orkney Library & Archive

44 Junction Road

Kirkwall

Orkney

KW15 1AG

UNITED KINGDOM

<www.orkneylibrary.org.uk/archive.htm>

PEEBLES

Heritage Hub

Kirkstile

Hawick, Roxburghshire

TD9 0AE

UNITED KINGDOM

<www.liveborders.org.uk/localhistory>

PERTH

Perth & Kinross Archive

A K Bell Library

York Place

Perth

PH2 8EP

UNITED KINGDOM

<www.culturepk.org.uk/
archive-local-family-history>

RENFREW

Inverclyde Heritage Hub

75-81 Cathcart Street

Greenock

PA15

UNITED KINGDOM

<www.inverclyde.gov.uk/community-
life-and-leisure/heritage/
family-history>

RENFREW (EAST)

Williamwood High School

Eaglesham Road

Clarkston

East Renfrewshire

G76 8RF

UNITED KINGDOM

<www.eastrenfrewshire.gov.uk/archives>

ROSS

Highland Archive Centre

Bught Road

Catherine Street

Inverness

IV3 5SS

UNITED KINGDOM

<www.highlifehighland.com/
highland-archive-centre>

ROXBURGH

Heritage Hub

Kirkstile

Hawick, Roxburghshire

TD9 0AE

UNITED KINGDOM

<www.liveborders.org.uk/localhistory>

SELKIRK

Heritage Hub

Kirkstile

Hawick, Roxburghshire

TD9 0AE

UNITED KINGDOM

<www.liveborders.org.uk/localhistory>

SHETLAND

Shetland Museum and Archives

Hay's Dock

Lerwick

Scotland

ZE1 0WP

UNITED KINGDOM

<www.shetlandmuseumandarchives.org.
uk>

STIRLING

Stirling Council Archives

5 Borrowmeadow Road

Stirling

FK7 7UW

UNITED KINGDOM

<my.stirling.gov.uk/archives>

SUTHERLAND

Highland Archive Centre

Bught Road

Catherine Street

Inverness

IV3 5SS

UNITED KINGDOM

<www.highlifehighland.com/
highland-archive-centre>

WIGTOWN (GALLOWAY)

Ewart Library

Catherine Street

Dumfries

DG1 1JB

UNITED KINGDOM

<www.dumgal.gov.uk/article/15308/
local-archives>

Religious Archives

Scottish Catholic Archives

Columba House

16 Drummond Place

Edinburgh

EH3 6PL

UNITED KINGDOM

<www.scottishcatholicarchives.org.uk>

Scottish Jewish Archives Centre

129 Hill Street

Garnethill

Glasgow

G3 6UB

UNITED KINGDOM

B

Societies

IN SCOTLAND

Scottish Genealogy Society
15 Victoria Terrace
Edinburgh
EH1 2JL
UNITED KINGDOM
<www.scotsgenealogy.com>

Aberdeen and North-East Scotland Family History Society
158-164 King Street
Aberdeen
AB24 5BD
UNITED KINGDOM
<www.anesfhs.org.uk>

Anglo-Scottish Family History Society
3rd Floor, Manchester Central Library
St. Peter's Square
Manchester
M2 5PD
UNITED KINGDOM
<www.anglo-scots.mlfhs.org.uk>

Association of Scottish Genealogists and Researchers in Archives (ASGRA)
41 Meldrum Road
Kirkcaldy
Fife
KY2 5HY
UNITED KINGDOM

Borders Family History Society

52 Overhaugh Street

Galashiels

TD1 1DP

UNITED KINGDOM

<www.bordersfhs.org.uk>

Caithness Family History Society

<caithnessfhs.org.uk>

Central Scotland Family History Society

4 Fir Lane

Larbert

Stirlingshire

FK5 3LW

UNITED KINGDOM

<www.csfhs.org.uk>

Dumfries and Galloway Family History Society

9 Glasgow Street

Dumfries

DG2 9AF

UNITED KINGDOM

<dgfhs.org.uk>

East Ayrshire Family History Society

The Dick Institute

Elmbank Avenue

Kilmarnock

KA1 3BU

UNITED KINDOM

<www.eastayrshirefhs.co.uk>

Family History Society of Buchan

22 Harbour Street

Peterhead

Aberdeenshire

AB42 1DJ

UNITED KINGDOM

<www.buchanroots.scot>

Federation of Family History Societies

PO Box 62

Sheringham

NR26 9AR

UNITED KINDOM

<www.ffhs.org.uk>

Fife Family History Society

33–35 Crossgate

Cupar

KY15 5AS

UNITED KINGDOM

<fifefhs.org>

Glasgow & West of Scotland Family History Society

Unit 13, 32 Mansfield Street

Glasgow

G11 5QP

UNITED KINGDOM

<www.gwsfhs.org.uk>

Guild of One-Name Studies

Box G, 14 Charterhouse Buildings

Goswell Road

London

EC1M 7BA

UNITED KINGDOM

<one-name.org>

The Heraldry Society of Scotland
25 Craigentinny Crescent
Edinburgh
EH7 6QA
UNITED KINGDOM
<www.heraldry-scotland.co.uk>

Highland Family History Society
Highland Archive and Registration Centre
Bught Rd
Inverness
IV3 5SS
UNITED KINGDOM
<www.highlandfamilyhistorysociety.org>

Lanarkshire Family History Society
North Lanarkshire Heritage Centre
High Road
Motherwell
ML1 3HU
UNITED KINGDOM
<www.lanarkshirefhs.org.uk>

Lochaber & North Argyll Family History Group
<www.lochaberfamilyhistory.org.uk>

Lothians Family History Society
c/o Lasswade Centre Library
Eskdale Drive
Bonnyrigg
Midlothian
EH19 2LA
UNITED KINGDOM
<www.lothiansfamilyhistorysociety.co.uk>

Moray & Nairn Family History Society
3 Dunbar Lane
Duffus
Elgin
IV30 5QN
UNITED KINGDOM
<www.morayandnairnfhs.co.uk>

The Moray Burial Ground Research Group
<www.mbgrg.org>

North Ayrshire Family History Society
c/o Largs Library
Allanpark Street
Largs
KA30 9AG
UNITED KINGDOM
<northayrshirefhs.org.uk>

Orkney Family History Society
Orkney Library & Archives
44 Junction Road
Kirkwall
Orkney
KW15 1HG
UNITED KINGDOM
<www.orkneyfhs.co.uk>

Renfrewshire Family History Society
51 Mathie Crescent
Gourock
PA19 1YU
UNITED KINGDOM

The Robert Burns World Federation

3A John Dickie Street

Kilmarnock

KA1 IHW

UNITED KINGDOM

<www.rbwf.org.uk>

The Scottish Association of Family History Societies

<www.safhs.org.uk>

The Scottish Military Research Group

<www.scottishmilitaryresearch.co.uk>

Shetland Family History Society

6 Hillhead

Lerwick

Shetland

ZE1 0EJ

UNITED KINGDOM

<www.shetland-fhs.org.uk>

Society of Genealogists

14 Charterhouse Buildings

Goswell Road

London

EC1M 7BA

UNITED KINGDOM

<www.sog.org.uk>

Tay Valley Family History Society

179–181 Princes Street

Dundee

DD4 6DQ

UNITED KINGDOM

<www.tayvalleyfhs.org.uk>

Troon @ Ayrshire Family History Society

c/o MERC, Troon Library

South Beach

Troon

Ayrshire

KA10 6EF

UNITED KINGDOM

<www.troonayrshirefhs.org.uk>

West Lothian Family History Society

21 Willow Park

Fauldhouse

Bathgate

West Lothian

EH47 9HN

UNITED KINGDOM

IN AMERICA

The American-Scottish Foundation, Inc.

Scotland House

575 Madison Avenue, 10th Floor

New York, NY 10022-2511

<americanscottishfoundation.com>

Association of Scottish Games and Festivals

<www.asgf.org>

Council of Scottish Clans and Associations

<www.cosca.scot>

List of St. Andrew's, Caledonian, and Scottish societies

<www.rampantscotland.com/features/societies.htm>

Robert Burns Association of North America

<www.rbana.org>

The Scottish-American Military Society

<www.s-a-m-s.org>

Scottish Heritage USA, Inc.

PO Box 457

Pinehurst, NC 28374-0457

Latin Word Lists

Most records that you encounter while researching your Scottish ancestors will be in English. However, a few may be in Latin. The Service of Heirs records were written in Latin until 1847, and some sixteenth-century Old Parish/ Parochial Registers (OPR) were in Latin as were university student lists until the mid-nineteenth century.

The lists on the pages that follow should help you identify dates and relationships in these documents.

NUMBERS

English	Cardinal (one, two, etc.)	Ordinal (first, second, third)
one	unus	primus
two	duo	secundus
three	tres	tertius
four	quattuor	quartus
five	quinque	quintus
six	sex	sextus
seven	septem	septimus
eight	octo	octavus
nine	novem	nonus
ten	decem	decimus
eleven	undecim	undecimus
twelve	duodecim	duodecimus
thirteen	tredecim	tertius decimus
fourteen	quattuordecim	quartus decimus
fifteen	quindecim	quintus decimus
sixteen	sedecim	sextus decimus
seventeen	septendecim	septimus decimus
eighteen	duodeviginti	duodevicensimus
nineteen	undeviginti	undevicensimus
twenty	viginti	vicensimus
thirty	triginta	tricensimus
forty	quadraginta	quadragensimus
fifty	quinquaginta	quinquagensimus
sixty	sexaginta	sexagensimus
seventy	septuaginta	septuagensimus
eighty	octoginta	octogensimus
ninety	nonaginta	nonagensimus
hundred	centum	centensimus
thousand	mille	millensimus

MONTHS

English	Latin
January	Januarius
February	Februarius
March	Martius
April	Aprilis
May	Maius
June	Junius
July	Julius
August	Augustus
September	September
October	October
November	November
December	December

DAYS OF THE WEEK

English	Latin
Sunday	dies dominuca
Monday	dies Lunae
Tuesday	dies Martis
Wednesday	dies Mercurii
Thursday	dies Jovis
Friday	dies Veneris
Saturday	dies Saturni

GENEALOGY TERMS

Latin	English
amita	paternal aunt
anno	in the year of
anno domini	in the year of our Lord
avia	grandmother
avunculus	maternal uncle
avus	grandfather
defuncti	dead
discipulorum	student
filia	daughter
filius	son
frater	brother
germana	birth sister
germanus	birth brother
haeres, heres	heir
hoc anno	this year
hoc inquisition	this investigation

Latin	English
in baronia de	in the barony of
in terries de	in the land of
insula	island
mater	mother
matertera	aunt (mother's sister)
maximus	the biggest, eldest
mensis	month
mercatoris	merchant
minimus	youngest
optimus	best
pater, patris	father
patruus	paternal uncle
soror	sister
terra	land/earth
unicus	only
uxor	wife

D

Worksheets

With so many genealogy records and websites to comb through, it can be easy to feel overwhelmed. That's why genealogy worksheets can be such useful tools in your research toolbelt. We've pulled together a few of the most useful genealogy forms for those researching Scottish ancestors:

- **Five-Generation Ancestor Chart**: Document your family back to your great-great-grandparents.

- **Scottish Census Questions at a Glance**: Learn what questions were asked in which census(es) between 1841 and 1911.

- **Name Variation Worksheet**: Track your surname searches and brainstorm alternate spellings for your ancestors' Scottish names.

You can find and download more free genealogy worksheets at <www.familytreemagazine.com/familytreefreebies>.

FIVE-GENERATION ANCESTOR CHART

4

birth date and place

marriage date and place

death date and place

2

birth date and place

marriage date and place

death date and place

5

birth date and place

death date and place

1

birth date and place

marriage date and place

death date and place

spouse

6

birth date and place

marriage date and place

death date and place

3

birth date and place

death date and place

7

birth date and place

death date and place

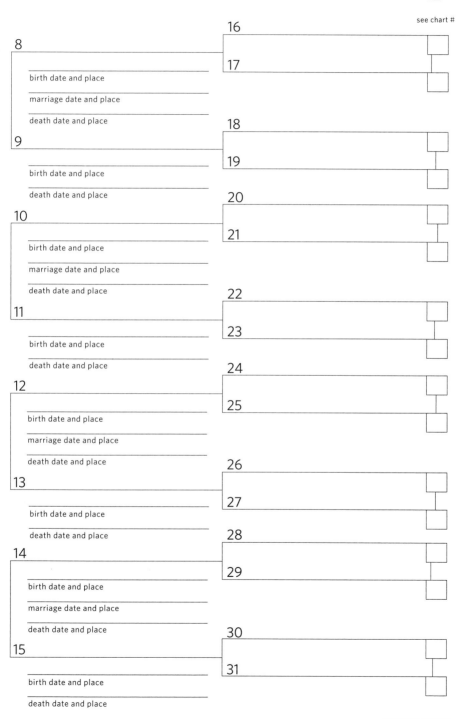

Chart # ___

1 on this chart =___ on chart #___

see chart #

16

8

_____
birth date and place

_____
marriage date and place

_____
death date and place

17

18

9

_____
birth date and place

_____
death date and place

19

20

10

_____
birth date and place

_____
marriage date and place

_____
death date and place

21

22

11

_____
birth date and place

_____
death date and place

23

24

12

_____
birth date and place

_____
marriage date and place

_____
death date and place

25

26

13

_____
birth date and place

_____
death date and place

27

28

14

_____
birth date and place

_____
marriage date and place

_____
death date and place

29

30

15

_____
birth date and place

_____
death date and place

31

SCOTTISH CENSUS QUESTIONS AT A GLANCE

	1841	1851	1861	1871	1881	1891	1901	1911
Place								
Name of village, square, close, court, etc.	●							
Name of street, place, road and number of house		●	●	●	●	●	●	●
Names								
Names of all household members	●	●	●	●	●	●	●	●
Birth Information								
Rounded down to the nearest five years	●							
Whether or not born in Scotland and county of residence	●							
Age		●	●	●	●	●	●	●
Born in England, Ireland, or foreign country	●							
Place of birth (county and town or parish		●	●	●	●	●	●	●
Marriage and family information								
Marital status ("condition")		●	●	●	●	●	●	●
Number of persons in the house								●
Relationship to head of household		●	●	●	●	●	●	●
Number of children aged 5–15 attending school or being educated at home			●					
Number of children aged 5–13 attending school or being educated at home				●				
(for married women) Duration of marriage								●
(for married women) Children born alive								●
(for married women) Children still living								●

	1841	1851	1861	1871	1881	1891	1901	1911
Occupation								
Profession, trade, employment, or of independent means	●							
Rank, profession, or occupation		●	●	●	●			
Profession or occupation						●		
Employer, employed, or neither but working on own account						●		
Employed, worker or on own account							●	●
If working at home							●	●
Personal occupation								●
Industry or service								●
Other Information								
Gaelic or Gaelic & English						●	●	●
Nationality (if foreign born)								●
Deaf, blind, or dumb		●	●					
Deaf and dumb, blind, imbecile or idiot, lunatic				●	●			
Deaf and dumb, blind, lunatic, imbecile or idiot						●	●	●
Number of rooms with one or more windows			●	●	●	●	●	●
Totally deaf or deaf and dumb, totally blind, lunatic, imbecile or feeble-minded								●

NAME VARIATION WORKSHEET

Family branch: _____

Surname			
Place of origin			
Phonetic variants			
Possible Anglicizations			
Surname prefixes (*Mc-*, *Mac-*, etc.) and suffixes (e.g., *-sen, -datter, -ova*)			
Other spellings/variants			

INDEX

PHOTO CREDITS

COVER

Top, left: Courtesy GoranQ/iStock, via Getty Images Plus

Right: Courtesy Library of Congress, LC-USZ62-96148

Bottom, left: Courtesy Library of Congress, LC-USZ62-120964

Back cover: Courtesy the David Rumsey Map Collection **<www.davidrumsey.com>**

INTRODUCTION

Title page: Courtesy the David Rumsey Map Collection

pp. 6–7: Courtesy the author and Patricia Hood Epperson

PART OPENERS

Courtesy the David Rumsey Map Collection

CHAPTER 1

Image A: Courtesy Patricia Hood Epperson

Image B: Courtesy Library of Congress, LC-USZ62-1512

Images C and D: Courtesy the author

CHAPTER 2

Images A, B, and C: Courtesy the author

Image D: Courtesy Ancestry.com **<www. ancestry.com>**

CHAPTER 3

Image A: Courtesy the author

Images B, C, E and G: Courtesy FamilySearch.org **<www.familysearch.org>**

Images D and F: Courtesy Ancestry.com

CHAPTER 4

Image A: Courtesy Wikimedia Commons **<commons.wikimedia.org>** by user NormanEinstein and reproduced under the Creative Commons license

Images B and D: Courtesy the author

Image C: Courtesy Wikimedia Commons

Regions of Scotland sidebar: Courtesy Jrockley

CHAPTER 5

Image A: Courtesy the David Rumsey Map Collection **<www.davidrumsey.com>**

Image B and Standardizing Gaelic Place Names sidebar: Courtesy the author

Making Sense of the United Kingdom sidebar: Courtesy *Family Tree Magazine* **<www. familytreemagazine.com>**

Image C: Based on map courtesy FamilySearch.org

Image D: Courtesy the National Library of Scotland **<www.nls.uk>**

Image E: Courtesy the Gazetteer of Scotland **<www.scottish-places.info>**

Image F: Courtesy ScotlandsPlaces **<www. scotlandsplaces.gov.uk>**

CHAPTER 6

Image A: 7/16/1749 Robertson, Janet (Old Parish Registers 360/30 173 Kenmore) (accessed via FamilySearch)

Image B: 8/8/1619 Gowrlay, Effie and 8/15/1619 King, Marjorie (Old Parish Registers Baptisms 359/10 5 Inchture) (accessed via FamilySearch)

Image C: Page 4 (Old Parish Records Baptisms 94/10 4 Croy) (accessed via FamilySearch)

CHAPTER 7

Image A: 1868 Hood, David (Statutory Register of Births 611/21) ©Crown copyright, National Records of Scotland **<www.nrscotland.gov.uk>**

PHOTO CREDITS

Image B: 1890 Hood, David (Statutory Register of Marriages 611/2 15) ©Crown copyright, National Records of Scotland

Image C: 1913 Clark, Martha (Statutory Register of Deaths 611/2 10) ©Crown copyright, National Records of Scotland

Image D: 1855 McIntosh Ann (Statutory Register of Deaths 105/16) ©Crown Copyright, National Records of Scotland

Image E: Courtesy ScotlandsPeople

CHAPTER 8

Learning About Your Parish sidebar: Courtesy the author

Image A: Page 48 (Old Parish Registers Births 597/7 48 Kilmarnock) (accessed via FamilySearch)

Image B: Page 263 (Old Parish Registers Marriages 598/20 263 Kilmaurs) (accessed via FamilySearch)

Image C: Page 8 (Old Parish Registers Deaths 685/1 920 8 Edinburgh) (accessed via FamilySearch)

Image D: Drainie kirk session minutes, CH2/384/2, p. 101, National Records of Scotland and the Church of Scotland

Image E: Courtesy ScotlandsPeople

CHAPTER 9

Image A: 1821 Census of Moy and Dalarossie Parish (Old Parish Register of Baptisms 105/2) (accessed via FamilySearch)

Image B: 1841 Muir, John (Census 706/7 3) (accessed via FamilySearch)

Image C: 1851 Stevenson, Robt. LB (Census 685/2 214/3) ©Crown copyright, National Records of Scotland

Image D: 1891 Baird, J.L. (Census 503 9/2) (accessed via FamilySearch)

Image E: Courtesy ScotlandsPlaces

Image F: Hearth Tax Cowall Division, Argyll and Buteshire, E69/3/1 Pg. 3 ©Crown copyright, National Records of Scotland

Image G: Poll Tax from Aberdour, Fifeshire, E70/5/1/1, National Records of Scotland (accessed via FamilySearch)

Image H: Courtesy the author

CHAPTER 10

Image A: John McBride, Testament Dative 1844. Register of Confirmations, Paisley Sheriff Court, SC58/46/9, p. 1 (accessed via FamilySearch)

Image B: Courtesy the author

Image C: Courtesy ScotlandsPeople

Image D: General Retours for John Macadie, No. 25. Record of Services of Heirs 1849-1850, C28/8, p. 2, National Records of Scotland (accessed via FamilySearch)

Image E: Minute Books of Sasines for the Burgh of Ayr, 1713–1729, B6/3/3 Folio 1, National Records of Scotland (accessed via FamilySearch)

Image F: Alexander McGillivray, Register of Sasines abridgements for Inverness-shire 1781–1820, vol. 1, no. 1079, RS173/AI/1781/1, National Records of Scotland (accessed via FamilySearch)

CHAPTER 11

Image A: Courtesy Commonwealth War Graves Commission **<www.cwgc.org>**

Image B: Courtesy Archive.org **<www.archive.org>**

Image C: Courtesy Ecclegen **<ecclegen.com>**

Image D: Courtesy University of Glasgow **<www.gla.ac.uk>**

Image E: Thomas MacAllen, 13 January 1791, from index card biographies of members of Excise Department, 1707-1830, compiled by J.F. Mitchell, RH4/6/2, National Records of Scotland (accessed via FamilySearch)

PHOTO CREDITS

ACKNOWLEDGMENTS

While I often felt that I labored on this book alone, I did, in fact, have help. This work would have been impossible without the countless publications—both in print and online—written by specialists in Scottish history, family history, local history, genealogy, and documents. Many thanks to my mother, Patricia Epperson, for helping me find family photographs and sharing her research. Samantha Smart and Robin Urquhart, both of the National Records of Scotland, provided images and citations; illustrating a book on Scottish genealogy would be impossible without the cooperation of the NRS. From the National Library of Scotland, I received valuable assistance from Louise Speller and Laragh Quinney. Much of the research for this book was done at the Westlake (Ohio) Family History Center—their generous hours and numerous computers proved invaluable. The digital resources provided by ScotlandsPeople and FamilySearch.org made it possible to successfully research and examine documents without travelling to Scotland.

My editor, Andrew Koch, deserves a medal for his patience and his kindness in guiding me through the process of writing and preparing this book. I also wish to thank the production staff for presenting my work in such a visually appealing way.

Finally, I'm incredibly grateful to my family for making sure I was fed while writing and teaching.

All mistakes are my own.

ABOUT THE AUTHOR

Amanda Epperson spent her childhood participating in many activities common in Scottish emigrant families: listening to her grandfather play the bagpipes and to Andy Stewart records; attending Highland Games; and wishing her family tartan were different. Then she grew up to obtain a Ph.D. in Scottish history at the University of Glasgow. For her dissertation, she examined the experience of a Scottish emigrant community in Ohio. This dual experience (as a grandchild of a Scottish immigrant and a resident of Glasgow) has given her an appreciation for both historic and modern Scotland.

Since completing her doctorate, she has taught history at the college level, researched and edited family histories (most recently for Genealogists.com), and written articles for a variety of publications including *Family Tree Magazine*. She blogs occasionally at the Scottish Emigration Blog <scottingemigration.blogspot.com>.

DEDICATION

To my grandfather, William Keir Hood, who is the reason I became interested in Scotland.

To my parents, Joseph and Patricia Epperson, who are the reason I am interested in anything at all.

THE FAMILY TREE SCOTTISH GENEALOGY GUIDE: HOW TO FIND YOUR ANCESTORS IN SCOTLAND.

Published by Family Tree Books, an imprint of F+W Media, Inc., 10151 Carver Road, Suite 300, Blue Ash, Ohio 45242. (800) 289-0963. First edition.

ISBN: 978-1-4403-5415-1

Other Family Tree Books are available from your local bookstore and online suppliers. For more genealogy resources, visit <www.familytreemagazine.com/store>.

22 21 20 19 18   5 4 3 2 1

DISTRIBUTED IN THE U.K. AND EUROPE BY
F&W Media International, LTD
Brunel House, Forde Close,
Newton Abbot, TQ12 4PU, UK
Tel: (+44) 1626 323200,
Fax (+44) 1626 323319
E-mail: enquiries@fwmedia.com

a content + ecommerce company

PUBLISHER AND
COMMUNITY LEADER: Allison Dolan

EDITOR: Andrew Koch

DESIGN/LAYOUT: Julie Barnett / Michelle Thompson, Fold and Gather Design

PRODUCTION COORDINATOR: Debbie Thomas

4 FREE Family Tree Templates

- decorative family tree posters
- five-generation ancestor chart
- family group sheet
- relationship chart
- type and save, or print and fill out

Download at <www.familytreemagazine.com/familytreefreebies>

MORE GREAT GENEALOGY RESOURCES

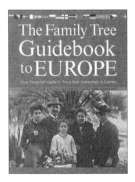

THE FAMILY TREE GUIDEBOOK TO EUROPE

By Allison Dolan and the Editors of Family Tree Magazine

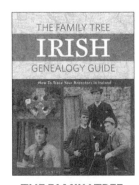

THE FAMILY TREE IRISH GENEALOGY GUIDE

By Claire Santry

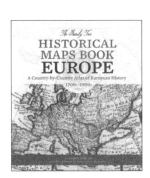

THE FAMILY TREE HISTORICAL MAPS BOOK: EUROPE

By Allison Dolan